Reading Apollinaire

READING
APOLLINAIRE

Theories of poetic language

TIMOTHY MATHEWS

Manchester University Press

Published by Manchester University Press
Oxford Road, Manchester M13 9PL, UK
27 South Main Street, Wolfeboro, NH 03894-2069, USA

British Library cataloguing in publication data
Mathews, Timothy
    Reading Apollinaire: theories of poetic language.
    1. Apollinaire, Guillame—Criticism and interpretation
    I. Title
    841'.912   PQ2601.P6Z/

Library of Congress cataloging in publication data

Mathews, Timothy.
    Reading Apollinaire.
    Bibliography: p. 237.
    Includes index.
    1. Apollinaire, Guillaume, 1880–1918—Criticism
and interpretation.   I. Title.
PQ2601.P6Z6986   1987   841'.912   87–7898

ISBN 0 7190 2220 7 *cased*

Typeset by Williams Graphics, Abergele, North Wales, UK
Printed in Great Britain by Bell and Bain Ltd., Glasgow

Contents

Chapter 2—POETRY, PAINTING, THEORY

Chapter 3—*ONDES*

Chapter 4—CONCLUSION

Contents

Preface

De Chine sont venus les pihis longs et souples
Qui n'ont qu'une seule aile et qui volent par couples

There certainly would be a poem to write about these obscure birds and the lines they fly in — as is suggested in 'Les Fenêtres' with the kind of cross-contextual irony from which Apollinaire derives so much expressiveness: 'Il y a un poème à faire sur l'oiseau qui n'a qu'une aile'. And it certainly should be a poem, perhaps, rather than a book. The birds' flight suggests a range of questions that re-emerge, wanting refinement, with each exposure to Apollinaire's images and rhythms: is there a power in Apollinaire's language to explore our sensuality, to make a common ground of it and penetrate our very sense of self? Or is it a writing that deals in a sequestration of language and an unbreached privacy in experience? Is it a writing that is lopsided and that falls over, as the one-winged birds seem destined to do? Or is it a writing built of immense flights of imagination, able to carry obscurity and impenetrable objects in its wake and endow them with meaning? Such questions may indeed seem to invite discussion in book form.

But even with these questions consistently in mind, writing purposefully about Apollinaire remains a daunting task. How do we respond to a biography that borders on the mythical? The events in his life are dramatically diverse — an existence open to all stimuli, displaying a capacity to sense the new kind of creativity at work in one of the greatest concentrations of intellectual and artistic activity since the Renaissance. During the tumultuous years of his time in Paris, his life developed strands and feelers that wove him into a collaboration so immensely powerful that it changed the course of Western art. In 1902 and 1903, he was attending the weekly gatherings of the Symbolist review *La Plume* and making controversial and sometimes alarming interventions there along with Jarry and Salmon, with whom he became friends immediately. He met Picasso for the first time in 'Le Critérion', the bar that Huysmans's *Des Esseintes* had put on the literary map. Simultaneously, as the chance result of his mother and her lover having taken a house in Le Vésinet, outside Paris, he became involved with the Fauvist painters Vlaminck and Derain, who were staying there. For a while, his time was divided between Le Vésinet, Le Bateau Lavoir, where Jacob, Jarry and Salmon, among others, gathered in Picasso's studio, and La Closerie des Lilas, where he met Paul Fort and the Symbolist revival group 'Vers et Prose', to which he ultimately introduced Picasso. From 1908, with his notes to the Fauvist exhibition in Le Havre, and to Braque's in Paris, and the beginnings of what was to become a regular column in L'Intransigeant, Apollinaire embarked on an almost uninterrupted parallel career in art criticism that put him in the forefront of avant-garde activity. He played a major role in forcing Cubism in 1907, Futurism in 1909, and Orphism in 1912, into the arena of public debate.

It is in response to the mythical quality of this diversity and this concentrated activity that Roger Shattuck calls Apollinaire's existence enchanted, borrowing the adjective from L'Enchanteur pourrissant, Apollinaire's first published work. The physiognomy of his existence is made up of an endless stream of activity that might otherwise have used up the time of at least three people. Moreover, this activity develops links between artistic events and private, biographical ones, making its reading and interpretation more complex. Not only are events in his personal life often involved with events that have their place in the history of twentieth-century Western culture, but both quotidian occurrences and highly charged personal situations find their way directly into writing aimed at public consumption. It is a matter of Apollinairian folklore that the ending of his frustrating relationship with Annie Playden 'produced' 'La Chanson du Mal-Aimé', although it was not printed until some five years later, and that the departure of Marie Laurencin 'produced' the elegiac 'le Pont Mirabeau', one of the best known poems in the French language.

This complicates rather than settles the problem of Apollinaire's credentials as a strong, ubiquitous man of letters, enchanting the world into poetry and the arts into progress; they were by no means unchallenged in his own lifetime. His explorations of Symbolist 'nuance', his predilection for medieval myths dear to the belle époque, and his idiosyncratic allusiveness and breadth of reading, all earned him the reputation of being a kind of mystificateur and confidence trickster. Georges Duhamel wrote a destructive review of Alcools when it appeared in 1913, qualifying its author's activity as 'de la brocante'. He was greeted with suspicion for his defence of young painters in 1905, and particularly of the Cubists in 1908. In fact, Apollinaire espoused the jibe 'cubiste' and transformed it systematically into a positive term in his own writing, denoting a new kind of painting, an analysis of painting, and the pursuit of a new creativity — even though the messianic tone of many of the pieces on Cubism may still leave readers unconvinced today, and Cubism itself is still often popularly regarded as a hoax at the expense of academic art. In the early days of Apollinaire's poetic production, the poems he would read aloud often earned him the response 'Trop symboliste! Encore trop symboliste!' from Salmon or Jacob. In the decades after his death, several of his painter friends seemed to imply that Apollinaire understood nothing about the plastic arts. And then there are the apparently trivialising and inappropriately ecstatic war poems.

There seems, then, to be a polarisation in the reactions that Apollinaire's work produces. The response ranges from respecting Apollinaire as a generator of novelty and creativity in expression to dismissing him as a trickster demeaning the status of art. Apollinaire himself is acutely conscious of such criticisms directed at his work (despite inviting, to some extent, a 'superhuman' quality of response). He is never more conscious of them than in his reaction to Billy's review of *Calligrammes*: 'En ce qui concerne le reproche d'être un destructeur, je le repousse formellement, car je n'ai rien détruit mais au contraire, essayé de construire.... Si je cesse un jour ces recherches, c'est que je serai las d'être traité en hurluberlu justement parce que les recherches paraissent absurdes à ceux qui se contentent de suivre les routes tracées.' But despite Apollinaire's persistent confidence in his work, his is a writing marked by a tension between an enlargement of the scope of language and an isolation within it, between creativity and sequestration. Why is *L'Enchanteur* 'pourrissant'? Why does Merlin, sorcerer-son of the devil, sleep with a woman he never touches, whose domain is the water in the lake, to whom he reveals his secrets without realising it, and by whom he is tricked and locked in a cave? Why are falsehood and illusion such dominant themes in Apollinaire's thinking and writing — false divinities, false magi and false magicians in *L'Enchanteur pourrissant*, false centurions in 'Les Fiançailles', a false river of blood in *Vitam Impendere Amori*?

Critics have approached the problem in various ways. Clearly, the relation between fiction and sensuous reality is a dominant source of enquiry and anxiety in nineteenth-century thinking and literature from Symbolism and Rimbaud, back through Baudelaire and Poe, and on to the drama of Musset. But literary historians have been more interested in grasping the nettle of the 'brocanteur' challenge by seeking to give depth to the breadth of allusion and the patchwork of private references that characterise Apollinaire's writing. Attempts have been made to trace the sources of his images and poetic structures through the intricate network comprising his reading, and his private and public lives. Biographies of Apollinaire have been produced that weave Apollinaire's personal anxieties and aspirations into the context of the cultural events he helped to shape.

Such an approach runs the risk of ignoring that many of Apollinaire's poems have a complex textural surface that cannot be broken down into individually assimilable parts. This surface is one that involves the reader in at least two discrepant experiences. On the one hand, the poems of *Alcools* in particular, or the initial run of seven poems in 'Lueurs des tirs', create a seductive lyricism that appeals to a deep-seated sense of nostalgia, frustration and loss. On the other hand, the poems are genuinely impenetrable, full of difficult leaps, disconcerting surprises, shifts of tone and of register. This impenetrability *is* the poem. To search for biographical or thematic progressions that 'explain' elements in the poem individually is to falsify the reading experience that Apollinaire's verse creates.

But penetrating synchronic analyses have been produced. Scott Bates's *Apollinaire* takes dominant, obsessive themes or myths in Apollinaire's psyche — Antichrist, the death of love, anxiety and incest, the Traveller, the City — and shows how they are incarnated in poems. Renaud's *Lecture d'Apollinaire* starts from the imperative that Apollinaire's thinking on literature and art should be taken seriously, and relates the development of that thinking to stages crossed in Apollinaire's poetic output. In this way, Renaud arrives at an image of a deeply reflective Apollinaire, one who does not merely consume the cultural upheavals he was thrown into by an accident of history, but who attempts to control his involvement in these events positively, and to arrive at a responsible and progressive art.

Jean-Claude Chevalier's *'Alcools' d'Apollinaire* — *Essai d'analyse des formes poétiques* brings into powerful relief the pursuit of a reasoned, controlled intervention in experience and the sense of history in Apollinaire's writing. Chevalier evolves a flexible dialectic with which to present the poetic forms that incarnate Apollinaire's thinking and with which to understand his attempts to dominate the language he discovers he is using. Moving on from here — and this is one of the most interesting consequences of Renaud's work — Apollinaire's calligraphic, 'modernist' interventions have attracted steadily more serious and penetrating criticism. Georges Longrée, in his *L'Expérience idéo-calligrammatique d'Apollinaire*, attempts to give historical and intellectual depth to these artefacts by integrating them with Symbolist thinking on poetry and painting. In articles, Alain-Mary Bassy has attempted to describe Apollinaire's calligraphy structurally, and Jean-Pierre Goldenstein has sketched a semiotic theory of the calligram. More recently, Willard Bohn, in his *The Aesthetics of Visual Poetry*, and Gilberte Jacaret, in her *La Dialectique de l'ironie et du lyrisme*, have brought the perspectives of linguistics and rhetoric respectively to bear on our understanding of this mode in Apollinaire's self-expression.

Valuable as these studies are, they all (with the exception, perhaps, of the rhetorical approach) risk withdrawing from the rebarbative elusiveness of Apollinaire's writing as a whole, and of reducing the interpretation of it to a form of decoding. What I will be asking my reader to do is to follow me through a *reading* of the poems designed to reconstruct the process whereby the reading mind gropes for meaning and purpose in them. By concentrating on individual texts, I hope to confront the poetic process in Apollinaire at one of its most crucial stages: the point where he consigns his words to print, content with them as a provisional fragment of his self-reflection. Apollinaire as 'brocanteur' is not so much as insulting *aperçu* as an unconscious statement of the reality of Apollinaire's experience and anxiety, of a problem he creates for himself and knows about. Each object, each cherished souvenir in the pawnbroker's shop is 'un médaillon toujours fermé', just like the pawnbroker's own memory and future. The treasure-chest is closed, the gift constantly withdraws — this is the quality in Apollinaire's verse that I hope to preserve as I analyse and explore it.

My object is not to isolate the text from its historical moment, nor to attribute a self-contained value to it. What my study uncovers again and again is the moment of anxiety when the text is discovered as text — language uncoupled from its producer. This can take two forms. On the one hand, it is the moment when the language emerges as potentially closed and private, seeking exchange and entry into the world. On the other hand, the poem's contact with its readers can be a moment when intervention is swept aside, and expressiveness coming from memory and the world seems to invade awareness. One of the objectives of this work is to allow a sense of self fragmented in language and as language to emerge from the experience of Apollinaire's verse, and to allow us to move on from a vision of Apollinaire as heroic conqueror of the forms made manifest in word and image.

Nor is my intense concentration on individual poems intended to isolate them from the rest of language. Apollinaire reminds us that poetry is intensely human and endlessly applicable, in that it is a heightened sense of language itself, its power and its power to rebuff. Necessarily, an approach seeking to preserve this immersion of poems in the language at large will make hard work for the reader. The more a text is focused on, the less it belongs to itself; the more it is explored, the less its position or value in relation to others in Apollinaire's output can be highlighted. My approach will allow single lines to encroach on our consciousness; they may seize our attention and not release it; they will not remain the same as reading progresses. But the fact that lines in Apollinaire's poems behave in this way is itself an indication of the daunting experience of language that is Apollinaire's, and it is this that I shall attempt to describe. My premise in reading, like Breton's, is that I can learn nothing more about an author than what his words tell me. One of the consequences of this premise is the view that the action of isolated groups of lines — single images blurring their distinction from others, images in search of relation, progress and exchange — is one of the most intense incarnations of Apollinaire's experience. In reading and re-reading lines and images, I hope to open out a space wide enough to trace the anfractuosities of Apollinaire's expression and create a mobile image of the interpenetration in his verse of the communicable and the resolutely private.

This gives rise to a paradox, and one that will re-emerge throughout this work. There is a fundamental — and potentially stimulating — tension between the reading method I develop, and the reality of the texts themselves. Lines are between other lines and can be withdrawn only arbitrarily from the associative play that locks them in a text. Furthermore, readers may often find more to perplex them in my interpretation than in the often disarming simplicity of Apollinaire's poetic *trouvailles*. Any critical discourse must confront such a paradox. To hold up an effective mirror to the texts it faces, criticism needs to emphasise the difference between its own discourse and the discourse of the text. So I ask my readers to bear with the discrepancy they will frequently come across in the following chapters between a line or a short group of lines quoted in the middle of the page and an extensive commentary that seeks to catch up with the diverse repercussions of this apparently small instance of writing. In return, I hope readers will ultimately find the lines re-situated in the text as a whole, epitomising the movement of the text and the direction it takes. For it is whole texts that I am interested in — their dissolving beginnings and endings. My intention is not to build up as broad a view as possible of Apollinaire's writing by relating to each other isolated images from different poems, but rather to give space over to the very process of reading a poem, and to see that process through.

But the gap between text and criticism, reading and meta-level, is not fixed. Moreover, the success or failure of a poet is implicated in this mobile and unmeasurable gap. The heroism that is so often discerned in Apollinaire's poetic gestures dissolves in the diversity it aspires to — the diversity of stimuli that remain on the other side of identification, and to which Apollinaire's writing is endlessly open. His writing confronts a fundamental tension between encapsulation and transcience — and it is for this reason that the following readings, though they are given over to 'whole' texts, arrive at conclusions about them only indirectly and serially. This crucial tension in Apollinaire's poems is one that brings his suffering into play — the anxiety of undermined control, valueless possession, gifts transformed into mere images. In turn, it is to this tension between encapsulation and transcience, to the anxiety of identification and of isolation within images, that the following pages are devoted — in so far as this tension is present *in and as poems*, and in so far as it is crucial to the understanding of objects that are read. Apollinaire himself is alive to the relation of grief to poetry in his own experience. One of the climatic periods of his involvement in the visual arts, when *Alcools* was also in an advanced stage of completion, coincided with the departure from Paris and from his life of his collaborator and lover Marie Laurencin; of this period he wrote in a letter to Robert Delaunay: 'je ne pense qu'une chose, cher ami, que je suis la tristesse même, mais non la vilaine et pauvre tristesse qui assombrit tout. La mienne brille comme une étoile, elle illumine le chemin de l'Art à travers l'effroyable nuit de la vie'.

Before we begin, I should like to include a word or two about terminology. In discussion of the basic tension between what I have been calling 'encapsulation' and 'transience', two groups of words will emerge repeatedly and readers might find it useful to bear them in mind from the very start. In describing the level in Apollinaire's writing at which creative intervention is established and communication with his readers is seen to operate through his images, I use three terms: articulation, expression, representation. On the other hand, for the level in his writing where experience eludes his poetic structures, in which it is absent *in* his images and identified *as* image, three different terms are useful: substitution, effacement, displacement. It is not for me to define these terms more closely here. This is not a work whose theory can provide at the outset the answers to the questions it poses. Indeed, it is not terminology that is the issue here, but writing at large, the sense that writing can only be responded to in writing, that its secrets cannot be untangled nor its value indicated or affirmed. The relations binding us to our expression and painting image onto us, and the capacity of theory to plough understanding, are active because they are de-centred and de-centering. No words can define without enacting or repeating. This is intensified in any attempt to pre-empt the action of words and terms, or to dominate in advance the associations they bring to bear. Nothing is more strongly laid bare than this in Apollinaire's writing. His involvement with the modern and his pursuit of progress take on the life-and-death risk of creativity and humanity — to dismantle the perimeters of the self, to be absent within them, to take apart the censorship of the invasion incessantly dramatised by word and sensation.

Abbreviations

C: *Calligrammes, poems of peace and war*, a parallel text translated by Anne
Hyde Greet, with an introduction by S. I. Lockerbie, and commentary by
Anne Hyde Greet and S. I. Lockerbie, University of California Press (Berkeley
and London, 1980)

CA: Guillaume Apollinaire, *Chroniques d'art*, edited by Leroy C. Breunig,
Gallimard (Paris, 1960)

CAA: *Du Cubisme à l'art abstrait*, les cahiers inédits de Robert Delaunay,
edited by Pierre Francastel, Bibliothèque générale de l'école pratique des
hautes études (Paris, 1957)

OC: Guillaume Apollinaire, *Oeuvres complètes*, preface by Max-Pol Fauchet,
introduction and notes by Michel Décaudin, iconography assembled by
Marcel Adéma, André Ballard and Jacques Lecat (Paris, 1965)

OP: Guillaume Apollinaire, *Oeuvres poétiques*, edited by Marcel Adéma and
Michel Décaudin, Bibliothèque de la Pléïade, Gallimard (Paris, 1965)

Acknowledgements

This book has been produced with the assistance of a loan from Lady Margaret Hall, Oxford, and a grant from the British Academy, and to these bodies I extend my warmest gratitude.

Many people, with numerous acts of friendship and encouragement, have given me the impetus to see this book through. I am sure none of them will mind that I select the following for mention here: Margaret Davies and David Shepheard for their penetrating suggestions for improvements on the typescript; David Kelley, for putting me in contact with Manchester University Press; Verity Ridgman for her sensitive copy-editing; Eiichi Kono for providing the line prints of Apollinaire's *idéogrammes*. I am especially indebted to Malcom Bowie for his insight and his generosity, and in nameless ways to Patti White, to whom this book is dedicated.

Apollinaire's texts are quoted here by kind permission of Editions Gallimard, © E. G.. 'Lettre-Océan', Coeur couronne et miroir' and 'Voyage' are reproduced by kind permission of the Bibliothèque littéraire Jacques Doucet, Paris.

1—ALCOOLS

INTRODUCTION— 'L'ADIEU'

One of the major achievements of *Alcools* is Apollinaire's ability to take us along the knife-edge of failed hope, unrealised desires, separation and transcience.[1] What better way to start an appreciation of the work than with a farewell?

L'Adieu

J'ai cueilli ce brin de bruyère
L'automne est morte souviens-t'en
Nous ne vous verrons plus sur terre
Odeur du temps brin de bruyère
Et souviens-toi que je t'attends

The poem seems dominated by a glowing fusion, in the fourth line, of the senses, of memory and of objects.[2] The coupling of internal and tactile experience is portrayed with such masterly simplicity that the critic might feel justified in drawing attention to it and leaving it to reverberate on its own. But to do so would be to disengage from the poem at the very beginning. For the confusion of experiences on which the elegiac appeal of the poem greatly depends is itself problematic. The reader's control of the text is undermined, and ultimately no single line has pride of place. No difference emerges between feeling and writing, or between reading and interpreting, and in this the poem brings us into contact with some of the most familiar experiences in word and gesture. But this does not settle the uncertainties of the poem — indeed, we positively relish their potency. The characters elude our grasp, and the relatively rare occurrence of words referring to concrete objects and phenomena — 'brin de bruyère', 'automne', 'terre' — seems to make the poem hover tantalisingly on the other side of familiarity and precision. The 'ce' qualifying 'brin de bruyère' is ironic; it adds no element of definition, we do not see 'ce brin de bruyère' as distinct from any other. 'J'ai cueilli', despite being in the perfect tense, does not place the action in a precise moment, or uncover a distinct area in memory. The voice in the poem and the voice in our head as we read and think interact in a space set in motion in reading itself, in an emphasis on the language as writing, or as inscribing. The poem's relation to the experience that prompts it, and to our own, is undefined. In our first contact with them, the images have a power we cannot circumscribe, the whiteness of the page surrounding the verse seems to bury this power and to confront us with it at the same time.[3] We are concentrated on the very activity of *reading*; the language invades our attention, its relation to others and to sensation remaining unknown and part of a search.

The title itself is a question — goodbye to what? From now on, isolation from what? Biographical input is displaced in the writing in favour of a crucial confrontation: the development of individuals, each sequestered in their own unrevealed context, is dramatically discovered in terms of difference and irreconcilable, irreducible opposition. The expression of separation in 'L'Adieu' is one in which the alien and the familiar coexist, in which the distinction between them is eroded, and in which each is presented as all-exclusive. In reading, the reader is disoriented; the writer's presence is dismantled and effaced in writing, in his self-expression, and in the very sense of familiarity that the poem explores.

In this way, 'L'Adieu' folds a concrete experience into a more conceptual one that remains resolutely unspecified. In doing so, it involves us in an attempt to discover an attitude to language itself, and to the past — 'adieu'. But such an attitude cannot be maintained in either the concrete or the conceptual levels that structure the poem. Both are expanded to the point where they incorporate each other, both express an attitude in relation to time, but neither locates this attitude nor dominates it — 'L'automne est morte souviens-t'en'. The definite and the unspecified displace one another, enacting the movement of memory eluded in language, added to in language. Nostalgia and intangibility, the clichéd images of time passing, are expanded and exploited; they set up a question asked about time and the experience of time in language.

In this way, 'L'Adieu' delves into the non-representational behaviour of language. In fact, Apollinaire seems to come to terms with some crucial consequences of this quality. The overthrow of 'natural' subject–object relations, a feature of French poetry since Hugo's *Les Orientales*, reaches a climax in the Symbolist drive and develops into the anti-idealist rejection of Symbolism that occurred after 1895.[4] But in 'L'Adieu', a non-representational mode of expression is not part of a quest for a language able to evoke the sources of sensibility and

2

provoke an interpenetration of the concrete and imaginary, the actual and potential. The unrepresented is the raw material of experience itself. The poem does not stop at dissolving distinctions between past and present; it focuses on expression as an act bringing together memory and the fact of language. By undermining a stable relation of words to sensation, Apollinaire, on one level, concentrates our attention all-exclusively on the poem context, the context established in reading. But key words such as 'bruyère' and 'odeur' do not open any doors. Apollinaire uses them to confront questions about the experience of memory in relation to expression, and to unearth imprints of the subject left in the movement between the two.

These questions come into evidence at one of the most immediate levels on which the poem presents itself: its aural impact. One of the elements that distinguishes sound-pattern in 'L'Adieu' is the simplicity of the rhyme scheme, partly dictated by the five-line length of the poem: there are only two rhyming sounds — 'erre', and 'ten'. The act of rhyming one word with another is a metaphoric act of desire to understand, for it expresses the desire to relate experience — or experience of language — from one context to another. Rhyme can be understood as an attempt to understand an event in terms of another event in the past, where events are linguistic and the passage of time is circumscribed in the duration of the poem. But in a five-line poem with two rhyming sounds, a rhyme scheme is a pattern of repetition and undermines its own search for structure in diversity. The use of rhyme in 'L'Adieu' progressively to emphasise repetition heightens the independence it shares with any poetic text, its withdrawal of reference to contexts other than the one in which it is read, and its power to discover and produce its *own* terms of reference. But this achievement is a problematic one; the relation of the poem context to other contexts in experience becomes blurred, the poem is secluded in its own terms of reference, its 'content' is separated from being closed off and communicated:

> J'ai cueilli ce brin de bruyère
> . . .
> Nous ne nous verrons plus sur terre

This is grounded in Apollinaire's treatment of memory, references to which are consistently woven into the poem: 'souviens-toi', 'je t'attends', 'temps', 'Nous ne nous verrons plus', 'morte', 'souviens-t'en'. In 'L'Adieu', Apollinaire approaches memory as a representation of thinking, of coming to terms with it. Like Orpheus, he uses sound to disrupt distinctions he finds meaningless or unacceptable: the categorisation that separates he and she, death and life, absence and presence, the stated and the inexpressible.[5] Orpheus gathers all species of animal, Apollinaire seeks to gather as many significances as may be associated with an event, or as are secluded in the memory of an event. At the same time, neither can overcome or incorporate death; neither can locate or accept difference. Eurydice and the power of music to charm remain part of another world. Apollinaire's disruption of context is the death of all context — it is the beginning of the repeated desire for context, and the desire to circumscribe and possess the expressiveness of language. The rhyme scheme and the so-called musical qualities in the verse of 'L'Adieu' are musings on the experience of language. They are musings on the paradox of an associativeness that is the creative potential of language, but that prevents the poet dominating language, and dominating experience through it.

Apollinaire's emphasis on the basic element in the experience of words and of reading them — phonetics — does not only take place in terms of rhyme. For throughout the poem Apollinaire creates a pattern of alliterative and assonantal echoes. 'Bruyère' is phonetically related to 'Odeur', 'morte', and 'verrons'; 'attends' to 'automne' and 'temps'. Apollinaire is evoking the desire, pursued by predecessors such as Verhaeren and Verlaine, of relating a patterning in the aural impact of words to a developing pattern of signification in the writing, as well as to the hidden structures in the sensibility of reader and writer. But rather than realising this desire, Apollinaire seems to intensify the tautological structure of the poem initiated by the rhyme sheme. To remain within a restricted phonetic structure in a short piece of writing is to suggest an effacement of the difference between verbal contexts. The relating of sounds to letters, expression to context, user to receiver of language is presented as an unended process of questioning.[6] Experience itself is an unanswered question, a continuous fragmentation, a continuous articulation of separateness: the experience of experience ('Odeur du temps'), the sense of being, but a sense of distance in being.

The tantalising simplicity of this poetic 'Odeur' from the line that attracts so many glances supports this level of reading. 'Odeur' refers to the sense of smell as a whole; it is able to abstract sense experience, to express its irreducible, acontextual presence. It expresses the experience of a moment in time, undifferentiated from the passage of time: difference without change, then. Equally, 'Odeur' and the sense of smell are an incomplete expression of time, of its action in experience and in language. This incompleteness is a synecdochal expression of distance *from* being, *in* the sense of being itself. The language of the poem, the structuring of memory it creates, seeks and fails to locate a context, a point in time, a point of contact. It replaces the experience that produces it, and this tautology presents the point of contact with the world, with others, with identity, as disintegrated, and as a function of nostalgia.[7]

The action of rhyme in the poem extends its reading still further. Rhyming a word with itself in a different context —

> J'ai cueilli ce brin de bruyère
> ...
> Odeur du temps brin de bruyère

transforms expression into a circular process. Within the restrictions of 'L'Adieu', it emphasises unification at the cost of the sense of difference that provokes the need for it, and that fires the desire to bring disparate elements together and construct a momentary sense of the specific and the subjective. The rhyme of the poem threatens to reduce the disparate to the same, and this goes beyond emphasising the artificiality of the writing, and hence its poetic quality. Rather, we are left with a poetic outcome that puts under wraps the process or the experience that gives rise to it. The poem takes the place of what it seeks to isolate. It explores a moment in awareness, at the expense of locating a moment of exchange or a moment in consciousness. Readers are confronted with an effort to maintain difference and shape, always in danger of suppression. Perception takes form as sourceless, dismantled in the terms that express it. The present — 'ce brin de bruyère' — disintegrates in its mobile relation to memory and the experience of time.

In this way, the poem increasingly involves the senses in what is made unavailable to them. This is one element in the poem that presents waiting as irreducible to a specific moment, and recasts it as an experience of time, of passage, and of distance in the face of the here and now. Waiting in 'L'Adieu' is a form given to the relation of experience to memory, and to expression itself. Reading the poem traces the invisible dividing line between sensual and conceptual experience along which memory appears. 'Odeur du temps brin de bruyère' does not express the sensual and the conceptual, or experience and image, in terms of difference discovered between them. The poem suggests a continuity that extends indefinitely. A paradox emerges by which the so-called immediacy that incarnates our awareness of the world is in fact continuous, and articulates perception in terms of an indefinite range of continuous, contourless fragments. The hand touches and the pen writes, but both are neither seen nor read other than in a moment in time in which touch and touch, word and reader, do not come together. 'L'Adieu' presents the immediacy of perception and of sensual experience in terms of the all-exclusiveness of the fragment: in terms of the experience of a seamless difference that does not locate differentiation, but that articulates repeated succession and continuous disappearance:

> Nous ne nous verrons plus sur terre
> ...
> Et souviens-toi que je t'attends

Time provides the structure in terms of which Apollinaire adopts an attitude to the various elements in his poem. The farewell presents thought and the appropriation of experience in terms of memory and the fact of metaphor. 'Nous ne nous verrons plus sur terre' — an objective, repossessed world, in which we could lay hands on a shared experience and create communication, is lacking. Communication and shared experience are articulated in 'L'Adieu' exclusively in interpretation and in reading — a reading that is itself a continuous waiting for the object of nostalgia to emerge, for language itself to be specified, for human beings to speak in it and to invade it with themselves.

This waiting is, then, an experience of time crucial to reading the poem and interpreting it. But interpretation is continually undermined and does not take definite shape. Time cannot be encompassed and wrenched from the continuous; 'L'Adieu' is a text whose contours dissolve. A defining element in consciousness is undermined. Self-consciousness is not in evidence, differences are not articulated. The past is discovered at every juncture, and changes everything in its passage.

1—'AUTOMNE MALADE': IMAGE, ABSTRACTION

One of the features that distinguishes 'L'Adieu' from the longer poems of *Alcools* is that it has no central persona, and that its protagonists are obscured. 'La Chanson du Mal-Aimé', 'L'Emigrant de Landor Road', for example, do present us with a central persona, however fragmented, and Apollinaire uses it to explore, among other things, the relation between images and the past.[8] Even poems such as 'Marie', or 'La Tzigane', similar to 'L'Adieu' in length and metre, bring poetic identities into sharper relief.[9] I want to go on to explore 'Automne malade', another short poem with an authorial persona as minimal and elusive, if not more so, as it is in 'L'Adieu'.[10] Such poems offer us a unique opportunity to explore at close quarters some essential Apollinairian experiences, which I have so far presented in introductory and concentrated form in my reading of 'L'Adieu'.

(i) LYRICAL APPEAL

First, let us reread the poem:

> Automne malade et adoré
> Tu mourras quand l'ouragan soufflera dans les roseraies
> Quand il aura neigé
> Dans les vergers
>
> Pauvre automne
> Meurs en blancheur et en richesse
> De neige et de fruits mûrs
> Au fond du ciel
> Des éperviers planent
> Sur les nixes nicettes aux cheveux verts et naines
> Qui n'ont jamais aimé
>
> Aux lisières lointaines
> Les cerfs ont bramé
>
> Et que j'aime ô saison que j'aime tes rumeurs
> Les fruits tombant sans qu'on les cueille
> Le vent et la forêt qui pleurent
> Toutes leurs larmes en automne feuille à feuille
> > Les feuilles
> > Qu'on foule
> > Un train
> > Qui roule
> > La vie
> > S'écoule

'Automne malade' exploits the silent voice of solitary reading. Language, clearly, is everywhere, all-invasive. At the same time, the poem creates an experience of language being awaited — continuously awaiting specification or the moment of an exchanged word. We saw that in 'L'Adieu' Apollinaire sets up two distinct structuring levels of metaphor — the recognisable and the indefinite. 'Automne malade' operates two similarly distinct levels of reading that Apollinaire again reveals in terms of each other, while problematising the distinction between them. In this way, as we shall see, the text erodes the 'object-ness' of things, along with their stability as metaphoric elements. As we respond to its invitation to reread, the poem seems continually to give new breath to that solitariness of reading, miming the movements of memory and creating the marks it leaves in the effort to locate.

But firstly, what are these two distinct metaphoric levels that contribute to the structuring of the poem? An accessible way of approaching the text is in terms of an appeal to familiar elements in French poetry. In 'Automne malade' Apollinaire transforms into expressions of perception poetic *leit motifs* that are in evidence in French poetry from the Romanticism of Lamartine through Symbolism and Verlaine, and on later to Carco and the 'fantaisiste' group.[11] In these terms it appears straightforward to interpret the poem as a rendering of melancholy experienced at the approach of autumn. 'Et que j'aime ô saison que j'aime tes rumeurs' can be interpreted as an enjoyment of the vagueness and transience autumn suggests. According to such a reading, the transience involved in the changing seasons is presented as non-threatening; it carries a richness of immanent expressiveness and ambiguity. The images expressing the fertility of the season — 'richesse', 'fruits mûrs' — contribute to the appearance woven by Apollinaire's text according to which transformation and transience do not imply the destruction involved in the passage of time, but rather imply a beauty inherent in the process itself, and a satis-faction to be gained from it: the wind blowing in the rose-garden, the fruits falling before there is time to pick them, the sound of leaves in the wind.

But on the other hand, it is possible to read these images more innocently, and as being much more threatening in relation to expec-tations of Romantic lyricism and Symbolist decorativeness. For in using a description that engages in a sentimentalising appropriation of transience and of death, Apollinaire simultaneously dismantles it by using terms of comparison that are inappropriate — though this does not interrupt the flow of the language that is one of its distinctively 'lyrical' features. Apollinaire describes autumn in terms of natural elements not connected with autumn, or not exclusively, '...quand l'ouragan soufflera dans les roseraies' — this image combines associ-ations of summer (rose bushes, rose blooms) and of winter ('ouragan'). Or again:

> Quand il aura neigé
> Dans les vergers (1. 3)

where autumn — the season of orchard fruits in Europe — is implied
by reference to winter and to snow. These 'inappropriatenesses' have
the result that the lyricism to which the text appeals is shown to be
incapable of accounting for, of responding semantically to, the experience incarnated by the text itself. In relation to this experience,
'lyricism' is a receptacle that leaks; it suggests ironically an unmeasurable gap between the categorisation offered by interpretation,
and the articulation of experience in language.

So the second of the two structural levels of the poem I mentioned
earlier is in fact a mobile space; it exists in relation to a poetic lyricism
from which the text ultimately disengages itself. The lyricism to which
the poem appeals is unlocatable, is made unavailable by the poem itself,
in that it is being responded to, remembered and reacted to *in* the poem.
The image

> Quand il aura neigé
> Dans les vergers

is a nexus at which appropriation is outmanoeuvred at every juncture
that reading invents. An orchard covered in snow refers to autumn in
terms of its having been superseded, in terms of its absence. To this
extent, it is an image that confronts transience, but in the form of the
movement that thinking about time involves. The image creates a
fusion — or a 'con-'fusion — of disparate elements: orchard fruits and
snow. The possibility of giving shape to perception and of taking it in
is challenged here, in that these elements are brought into a context
made up in a reading space encroaching on all others and engulfing
them; so that within this context the elements in the image do *not* give
form to movement or imply development. They do *not* represent
thought or its engagement with itself, and with a changing world.
Instead, the reader is threatened with immobility and stasis. The future
perfect is undermined, the nexus does not present itself as the culmination of a development. Indeed such a development is made inaccessible in this image/artefact.

So the image 'Quand il aura neigé/Dans les vergers' confronts a
continuous process of transformation with a spectre of stasis. On the
one hand, Apollinaire presents the reader with autumn passing through
to winter — with the erosion and the absence of autumn itself. On the
other hand, Apollinaire's image suggests all the seasons through which

autumn has passed now contained, formlessly, under the snow. Once again, this can be read as a suggestion of innocuous transience, or a sense of pregnant expectation. But the text is not being read comprehensively if we settle for a simplistic attitude to the concept of immobility. The seasons are not contained as such under the snow, but eroded, made invisible in the whitenes of the snow. The transformation evoked by the poem now takes the form of the shapes invented in the reading or the writing of a single image. This implies a precarious balance with which a straightforwardly 'lyrical' response cannot cope: a balance between flux and the static object — between memory and a moment in perception. But is it a balance or, once again, a confusion? Does the image not confront us with the problem of establishing the distinction between those two kinds of awareness? If the distinction between perception as process, and the identification of objects, i.e. seasons, is dissolved, where does this leave the reader, and what does it tell us about Apollinaire's experience of writing?

We are far removed from reading the words as a 'poetic' rendering of a remembered or imagined situation, or from discussing the significances presumed to be latent in the idea of snow. We are not talking about snow, but about something at once more specific and more abstract. The image 'Quand il aura neigé/Dans les vergers' is a representation of an object or a season in perception, rather than its identification. The images of 'Automne malade' express an experience by which static, object-like qualities are unavailable, and placed in the domain of metaphor — and of nostalgia. In the images of this poem, perception of the object is represented in terms of a process that emphasises the object as a kind of matter — a reading matter, or a thinking matter. The naming of the object ('Automne malade') is the context of its inaccessibility. Apollinaire is at once referring to a concrete object (an autumn with fixed spatial and temporal limits) and creating a dissolved object. The object is not described, but implied in its transparency, in the mobility of the eye and the pen that pass over it, in the continuous process of its coming into and out of being. Through its absence the object comes into being, and traces artificial contours around the memory of the reader.

(ii) READING

But the claims I am making for 'Automne malade' as an intellectually challenging, anti-nostalgic poem of absence and being need more support than the single image on which much of the argument has been

10

based so far. The poem is in fact a network of images dismantling their own contours as images.

> Au fond du ciel
> Des éperviers planent (1. 8)

And again:

> Aux lisières lointaines
> Les cerfs ont bramé (1. 12)

These are images that defy searches for references to a framework outside the one created in the poem itself. They are word-constructs that emphasise their artificiality.[12] In these images, the objects that are obviously associated with the words are not important as such, in any sense of pictorial or symbolic reference:

> Au fond du ciel
> Des éperviers planent

The image of sparrow-hawks silhouetted against the sky is not reducible to a specific context. Nor does it imply a poetic or stylistic framework in terms of which it can be interpreted. The image is a juxtaposition of material elements, neither of which is defined conceptually. They lack a context in terms of which they would be immediately tangible. One is presented in terms of its vastness — 'le ciel' — in opposition to the other, which is presented in terms of its fragility — the sparrow-hawks' smallness in perspective, their constant movement. In effect, the image removes the power of perspective to identify and to locate in space. Apollinaire is playing on and dissolving the opposition between flatness and depth: 'Au fond du ciel' does not only mean 'on the horizon', but also 'at the bottom of', 'in the depths of' the sky — although the sky, in terms of the horizon in visual perception, is flat. In terms of perspective, the sparrow-hawks are impossibly placed.

Something similar is happening in the image

> Aux lisières lointaines
> Les cerfs ont bramé

'Une lisière' is commonly used to refer to the edge, the frontier of something extensive: a forest, the sea, sleep. But here it is the frontier of something that remains unnamed. So the image of 'les cerfs' — with its ironic definite article that does not distinguish these stags from others or place them in the reader's recollection — standing at 'lisières' is not one that sets the extensive against the specific, but more one that presents the object — the stags — as indistinct and unlocated. The object is placed in an unspecified space, an area of non-objective imagination where thought is mobile, uncategorised, all-exclusive in the discourse of the poem. The terms of relation between object and imagination are unavailable. Even the distance ('lointaines') at which the stags are placed in space or in imagination contributes to their presentation as non-objective, since it is a distance that is both extensive and indefinite. These images place objects in a context in which they acquire significance neither through their power to refer, nor through being intentionalised symbolically. As they are named, or as they appear in the lines of the text, so the objects dissolve in the material itself of reading — the reading matter I mentioned earlier.

This 'reading matter' does not comprise an abdication of the power of language over experience on the part of the writer; Apollinaire is clearly not entrusting words to the free association of the reader. He is presenting us with the material of an abstract expression that articulates a desire for specificity, for location, for punctuality. Simultaneously, in a space where perspective and identification are dissolved, the material created in the reading of these images is an appropriation of perception; in so far as it represents, it represents the erosion *in* perception of the terms that relate memory to experience and to language.

The activity of creating these images emerges as an attempt to locate language in space — the language of the writer in the space in which he uses it. The images we are looking at both represent and create the fluidity of this space. The objects in them do not break up the space in which they operate into sections that can be set in opposition, compared and defined. The sequence of images of which 'Automne malade' is made is a kind of understated dream-sequence, where objects move as the result of an undefined volition and in an undefined context. As in dream, both perspective and context are dissolved and produce a 'space'; they do not reflect and are not reflected. 'Space' in Apollinaire's poem is an ironic transparency, a unity never at one with itself, a plastic continuity created in reading. Each image is a dissolved and dissolving object, the material of absence. The space in terms of which the writer and the language that he uses could be identified is written out as the words emerge in lines across the page, and in the reworkings they undergo. This is the experience, 'the space' that the text invites us to share.

(iii) THE OBJECT

The 'space' in Apollinaire's poem escapes definition. It cannot system-atically be perceived as static, and the attempt to locate it in language — and to appropriate language itself within it — is endless. To this extent space (or 'space'), and the effort of language to describe it is inconceivable without recourse to a notion of time, references to which abound in the peom's expressions of transience and seasonal change. But the poem goes further than this, and it directs language at a rep-resentation of time in the forms in which it is experienced. In this way, the text allows us to approach the mobility of its writing space — the space where the writer seeks to identify with his language.

Just as in 'L'Adieu', we are once again a long way from seeing Apollinaire's references to the passage of time and the passing of the seasons in terms of a naïve expression of nostalgia. It is an approach that involves us as readers in accepting that Apollinaire's writing needs to be confronted conceptually — perhaps in the hope of dismantling any distinction between conceptualisation and immediacy in experi-ence. But even accepting this, to suggest that the writing space, which remains uncircumscribed, presents itself in terms of a relation to time evidently raises as many problems as it attempts to solve. It is designed, however, to respond to the fact that Apollinaire's images direct the reader's attention to the very activity of inventing images — of rep-resenting and exploring a relationship between expression and percep-tion. What the treatment of time in the poem adds to the penetration of this relationship is its own confrontation with difference. Here is one of its forms. Language is inconceivable without time, even if only because language is sequential. But the sequentiality of language does not mean that language dominates time, or the movements of thought in time. This sequentiality, and the images it enunciates, amount, in reading, to a *substitute* for an appropriation of time and of our develop-ment in relation to it. The suggestion is created that the unfolding of perception can only be grasped in terms of this substitution. Apollinaire's images dissolve context, dissolve an object or a season, and are themselves a dissolved object in reading; equally they are also a substitute object.

Substitution implies negation. In 'Automne malade', the absence of the negated, original object is complete. It is indistinguishable from the unfolding of images, from the expression on offer. The notion of substitution presents experience as continuously, and repeatedly, 'other'. The dissolution of the object is not only continuous, but complete. It suggests that there is no source object in perception — even in immediate perception. Instead, there is an experience of our involvement in language as an effaced point of reference. The activities of reading, interpretation and identification are dissolved in the relation that binds them together.

But this dissolving cannot be seen as the blurred edges of an approximation or a presumed equivalence. What is being radically questioned is the assumption of an unproblematic access, within the continuity of perception, of objects to expression. In Apollinaire's text, each of these three elements represents an uncompromising displacement of the others. There are no degrees, or divisible contexts existing separately in relation to others. As for the involvement in language, perception and the object — each is a 'space' excluding the others in and as expression.

> Pauvre automne
> Meurs en blancheur et en richesse
> De neige et de fruits mûrs   (l. 5)

In these non-figurative and abstract lines, the incompleteness of autumn in expression ('Meurs') substitutes itself for the endless continuation of autumn in memory, or in the ways perception is structured. Autumn is alive in the abstract 'space' that colours *in* ('richesse') experience and colours *out* ('blancheur') the identification of experience and its domination. The expression of time (of incompleteness) through substitution ('Meurs') is an expression of a conceptualised anxiety, a galvanised nostalgia, which locates experience in a world that eludes being identified with, and that extends itself before us, as we read, in the abstract image on the page.

2—LITERARY EXCHANGE

We have reached a stage where the notions of language as process as opposed to language as the exchange of information, of language as 'other' as opposed to language as identification, need further definition to remain working concepts, and for the difference between them to remain operative. Roland Barthes has developed a terminology that is useful in attempts to do this.

In his essay 'Ecrivains et écrivants', he defines the two categories announced in his title in relation to the French language as a whole, and to the cultural and intellectual assumptions that inform its literature.[13] Barthes locates an approach to literature whose dominance he regards as having remained intact, protected by the institutions of literature itself:

> ...et cette sorte de monopole du langage produisait curieusement un ordre rigide, moins des producteurs que de la production: ce n'était pas la profession littéraire qui était structurée (elle a beaucoup évolué pendant trois siècles, du poète domestique à l'écrivain homme d'affaires), c'était la matière même de ce discours littéraire, soumis à des règles d'emploi, de genre et de composition, à peu immuable de Marot à Verlaine, de Montaigne à Gide (c'est la langue qui a bougé, ce n'est pas le discours).[14]

The *écrivant* is the custodian of this monopoly, the curator of these unchanged rules of composition and institutionalised boundaries. The 'langue' Barthes refers to here as having shifted the terms of its performance is an application of Saussure's 'langue/parole' distinction, and Barthes is evoking the range of literary possibilities existing implicitly at any one historical moment, the invisible but all the more insidiously operative boundaries of the possible in literature. Despite the different terms that have policed these boundaries since the development of Classicism and the system of patronage on which it was based, the literary discourse itself, Barthes argues, has continued to fulfil the same socio-cultural demands and to respect the same vested interests. For the literary 'parole' is the raw material of *writers*, that is, *écrivains*, whose names and reputations are the property and the support of the institutions of literature, the evidence of their contribution to its power to remain intact. 'Parole', rather than 'langue', is here the entry of the *écrivain*'s language into the institution of literature, the binding of his language to a literary audience. This is the tension under which the *écrivain* operates, for his objective and his experience are a subversion of the practices and modes of self-presentation organised by the literary 'discours'.

But alongside the *écrivain* emerges Barthes's other category of involvement with language and literature, the writing engaged in by the *écrivant*, whose concern is to dissolve any incompatibility between the *écrivain*'s activity and the interests of Literature:

> ...mais les fonctions changent... les écrivains eux-mêmes, de Chateaubriand ou Maistre à Hugo ou à Zola, contribuent à élargir la fonction littéraire, à faire de cette parole institutionnalisée dont ils sont encore les propriétaires reconnus, l'instrument d'une action nouvelle; et à côté

15

des écrivains proprement dits, il se constitue et se développe un groupe nouveau, détenteur du langage public. Intellectuels? Le mot est de résonnance complexe; je préfère les appeler ici des *écrivants*.[15]

The *écrivant*'s commitment to language consists in the preservation of the category of literature, in ensuring that its boundaries are not distinguished or questioned in the experience of the world through literature, in commenting on experience, and in the business of communicating thought. To achieve this, the *écrivant* has the support of a mythology of thought, and a mythological account of the relation of thought to language: language is a vehicle for thought, which has its own literary aesthetic, that of 'la clarté': 'Institutionnellement, la littérature de la France, c'est son langage, système mi-linguistique, mi-esthétique, auquel n'a même pas manqué une dimension mythique, celle de sa *clarté*.'[16] This is the situation the *écrivant* exploits to distinguish language from experience, and to colonise both with his craft: 'Voilà donc le langage ramené à la nature d'un instrument de communication, d'un véhicule de la "pensée".'[17]

But the *écrivain*, on the contrary, expresses his commitment to language through questioning its categories, and resisting the institutionalisation of experience. The questions he asks are endless, and their beginning is the language he writes. For the *écrivain*, questions about existence are questions about language, and it is his experience of language that he seeks to penetrate and to enrich his involvement with. To this extent, the *écrivain*'s activity brings him face to face with a tautology: 'Le paradoxe c'est que, le matériau devenant en quelque sorte sa propre fin, la littérature est au fond une activité tautologue, comme celle de ces machines cybernétiques construites pour *elles-mêmes* (l'homéostat d'Ashby): l'écrivain est un homme qui absorbe radicalement le *pourquoi* du monde dans un *comment écrire*.'[18] The problems of coming to grips with existence and memory are represented by the *écrivain* in a dismantled distinction between experience and comment, perception and analysis; between the structures of sense and the operations of exchange.[19] But this approach is not fixed by the language it produces, since the questions it raises do not exist before the first word appears on the page, or before the source of questions about existence is both buried and articulated in the interplay of signs. In the relation of word to unwritten word, the appropriation of experience is a process of endless addition to experience, and to memory unconfronted as memory. Moreover, for the *écrivain* the written word itself is a repeated and extending instance of this relation. For reader

16

as well as writer, its terms are questions asked of experience — extending terms, heavy with experience: whose? where from? why? The words are the experience of question, the erosion of meta-level in reading and writing; writing itself is overrun by the readings, interpretations and memory-structures it gives rise to. The written word as question, re-presented as the written word as experience — it is in this sense that Barthes refers to the *écrivain*'s praxis of literature as 'une activité tautologue', in which the striking of an attitude and the dissolution of its contours coincide.

Barthes goes on to explore the paradox by which this anti-referential structure of language to which the *écrivain* is committed creates a product that is open to interpretation, and to being consumed as literature. Barthes is concerned with the involvement of the *écrivain* in the institutionalised literary 'parole', the articulation, re-presentation and burial of the structure of his identity in the 'parole' exchange system.

> En somme, c'est le moment même où le travail de l'écrivain devient sa propre fin, qu'il retrouve un caractère médiateur: l'écrivain conçoit la littérature comme fin, le monde la lui renvoie comme moyen: et c'est dans cette *déception* infinie, que l'écrivain retrouve le monde, un monde étrange d'ailleurs, puisque la littérature le représente comme une question, jamais, *en définitive*, comme une réponse.[20]

The *écrivain*'s experience of writing is an experience of question, which his writing does not encircle, but which it creates, articulates and explores. But in so far as he uses a literary langauge that is the property of a literary audience contributing to the history of literature and the shifts within it, the object of the *écrivain*'s pursuit is a question about literary discourse itself. The *écrivain*'s exploration of language and in language is a contribution to literature; it *is* literature. But the relationship between the praxis of the *écrivain* and his or the reader's recognition of literature is not a coincidence, but a tautology. Barthes argues that the consumption of what the *écrivain* produces as literature is the result of a misconception, or a misappropriation. The category 'literature', not only for the *écrivant*, but for readers, is one of many allowing language and experience to be divided and appropriated. But for the *écrivain* the category 'literature' is not available; it fails to present language as something he can identify with. His identity *is* the text he produces, and it is eroded in the textual transformation of memory into the literary object. The printed object the *écrivain* produces exists by virtue of a deception ('déception'), in that it appeals to the category 'literature' while attempting to create a separation from it, and its existence is also a disappointment ('déception'), in that it leaves unanswered the question of the relation of the writer to his language (literature), of the individual to history.

The reason the *écrivain* perseveres with this tautology of resistance and absorption is itself tautological. He seeks to manipulate desires and a motivation to write that literary objects at once suppress and articulate. For Barthes, these desires emerge in a process of rewriting, reading and interpreting:

> Or cette parole [the *écrivain*'s product] est une matière (infiniment) travaillée; elle est un peu comme une sur-parole, le réel ne lui est jamais qu'un prétexte (pour l'écrivain, *écrire* est un verbe intransitif); il s'ensuit qu'elle ne peut jamais expliquer le monde, ou du moins, lorsque elle feint de l'expliquer, ce n'est que pour mieux en reculer l'ambiguïté: l'explication fixée dans une *oeuvre* (travaillée), elle devient immédiatement produit ambigu du réel, auquel elle est liée *avec distance*; en somme la littérature est toujours irréaliste, mais c'est son irréalisme même qui lui permet de poser de bonnes questions au monde — sans que ces questions puissent jamais être directes....[21]

The process both articulated and petrified ('fixée') in the *écrivain*'s product is the very experience of the continuous attempt to appropriate language and to trace the development of ('expliquer') an involvement with the world. The publication of the *écrivain*'s work is its point of access to history and culture ('le réel'), but for the *écrivain* himself, this does not represent a stage in an increasing domination of his experience, but promotes a re-presentation of the question he asks about his relation to language ('produit ambigu du réel'). The difference between literary discourse and non-literary communication is not available to the *écrivain* in his writing process — it is a difference and a barrier that he both transgresses and dissolves in writing. His writing does not produce categories of expression by which he can appropriate his language and his relation to it. In the experience of the *écrivain* language is endlessly reworked and reworking: 'une matière (infiniment) travaillée'. The difference between language and experience is presented as unavailable; the questions asked of experience are questions articulated in an experience of language. The *écrivain*'s writing materialises as a search for confrontation with self, for a fixed exchange of meaning in the endless and instantaneous transformation of experience into memory. This materialisation is the experience with which the *écrivain* becomes familiar, the experience and the praxis of *intransitivity* in writing. At the same time, this is experience of an unexplained world, of intransitivity repeatedly transformed into a fixed object ('oeuvre fixée'). This 'space', in which process is dissolved into object and the production of language into its consumption, is the space that is, Barthes argues, intransitively inscribed in the praxis of the *écrivain*.

3—*MÉDITATIONS ESTHÉTIQUES*: READING AND SEEING

(i) CHRONOLOGY

Barthes, then, offers us an experience in which language is a problem and remains one. In tension with its consumption as a literary object, the language of the *écrivain* resists being identified, and in relation to it, the identity of reader and writer is steered into an open question. My discussion of this Barthesian experience was prompted by the need for a working distinction between language as process, as 'other', and language as exchange and identification. This aspect of Barthes's approach to language creates a firm foothold in the establishment of this distinction, in the form of the differing interests of the custodian (*écrivant*) and the practitioner (*écrivain*). Clearly, it is a distinction that operates an interaction between the two component elements, to the extent that the distinction between them is dynamically eroded. The artist's desire to seize the initiative is undermined by this interaction, and it remains a desire.

But in the case of Apollinaire, there is much to support the familiar critical image of his work as a fundamentally confident and enthusiastic espousal of all the artistic initiatives, traditional and innovatory alike, made available to him by his culture. At the beginning — and indeed throughout — he recognised Symbolism as the leading force in French poetry and in his own inspiration. At the same time, he involved himself in a radical questioning of the themes and aspirations of Symbolism: his decision to read 'L'Ermite' at his début in 1903 at a soirée of the Symbolist group 'La Plume' — a pastiche of Symbolist language and aspiration — testifies to this ambiguity.[22] Apollinaire was also anxious, along with Salmon, to participate in Paul Fort's project of rejuvenating the Symbolist impetus with his review *Vers et Prose*, which was finally launched in 1905.[23] On the other hand, as early as 1904, Apollinaire began to feel for a different understanding of artistic expression through his exposure to the visual arts and in particular his involvement with Fauvism and with Picasso.[24] This apparent eclecticism is easily, if superficially, interpreted as an eagerness to appropriate novelty for its own sake, and as a tendency to confuse it with liberation in expression and in thinking. But in his own writing on art Apollinaire presents his experience of art in terms of a desire that remains unrealised, or realised exclusively in the text or on the canvas and in its interpretation. In *Méditations esthétiques — les peintres cubistes*, Apollinaire writes about innovation as intellectual survival, as a confrontation with structures presented by expression itself, rather than as an unmediated embracing of language and of its assumed powers to liberate experience and to make it new.[25] Apollinaire writes about expression as though it were a resister, and I hope to show that his verse also deals with this experience, an experience that involves the artist or *écrivain* ever more deeply in the dynamics of artifice and representation.

But before exploring some of the language of *Méditations esthétiques* and the kinds of argument he conducts, a word about the problems arising from a discussion of it at this point. Firstly, it is a work that deals with an experience of painting, whereas we are in the process of discussing poetry, and 'Automne malade' in particular. Moreover, it might seem more appropriate to discuss Apollinaire's approach to painting in the context of the more obviously 'modern' texts of *Calligrammes*. But to think in this way is to disregard the way Apollinaire worked. *Alcools* is a heterogeneous body of poems, produced and reworked over a decade and more, and placed in a creative order that disregards chronology. *Méditations esthétiques* is an equally heterogeneous body of art criticism produced over the same period. The opening section is a minimally reworked version of *Les Trois Vertus plastiques*, which Apollinaire wrote as catalogue notes to the Fauvist exhibition in Le Havre in 1908. Other sections were written at various points in 1912, and *Méditations esthétiques* as an entity is an appraisal of a period in the plastic arts that coincides with the writing of many of the poems in *Alcools*.[26] The simultaneous development of Apollinaire as poet and Apollinaire as art critic suggests strong links between *Alcools* and *Méditations esthétiques*, and I want to try and explore some of the ways in which the two mesh illuminatingly in one another.

(ii) ANTECEDENTS

In *Méditations esthétiques*, Apollinaire writes of a form of expression which is irrecuperably non-figurative — a 'pure' or 'non-objective' painting, as Robert Delaunay terms it from about 1912 onwards.[27] It is a form of expression that cannot be limited to either painting or poetry, and is produced exclusively in neither mode. Apollinaire writes that the nature of poetry — verbal as well as plastic — is to resist 'un prolongement de la nature', by which nature and sensation continue to flower and to develop in language, as though language itself had the malleability and diversity of sensation.[28] By contrast, he defines the enterprise of the modern artist (poet and painter) not as an attempt to give nature access to expression and to transform it into something it is possible to reflect, but as a striving '*vers* la nature, et ils ['Les Jeunes', and Picasso in particular] n'ont avec elle aucun voisinage immédiat'.[29] The relation of an artefact to nature is a progressive one, open-ended and unfulfilled. It is a relationship of repeated discovery, both of 'la nature' and of expression itself. It is a relationship that articulates the *difference* between expression and the natural world, expression and sensation; a relationship that increasingly confronts the artist and others who engage with it with an irreducible 'otherness' in expression, the *displacement* in one another of expression and sensation.

Apollinaire's article entitled 'Les Jeunes', published in the Symbolist review *La Plume* in 1905, is his first major statement on a new non-representational art.[30] It deals with Picasso's blue and pink periods, and is included in *Méditations esthétiques*. The specificity of Apollinaire's rejection of mimesis would be blurred if we did not, however briefly, distinguish it from the Symbolist and Decadent efforts of the previous generation to reject mimetic approaches to nature.

Mallarmé dismisses mimesis and 'les hontes de la réalité' in pursuit of the essential impulses of thought itself.[31] Verlaine's subversion of mimesis takes place in the pursuit of an expression able to articulate the very sensation of existence. In the 1880s, the Decadents, by whom Verlaine's 'Langueur' was adopted as a seminal and model poem, also defined their enterprise in terms of a rejection of mimesis and of a passive naturalism.[32] The Decadent poet Baju puts it in this way:

> *Décadents* désigne un groupe de jeunes écrivains écoeurés du naturalisme et cherchant la rénovation de l'art. A la vérification plate et monotone des parnassiens, ils ont substitué une poésie vibrante et sonore, où l'on sent passer des frissons de vie. Ils ont supprimé le verbiage des vieilles littératures au profit de la sensation et de l'idée. Leurs livres sont des

quintessences. Etre décadent, c'est être sceptique, c'est accepter tous les progrès de la civilisation.[33]

The desire to develop a form of expression infinitely adaptable to the rhythms of 'progress', as well as providing access to the anfractuosities of sensation and thought, would certainly correspond to the obsessions central to Apollinaire's poetic development from about 1908 onwards. But the Decadents' appropriation of Verlaine implies an approach to expression that Apollinaire ultimately rejects. The simultaneous idealism and scepticism involved in the Decadent rejection of preceding art forms and rhetorical attitudes is magnetically attracted to the sense of 'langueur' that runs through Verlaine's work. In the case of the poem 'Langueur' itself, the sensation of failed poetic powers is delved into, and this is deemed valuable, for it justifies our engagement with it in so far as it provides an access in language to a sensation of the world, the sensation of impulse, of transience and the desire for novelty:

> L'âme seulette a mal au coeur d'un ennui dense.
> Là-bas on dit qu'il est de long combats sanglants.
> O n'y pouvoir, étant si faible aux voeux si lents,
> O n'y vouloir fleurir un peu cette existence!   (l. 5)

Verlaine's pursuit of sensation through expression is an exploration of the melodic in verse. 'De la musique avant toute chose' Verlaine demands of himself and of poetry in 'Art poétique', a kind of retrospective appraisal of some of his major works.[34] But at the same time, it is clear that Verlaine's entry into poetic discourse is involved with simultaneous developments in the plastic arts, and this provides a sharp comparison with Apollinaire's own involvement with the painting of his generation. Verlaine's poetic sensibility seems to participate in the creative initiative set up by the Impressionists in painting. Verlaine's success in dissolving formal constraint on poetic discourse, in ridding it of mythological references, allegorical purpose and philosophical speculation, puts him in the same ideological frame as Renoir or Monet. In reaction to the innovators they succeeded — Delacroix, Ingres, Courbet, who came to appear as producing the last chapter in the history of the representation of nature on canvas — the Impressionists developed a vocabulary of textures, a network of trapped light and intricate subdivisions, in which the quotidian, the anti-allegorical is at once explored and exploded. Controlled splashes of colour are exploited as the language of sensation itself.[35]

The initial impulse in Verlaine's work is, in a sense, a response to

22

the Impressionist creative space. His liking for the poetic sketch format, for open air rural scenes, for scenes from a kind of suburban 'bohème' and from street existence, reveals an objective he shares with the early Monet and Renoir: that of transforming and humanising the subject matter and purpose of art. For example, the 'La Grenouillère' paintings that Monet and Renoir both produced[36] — contrasting with Monet's later abstraction of light into texture in his treatment of waterlilies, and in the series of haystacks and of Rouen cathedral — can be seen as involving the kind of mysticism of the quotidian that emerges from some of the poems in *Jadis et naguère*:[37]

> O ce cri sur la mer, cette voix dans les bois!
> Ce sera comme quand on ignore les causes:
> Un lent réveil après bien des métempsycoses:
> Les choses seront plus les mêmes qu'autrefois
>
> Dans cette rue, au cœur de la ville magique
> Où des orgues moudront des gigues dans les soirs,
> Où les cafés auront des chats sur les dressoirs,
> Et que traverseront des bandes de musique.[38]

But to read Verlaine's verse in the same creative space as, for example, Monet's *Rue de la Banvolle à Honfleur* (1864) or his *Boulevard des Capucines* (1873) is ultimately to falsify the nature of Verlaine's poetic development, and to obscure the desire it expresses to arrive at a uniquely linguistic form of magic.[39]

> Car nous voulons la Nuance encor,
> Pas la Couleur, rien que la nuance!
> Oh! la nuance seule fiance
> Le rêve au rêve et la flûte au cor![40]

This emphasis on 'nuance', this demand for a dissolution of contrast between colours might appear to be a poetic response to the Impressionist treatment of colour in relation to light. But in fact, this 'nuance', in terms of Verlaine's poetic development and of the Symbolist-Decadent context to which he contributes, is a melodic one, and to this extent represents a rejection of the plastic and of the mimetic constraints it was perceived to impose on the artist. These lines from 'Art poétique'

> Rien de plus cher que la chanson grise
> Où l'Indécis au Précis se joint.   (1.7)

express the objective of Verlaine's poetry, and indicate the means it has at its disposal. 'Grise' is not emphasised for its neutrality, but expresses a kind of sensual ecstasy ('grise'/drunk), in which the stated and the unstated, the male and the female interpenetrate, dissolve the difference that constitutes them as separate, and *in doing so* rediscover language — a language of song and of melody.

In relation to such a power of expression, painting, within the Verlainian framework, emerges as a form of expression that restricts the power of the artist to expand experience and intervene creatively in the barriers he is confronted with. Despite the Impressionist exploration of colour and light, it was still not conceived of by its counterparts in poetry as producing a plastic language independent of representation. Octave Nadal puts it in these terms: having said that Verlaine is 'à la croisée des chemins, d'une poésie historiquement située entre l'impressionnisme pictural et l'impressionnisme musical', he comes to the conclusion that 'le pouvoir plénier reste de toute évidence celui de la voix et non de l'image, du chant et non de la représentation'.[41] 'Le chant', the creation and exploration of melody in verse, is envisaged as the source of pure poetry, of a poetry able to create, to penetrate experience, and magically to transform sensation into language. The plastic, by contrast, is regarded as spatial rather than temporal, as context-bound, as limited in the movement it can envisage and create. It imposes its own rhetoric, its own form on sensation, rather than opening itself to sensation and inventing the power to create an infinite access to it. The marrying of 'l'Indécis' to the 'Précis' is a process in which Verlaine hopes to succeed by dissolving a sense of other, by penetrating alienation in the discovery of a flexible, melodious language able to express the continuity and the texture of alienation itelf. The pursuit of interpenetration and of a melodic dissolution of difference is not only directed at sensations of ecstasy, but also melancholy, 'langueur' and defeat. Verlaine's desire is to create a melodic harmony of sensation and interpretation, a language moulded to the psychic textures of stimuli, a language that sublimates difference, and offers an indefinite access of self to other and to creativity.

Verlaine ultimately rejects the plastic in order to direct the creativity he pursues at a further dissolution of difference, and at a reconciliation of self with time. By contrast, in the development of his thinking from 1905 to 1913, which *Méditations esthétiques* represents, Apollinaire confronts the plastic as a renewal of the search for a genuinely non-mimetic form of expression, though rejecting Impressionism in the strongest terms.[42] The question arises as to whether Apollinaire's approach, as distinct from Verlaine's, involves an intensified confrontation with difference. Initially, this speculation seems unjustified, in that Apollinaire compares the new painting, the new art he is observing and striving for, to music — thus apparently appealing to the Verlainian, Symbolist-Decadent pursuit of a melodic language indefinitely open to the mobile world of sensation: 'On s'achemine ainsi vers un art entièrement nouveau, qui sera à la peinture, telle qu'on l'avait envisagée jusqu'ici, ce que la musique est à la littérature.'[43]

But compare Apollinaire's statement to Nadal's self-evidently less intense account of the operation of melody and harmony in the development of Verlaine's language:

> Le pouvoir plénier reste de toute évidence celui de la voix et non de l'image, du chant et non de la représentation. Verlaine devait appréhender l'intériorité du songe dans les structures les plus fluides et comme informelles d'une langue prête au chant plus qu'à l'idée. Son goût pour la chanson et la romance ne fut, comme chez Nerval et Apollinaire, que la reconnaissance du caractère organiquement rhythmique et gestuel de la parole accordée au sentiment même de la durée.[44]

The ambitious claims that Nadal makes for Verlaine's and Apollinaire's poetry are both all-embracing and specifically textured: poetry is a musical, non-speculating language, the domain of which is the experience of time and transience, decay and rejuvenation, spontaneous creation and death.[45] But Apollinaire's description of a new reality of expression is not non-speculating, nor does it deal unproblematically with the access of sensation to language or with the dissolution of barriers. It is a statement based on analogy; it constructs a series of hiatuses, either side of which no equivalences are established. The 'entirely new' art that Apollinaire perceives is articulated in the leap from 'old' to 'new' painting, from literature (constantly in movement) to music (pure movement). His statement 'about' new art is a description of no particular work of art; the repeated displacements it comprises are themselves an enactment of the new art.

The poetry of Verlaine, on the other hand, as characterised by Nadal and enacted in poems such as 'Chanson d'automne' and 'Crépuscule du soir mystique', represents, despite its claims to a disruption of mimesis, what in Apollinaire's terms is 'un prolongement de la nature'.[46]

> Le souvenir avec le Crépuscule
> Rougoie et tremble à l'ardent horizon
> De L'Espérance en flamme qui recule
> …
> Mêle dans une immense pâmoison
> Le Souvenir avec le Crépuscule.[47]

The Verlainian enterprise is not to confront self with other, but to *dissolve* self in other, where other *is* nature, the experience of self in sensations of nature and of the concrete.[48] Verlaine's emphasis on the senses, for which he was so admired, and even his liberation of the senses in a poetry aimed at its own radicalisation, are still passive responses to experience. They express both a plea for and an expectation of inclusion ('le sentiment même de la durée'), rather than a will to speculate on difference and otherness, or to confront the fact of inclusion in language and in otherness itself.[49]

(iii) PERCEPTION, PERSPECTIVE, INTERVENTION

It seems that it is to this kind of speculation that Apollinaire is addressing himself in his rejection of an art that willingly establishes itself as 'un prolongement de la nature'. He deals in a complex way with dissolving and mobile differences, whereas the art he exposes as static is one that attempts to transcend difference. It attempts to reduce the threat confronting any user of language, the threat created by the fact that experience — of the world, of sensation, of memory — is irreducible to the language it prompts, and in which it is not located or objectified:

> Il y a des poètes auxquels une muse dicte leurs oeuvres, il y a des artistes dont la main est dirigée par un être inconnu qui se sert d'eux comme d'un instrument. Pour eux, point de fatigue, car ils ne travaillent point et peuvent beaucoup produire, à toute heure, tous les jours, en tout pays et en toute saison, ce ne sont point des hommes, mais des instruments poétiques ou artistiques. Leur raison est sans force contre eux-mêmes, ils ne luttent point et leurs oeuvres ne portent point de traces de lutte. Ils ne sont point divins et peuvent se passer d'eux-mêmes. Ils sont comme le prolongement de la nature et leurs oeuvres ne passent point par l'intelligence.[50]

By strongly emphasising the action of thinking in the production of the worked ('travaillent') artistic artefact, Apollinaire is urgently repudiating the notion of art as springing from inspiration ('une muse'). Such art, he seems to suggest, abdicates the right to confront existence through expression. For Apollinaire, intelligence, directing thought at experience, is not a process of automatic exchange; instead, it produces a struggle. It does not establish the contours of the object it interprets, or uncover the experience occupying its attention; thus many writers remain victims: 'leur raison est sans force contre eux-mêmes'. In opposition to the approach to imagination and expression implied by these poets and artists from whom he dissociates himself, Apollinaire

26

suggests that the intellect is in conflict with attempts to understand experience, and that this conflict must be accepted and internalised if any progressive expression is to take place. But to confront reason and to accept the struggle it instigates is to work with a reason that, far from locating objects in space or appropriating experience, proliferates its own operations and confronts thought with itself.

For Apollinaire in *Méditations esthétiques*, human beings are confronted with their own mortality and, simultaneously, with their desire to dominate their experience of it. It is out of this conflict that a new painting arises, along with new demands made on thinking and its relation to the senses:

> La flamme est le symbole de la peinture et les trois
> vertus plastiques flambent en rayonnant.
> La flamme a la pureté qui ne souffre rien d'étranger
> et transforme cruellement en elle-même ce qu'elle atteint.
> Elle a cette unité magique qui fait que si on la divise,
> chaque flammèche est semblable à la flamme unique.[51]

In Apollinaire's presentation of the flame analogy, experience of self in relation to the world, is confronted in the artistic striving to move in between the rhetorical structures of mimesis, and to move through the limitations imposed by the status quo of sensation ('leur raison est sans force contre eux-mêmes'). Hence the flame is a process of purification; it establishes the independence of the artistic creation, which appears to move of its own volition and to be illuminated in its own light. On the other hand, this light, being a flame, is a purification of the material exactly in so far as it *is* material. The textuality of Apollinaire's analogy prevents his reader from envisaging a magical cooperation between experience and its domination in expression: this is not the experience of the text. The independent creativity envisaged *is* the internal relations in Apollinaire's analogy; the text as text displaces the purity it strives for. Moreover, 'la flamme' is an incarnation of this displacement: the diversity of experience is expressed in the repeated singularity of the flame. Each instance of the flame is not only 'semblable à la flamme unique', but, in time and in the dissolving contours of the analogy, it is the exclusive representation of purity and the pursuit of it. 'La flamme unique' realises purity by taking its place: 'la flamme ... transforme cruellement en elle-même ce qu'elle atteint'. Purity grapples with displacement in the most intense way.

Apollinaire does not treat thought as though it dissolved in language.

Instead, in relation to language, he represents thinking in terms of a continually unfolding desire: the desire to transform displacement into place, otherness into immediacy. This desire becomes increasingly intense as it becomes clear that the two cannot be isolated from each other in Apollinaire's text, or in relation to each other. Both are represented in the analogy of 'la flamme', which continually transforms itself into image. It is the unthinking acceptance of this apparent equivalence between name and image as the magical product of 'inspiration' that Apollinaire is characterising as oppressive.

In opposition to the notion of inspiration and to the way its apologists conceive of language, Apollinaire recognises language as a system producing resistance. Apollinaire confronts the artist with a choice, and categorises him according to his decision. Either, in the name of 'une muse', he can disengage his intelligence from the fact of language and the experience of it, and attempt to relish in the process of expression by transcending it. In this event, his work is merely passive: 'Ils peuvent être émouvants sans que les harmonies qu'ils suscitent se soient humanisées'.[52] Or he can strive to confront language as resistance, and as an intervention in experience. In this way, he strives to intervene in the terms of his experience ('humaniser'), and to be born, through this intervention, *in* the resistance proliferated by language. His desire, in doing this, is to involve himself with the process of language itself and to contribute to it, rather than producing mere instances of it. It is on this fine, potentially tautological distinction that Apollinaire pins his ambitions for the artist — just as Barthes does, in 'Ecrivains et écrivants', in his casting of difference and opposition as intransitive.

But Apollinaire's language is an incarnation of tautology and of speculation about it, of language confronting language. Following immediately on from the sentences on the attitude of the old art to intelligence and its role in expression, Apollinaire characterises the experience of Picasso and the new art generally in the following way:

> D'autres poètes, d'autres artistes au contraire sont là qui s'efforcent, ils vont vers la nature et n'ont avec elle aucun voisinage immédiat, ils doivent tout tirer d'eux-mêmes et nul démon, aucune muse ne les inspire. Ils habitent dans la solitude et rien n'est exprimé que ce qu'ils ont eux-mêmes balbutié, balbutié si souvent qu'ils arrivent parfois d'efforts en efforts, de tentatives en tentatives à formuler ce qu'ils souhaitent formuler. Hommes créés à l'image de Dieu, ils se reposeront un jour pour admirer leur ouvrage. Mais que de fatigues, que d'imperfection, que de grossièretés![53]

Apollinaire's Christian analogy is in tension, here, with his character-isation of genuinely creative art, even though it also supports it — hence his immediate and bathetic defusion of the analogy. In Apollinaire's dismantling of the Christian hierarchy of redemption, man, in the image of God, *is* the unattainability of God; man *is* image. It is con-tinually in terms of image that he comes to terms with his existence. But this is not a conventional, distinct poetic image. The image arti-culates the process itself of writing and of painting, of rewriting and reworking ('balbutié si souvent'). The poet/artist creates a world in the image of himself, and lays claims to an independent, 'divine' creativity. But it is not an image he can be satisfied with as he stands back and evaluates; it is not an image he can locate or even see as such. This image negates the notion of a source object, an original experience of the world emerging from its dialogue with the artist's artefact. The poet/artist, cast in the mould that Apollinaire envisages, expresses the fact that he sees, he is defined while the objects he creates take form.

Simultaneously, within these contexts, he is blind. Each image displaces others, and is invaded by them. The fact of seeing involves the artist/*écrivain* in a continuous, material image, dissolving distinct 'moments' of recognition. Turning the simultaneity another way, every point in this continuity incarnates a resumption of thought, a rebirth of memory, and opens the way to the creation of a meaningful novelty.

Summarising the argument so far, we can say that the activity of artistic expression consists, for Apollinaire, in the creation of an image of perception itself, in opposition to the object in perception. But it is clear that a difference between object of perception and image in per-ception cannot be definitely located, and that the rejection, or the dissolving, of the object of perception is not seen to be complete. The object is there, if only as paint. Yet the painting, or the poem, cannot be identified in terms of an experience independent of itself; nor, as a finished objct, can it be identified in terms of the process in which it is produced, although it is on this ground that it appeals to the viewer or the reader. So what is the painting or the poem? In its production as well as in its consumption, it confronts the spectator and the reader with difference, with the failure of interpretation to appropriate the art-object itself. As he interprets, the interpreter is confronted with a repeated failure and a continual desire to take possession of otherness, and this quest takes on the materiality of experience itself.

Apollinaire's comment about exhaustion, imperfection, and artistic atrocities, then, signals a desperate awareness of the incomplete. The experience of difference is not only ever-present, but elusive and unlocatable. An image of perception — an independent, 'divine' intervention in language and experience — is nowhere made definite. The image of perception is articulated *in* the process that seeks to establish its 'distinctness'. It is produced in expressing a desire for difference — a difference between image in the devalued sense of appearance, and the reality of experience ('la vérité'). Ironically, the production, the search for the image of perception threatens the artist in his 'divine' capacity to intervene creatively in experience. It seems it cannot be produced without functioning like the appearance-bound images it seeks to undermine. Apollinaire emphasises the impossibility of the new artists' objective — it is not only 'divin', but 'inhumain':

> Avant tout, les artistes sont des hommes qui veulent devenir inhumains.
> Ils cherchent péniblement les traces de l'inhumanité, traces que l'on ne rencontre nulle part dans la nature.
> Elles sont la vérité et en dehors d'elles nous ne connaissons aucune réalité.
>
> Mais, on ne découvrira jamais la réalité une fois pour toutes. La vérité sera toujours nouvelle.
> Autrement, elle n'est qu'un système plus misérable que la nature.
> En ce cas, la déplorable vérité, plus lointaine, moins distincte, moins réelle chaque jour réduirait la peinture à l'état d'écriture plastique simplement destinée à faciliter les relations entre gens de la même race.
> De nos jours, on trouverait vite la machine à reproduire de tels signes, sans entendement.[54]

In the first of these two units (which conclude the first section of 'Sur la peinture', and therefore the first part of *Méditations esthétiques*) Apollinaire writes as though searching for something other than a passive submission to observing nature were to be continuously groping for a distinction that is nowhere in evidence, and that his own terminology explicitly refuses to provide: 'l'inhumanité', 'la vérité', 'la réalité'. 'La vérité' — the third of 'les trois vertus plastiques' — is the reality of experience, and the sense that this reality cannot be named within the complex relations that involve our thoughts with appearance.[55] The paradox that Apollinaire repeatedly discovers is that the creative urge to rethink appearance and to remove the artist from its dominance can only be pursued in relation to appearance itself. The experience of difference in terms of which he strives to give shape to perception cannot be simplistically distinguished from the experience of what is *there*. This is implicit in Apollinaire's manipulation of a term as ambiguous as 'la réalité' — 'réalité' as authenticity as well as 'réalité' as the concrete world of appearance. Apollinaire is searching for a distinction between these two 'réalités', and this desire is a fundamental one, however tantalising, obscure and resolutely metaphoric this and the rest of the 'Sur la peinture' section may strike us. It is the desire to find forms flexible enough — 'abstract' enough — to give shape to the very experience of perception; and the vitality of this desire is that it remains unfulfilled. The experience of perception is not what is seen, even if the object we look at is a painting. The creative drive is maintained in that it is *not* recognised, *not* incarnated in the objects it produces. Thus the artist seeking a 'divin' and 'inhumain' intervention in the dynamics of perception and expression repeatedly encounters failure. The distinction between passivity, between non-humanised harmonies and an authentic, creative otherness, is not definitively established in a finished work of art. It is in the failure to establish this distinction that the artist develops the image of perception: 'Hommes créés à l'image de Dieu, ils se reposeront un jour pour admirer leur ouvrage. Mais que de fatigues, que d'imperfection, que de grossièretés!' [56]

It is the reality of this failure that Apollinaire goes on to confront in concluding the first section of 'Sur la peinture'. 'Les traces', the traces of the truth, the sense of difference in terms of which perception can be explored, are nowhere in evidence; 'la vérité' that Apollinaire seeks 'sera toujours nouvelle'. Apollinaire's use of the term 'trace' suggests an oscillation of the kind with which we are becoming familiar, and we can summarise it like this. On the one hand, Apollinaire discovers the fact of language, of experience overrun by passive approaches to expression: 'des harmonies non humanisées'. On the other hand, he strives for a creative, independent intervention in the relation of expression to experience: 'la vérité', 'les traces de l'inhumanité', otherness. It is the potential dissolving of the second in the first that constructs the failure that Apollinaire is confronting. For the distinction between perception and the object cannot be established, it is the object of a desire. In the same way, the barrier that makes the unconscious unavailable to consciousness cannot be located, even though the unconscious is banished by it, emerging as vestiges of memory and traces of the self.[57] Apollinaire is exploring the relation between failure and a creative consciousness, the sense of undermined creativity that is a crucial element in the experience for which he is seeking new forms. Let us remind ourselves of the expressions of failure that abound in the units we are reading and that draw the first section of 'Sur la peinture' to a close:

> la vérité sera toujours nouvelle
> un système plus misérable que la nature
> la déplorable vérité, plus lointaine, moins distincte, moins
> réelle chaque jour
> la peinture à l'état d'écriture plastique
> la machine à reproduire de tels signes, sans entendement[58]

The objective, perspective-bound status of the object is equated in Apollinaire's writing with the fact of language, of paint and canvas, along with the fact that in any perception and in any communication we *select*. This is the situation to be penetrated, 'seen' by the artist, transformed into the traces that structure it. But these traces are not available — either in perspective-bound nature or in expression. To assume an essential truth, essentially and absolutely hidden by nature and by the fact of appearance, would not be different from assuming 'objectivity' in nature and in appearance, or from using them to refer to truth in a framework of convention as the *écrivant* would. As Apollinaire recognises, 'la vérité' could turn out to be no different from 'la nature', or from the images produced in perspective — 'un système plus misérable que la nature'. What prevents this is its unavailability: 'Ils cherchent péniblement'; 'la vérité sera toujours nouvelle'. The image of perception is nothing other than the traces of its displacement. The reality of perception is that it is displaced as appearance; the truth of perception is that the traces of its displacement are *in* appearance — in light and in objects, in nature — the space of their absence.

To continue within Apollinaire's terminology, there can be no creative 'écriture plastique'. Read straightforwardly, it implies a transitionless access from writing to painting, object to perception, appearance to trace. But in effect, such an access exists only among producers and consumers who agree as to its function — 'gens de la même race'.[59] To assume such an access is to capitulate in the face of language and of its power to impose statements, images and signs — 'une machine à reproduire des signes'. It is to adopt a mechanistic and passive approach to language as opposed to a creative one. Apollinaire discovers this creative independence, an intervention in language and in himself, in 'Le Brasier':

> J'ai jeté dans le noble feu
> Que je transporte et que j'adore
> De vives mains et même feu
> Ce Passé ces têtes de morts
> Flamme je fais ce que tu veux[60]

In fact, Apollinaire's entire discourse in *Méditations esthétiques* is a rejection and a negation of 'écriture plastique'. There is no access from Apollinaire's writing to painting or to any particular painting; the dominant and overwhelming difference articulated in the text is the difference between the language Apollinaire invents and the painting he sees. The text denies the possibility of an 'écriture plastique' able to mould itself to the anfractuosities of experience. The difference between painting and text is not one that keeps the two distinct and opposed to one another; it is not a difference that can be measured or given the qualities of an object. The painting Apollinaire sees comes to life as text, and is absent in his text. The text operates in the same way as the art he sees: it transforms everything in its path into itself, like the flame transforming the world and experience of it into fire.[61]

The relation of Apollinaire's text to painting is the relation of Picasso's painting, as Apollinaire re-presents it, to the object. The whole of the 'Sur la peinture' section of *Méditations esthétiques* is so irrecuperably and profusely metaphoric that Apollinaire's discussions of particular painters in the following 'Peintres nouveaux' section may come as something of a relief to his reader. Even though Apollinaire refers to specific painters and works in 'Sur la peinture', his concepts of light, fire and illusion do not specify particular images but deal with a dynamic involving painting, seeing and writing. In fact, though, the opening paragraphs of the 1905 *La Plume* article I referred to earlier, which is included almost unchanged at the beginning of Apollinaire's long section on Picasso, are equally provocative. The images seem to occlude Picasso's work at the same time as encapsulating its development and projecting its desires. But Apollinaire does go on to present an experience of specific and recognisable Picasso features and images — children and grieving mothers, old men begging without humility, adolescents prematurely aged and with distant expressions, a tender and urgent eroticism. Having followed Picasso's development through to the pink period, Apollinaire comments more extensively on Picasso's harlequin series. Distinctions dissolve between humans and animals, male and female: 'Mais placés à la limite de la vie, les animaux sont humains et les sexes indécis.'[62] The boundaries of difference are both approached and sequestered in the space between Apollinaire's writing and Picasso's canvas: differences between female and male, language and silence, image and experience. Imperceptibly, Apollinaire's imaged narrative moves towards epistemological questions. This does not mean that the tone or the vocabulary of the narrative change: the seamlessness of its development from descriptive imagery to questions that elude the framework of imagery is characteristic of him. Apollinaire paves the way early on in his text, in his references to the figures in Picasso's blue period, for the transformation it is to enact: 'Ces enfants qu'on n'embrasse pas comprennent tant! Maman, aime-moi bien! Ils savent sauter et les tours qu'ils réussissent sont des évolutions mentales.'[63] Earlier, Apollinaire uses images of pathos and charity, and he develops them here. An image expressing a mythology of love and charity develops so as to express the psychological structures of insecurity and grief, and to give space to the abstract gestures of thought and sensation. Later on, in his comments on the harlequins, Apollinaire again distinguishes between the (Greek) mythological power that the spectator might associate with the images, and the obscure desires that, in his view, are expressed by these images:

> On ne peut pas confondre ces saltimbanques avec des histrions. Leur spectateur doit être pieux, car ils célèbrent des rites muets avec *une agilité difficile*. C'est cela qui distinguait ce peintre des potiers grecs dont son dessin approchait parfois. Sur les terres peintes, les prêtres barbus et bavards offraient en sacrifice des animaux résignés et sans destinée. Ici, la virilité est imberbe, mais se manifeste dans les nerfs des bras maigres, des méplats du visage et les animaux sont mystérieux.[64]

Apollinaire hints at a desire that is displaced in sensation, at the same time as articulated ('se manifeste') in a repeatedly incomplete ('mystérieux') exploration of sensation ('nerfs'), and in the impenetrably silent relations uncovered between memory and the world of objects.

As Apollinaire delves into these images that have structured his experience so dramatically, specific images are explored in such a way that they dissolve in the dynamics of the text itself. Moreover, the process Apollinaire is striving to locate remains 'mystérieux'; it is enacted, represented in the text, rather than being given a specific shape. Apollinaire's writing on Picasso in *Méditations esthétiques* develops, then, from engaging with images, however vestigially, to engaging in the kind of metaphoric writing we saw in 'Sur la peinture', which refers more and more exclusively to its own terminology and imagery. This development in Apollinaire's section on Picasso takes place as the text moves on from the 1905 *La Plume* article and confronts Picasso's later works. The process is completed when Apollinaire dramatically announces that his text, following Picasso's development, has taken us right up to the point where Picasso is drawn into Cubism: 'Alors, sévèrement, il a interrogé l'univers'.[65]

The kind of writing Apollinaire embarks on again at this point, in dissolving specific images and the specificity of works, presents Cubism and Picasso's part in it as residing essentially in the relation of expression to objects. The text takes the reader from Picasso's harlequin figures to a statement as general as 'un art étonnant et dont la lumière est sans limites', and in the process removes specific Picasso art-objects from the text.[66] But this removal is *not* an expression of disinterest in the object, either in Apollinaire's thinking or in Picasso's — quite the opposite. This is the tension in Picasso's Cubism that Apollinaire is drawn to and that his text enacts. Apollinaire makes the point by opening this new stage in his presentation of Picasso by making a paradoxical reference to specific objects, in particular to ones Picasso included unchanged in his works:

> Il [Picasso] s'est habitué à l'immense lumière des profondeurs. Et parfois, il n'a pas dédaigné de confier à la clarté, des objets authentiques, une chanson de deux sous, un timbre-poste véritable, un morceau de toile cirée sur laquelle est imprimée la cannelure d'un siège. *L'art du peintre n'ajouterait aucun élément pittoresque à la vérité de ces objects.*[67]

'La vérité de ces objets' is the crucial challenge thrown down to expression and to the desire to extend its scope. It is in the artist's response to this challenge that Apollinaire sees him developing the power to intervene creatively in the structures of perception. Equally, as Apollinaire watches Picasso respond to this challenge, he sees the object disappear on the canvas as well as in his own text. For it is not only the case that the new artist resolutely faces up to and accepts the irreducible 'object-ness' of the object — 'la vérité de ces objets'. The object is also the context in which 'l'immense lumière des profondeurs' is articulated. This light-in-depth is the playground of Picasso's creativity, and for Apollinaire, it gives him the scope to approach objects positively and 'humaniser' his experience of them.

Clearly, Apollinaire is approaching light in a way that is consistent with the metaphors he develops throughout.[68] Light expresses the urgency of experience, the involvement of memory with perception of the present. Equally, Apollinaire develops his metaphor of light-in-depth in order to represent the creative intervention in this involvement he is pursuing. But the metaphor is developed in terms of an unarrested continuum of dissolving obstacles and differences — an immensity consisting of light and depth, in which light and darkness interact and are not opposed, whereas the object itself is *discrete*. It articulates its difference from others. In Apollinaire's text, the object, which throws down the challenge to creativity and demands intervention, disappears in the continuity of light and depth. Equally, the perception of this continuity is displaced in the object itself. So the inclusion of objects in the painting, potentially an unproblematic extension of the scope of expression and imagination, is in fact presented by the dynamics of the text as a network of hinges, pivots and barriers. The vision of 'l'immense lumière des profondeurs', while referring to an opening out of potential in expression, equally represents the burial of this desire in what we see — objects and light itself.

The same ambiguity continues in Apollinaire's appraisal of Picasso's treatment of specific objects. On a first reading, the object in Picasso's work opens out in Apollinaire's text and reveals itself progressively; its structure as an object materialises as the viewer becomes involved:

> Imitant les plans pour représenter les volumes, Picasso donne des divers éléments qui composent les objets une énumération si complète et si aiguë qu'ils ne prennent point figure d'objet grâce au travail des spectateurs qui, par force, en perçoivent la simultanéité, mais en raison même de leur arrangement.
>
> Cet art est-il plus profond qu'élevé? Il ne se passe point de l'observation de la nature et agit sur nous aussi familièrement qu'elle-même.[69]

Apollinaire is responding to the Cubist volumetric practice, initiated by Braque and Picasso in particular, of presenting objects from diverse points in perspective simultaneously. This practice, which has the effect of dissolving the difference between angles in perspective, is designed to liberate viewer and painter from the illusion that appearance is meaningfully represented in the conventions that equate it with reality, with nature or with truth. The Cubist objective is to dismantle the illusion by which the object is specified as occupying a single point in space or in time. In the Cubist analysis, the totality of the object consists in the infinity of points of view in which it exists not only in space but also in memory — 'une énumération complète'. The Cubist engagement is not with the perception of objects as such; it is an intervention in the experience of perception — something not reducible

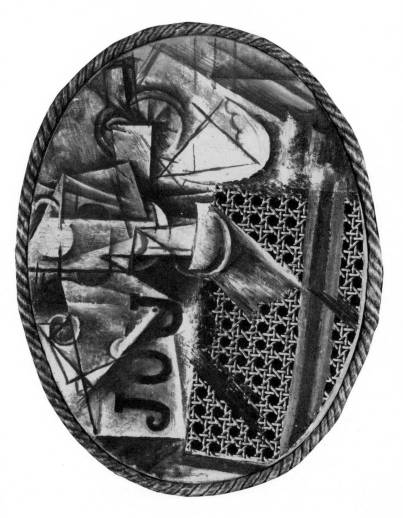

1 Pablo Picasso:
Nature morte à la chaise
cannée, 1912 (photograph by
courtesy of the Réunion des
Musées Nationaux, Paris),
© DACS 1987

to specific objects, but articulated by them. The specificity Cubist expression discovers in objects comes to grips with the viewer's or the painter's own experience of objects as such. Cubist painting articulates a relation to appearance, the experience of difference *and* familiarity that appearance produces: objects are presented in 'une énumération that is not only 'complète' but 'aiguë'.

In tension with this, Apollinaire implies that simultaneity is not itself the crucial element in the revelation of objects. He presents it rather as a self-evident, though none the less vital, aspect of the reality of perception and the object. The artist's creativity depends on the power of his 'arrangement' of diverse aspects of the object. Perhaps Apollinaire is implicitly recognising that the enumeration of aspects of the object, and of the angles in perspective in which it appears, is as indefinite as the divisibility of time itself. In any event, the paragraphs we are reading are constantly shifting, and are not only concerned with presenting simultaneity as an unproblematic source of creativity. The fact that Cubist art presents simultaneity as a self-evident reality of the object in perception means that the object is always there still, waiting to be explored, and to allow experience to be recognised in a different way.

This self-evident quality of simultaneity in perception could be expressed in the following linear reordering of Apollinaire's consciously ambiguous and multidirectional syntax: 'les spectateurs perçoivent *par force* la simultanéité des divers éléments de l'objet'. But 'par force' also suggests difficulty — the effort to penetrate a complex artefact or to come to terms with a worked surface. Apollinaire develops this difficulty by pointing out that it is the 'arrangement' of the object's fragmentation on which the artist relies in his pursuit of a creative engagement with the object. The entirety of the object in space and in perception shifts from being appropriated as a sum total ('une énumération complète') to being represented as an interplay of planes. An interplay of planes is viewed in terms of the discrete aspects of which it consists; but it is also viewed simultaneously as an entirety. On the level of the discrete elements in the represented object, each one in fact not only displaces the object, but effaces the others from view so that they materialise as the subject of a search. On the other hand, as an entirety, the Cubist interplay articulates objects in the movement of the eye between the elements in the painting. In the painting as interplay, the object, its depth in space and in perception, is constructed in a material that extends the present in space. Simultaneously, the object is displaced, for the same material confronts the viewer repeatedly with the two-dimensional. Creativity neighbours with impenetrability, and what is initially presented as an opening out is simultaneously presented as a network of barriers. This visual texture of displacement becomes increasingly expressive, increasingly familiar: 'un art ... qui agit sur nous ... familièrement'. It articulates the seamless interchange of memory and the present. And it is the traces of *this* interchange that are articulated in the movement of the eye between the elements in the 'arrangement' of the painting.

In these two short paragraphs on the Cubist disruption of perspective, Apollinaire presents us with two almost identical alternatives, 'la simultanéité' and 'l'arrangement', in order to confront us with difference as a problem. The part cannot be distinguished in the whole; an evaluation of the painting cannot be distinguished from the improvisatory movements of the eye as it 'interprets'. Moreover, the painting is not a representation of an object that can be distinguished from the painting itself, or located in terms of its relation to the painting. While Apollinaire conceives of progressive expression in terms of the discovery of a difference, this difference is a continuity in which identification disappears in the traces of perception. Yet Apollinaire is not imagining a seamless transition from perception to expression, but describing a process by which the object in perception is replaced and dismantled by the object in expression. It is this process itself that is continuously under definition and that the 'new' artist strives to assimilate and intervene in. The continuous difference emerging from Apollinaire's view of progressive painting is not a melting of barriers. It is a continuity of lack, and of the dissolving categories of past and present; the past exploding in a present that extends as it is desired. *This* is what is expressed in the Cubist abolition of perspective, and in the Cubist fiction of the total object. The Cubist artefact confronts the viewer with an experience of seeing that *is* the experience itself of seeing and reading the object — but an object locked into being seen repeatedly for the first time. For the object is not distinguished in a context, or in relation to one. Context resists being circumscribed and eludes being appropriated. It becomes the material of a search, and it extends the present indefinitely, as the eye discovers texture on the canvas. The eye's movement between the elements in the 'arrangement' of the painting constructs the central Cubist fiction: that the totality of angles in perspective on an object can be both experienced and expressed. But the eye's movement is only movement, it is never arrested and it is confined to a surface. The fiction it produces is one that allows the object to be transformed into an image of perception and set in *motion*. The creative potential of this fiction is both asserted and undermined. For the object-as-painting both incarnates *and* merely leaves traces of the bright, conceptual coincidence of perception and memory.[70]

This is the familiarity with the object or the natural world, and with experience as such, that Apollinaire discovers Cubism is dealing with and focusing on. It is the familiarity of the experience of difference, of the sourcelessness of identity, its articulation as uniquely *other* in every movement of the eye and in every group of objects fading and regrouping brightly in memory. The Cubist experience of the painting incarnates 'otherness' in that it is indistinguishable from the object, it acts on us like the object-in-perception. Cubism is a confrontation with expression that erodes the distinction Apollinaire seeks between the passive and the creative responses, for it brings the artist back face to face with objects. Cubism involves us in a *struggle*, the desire to represent the fact that objects *express*. It is *this* struggle that confronts Apollinaire with danger and with potential failure. As we saw, Apollinaire is made anxious by the spectre of an art transforming itself into a ritualistic, automatic exchange of signs dealing exclusively with the private experiences of a particular and ever more restricted group:

> ... la déplorable vérité, plus lointaine, moins distincte, moins réelle chaque jour réduirait la peinture à l'état d'écriture plastique simplement destinée à faciliter les relations entre gens de la même race.
>
> De nos jours, on trouverait vite la machine à reproduire de tels signes, sans entendement.[71]

The paradox that Apollinaire grapples with is that the spectre of the new art as well as the old lapsing into a shared but increasingly passive response to appearance is a consequence of the objectives of Cubism and the new art itself. It derives from the desire to replace the object in perception with an image of perception. But as we have seen, the distinction between the two remains the material of desire, and the representation of perception depends on a desire that is unfulfilled. Although in Cubism representation of objects is replaced with articulations of perception, objects are not simply removed, perception is not simply let loose and creative imagination uncovered. The object is *in* perception, it is the form that perception takes and in which it is displaced. This is the reality of the object — its 'vérité'. Neither perception nor the object is discovered in Cubist expression; both dissolve as they are focused on in an extending and textured present. As we have seen, Cubist expression operates on perception *just like* the object — a displaced object, a displaced context: '[Cet art] ne se passe point de l'observation de la nature et agit sur nous aussi familièrement qu'elle-même'.[72] In Apollinaire's appreciation of Cubism, perception *is* its articulation in the painting and in the eye's improvisation. Equally, perception is everywhere and nowhere in the painting, in the space between elements in the 'arrangement' of objects that proliferate in the painting and are not captured in enumeration. Cubist expression is intransitive, it sets the object in a *representation* of motion, producing the image of perception. Simultaneously, the Cubist artefact is autonomous, it presents us with its irreducible, *object-like* 'otherness' — 'la vérité des objets'.[73]

4—'L'ADIEU' AGAIN: DIALOGUE

I shall be returning to Apollinaire's approach to the visual arts, up to and through Cubism, in chapter two. But already we can see that *Méditations esthétiques* reveals much about the dynamics at work in *Alcools*. As I pointed out at the beginning of the discussion (p. 20), *Méditations esthétiques* is, from the point of view of the rhythm of its composition, contemporary with many of the poems in *Alcools*, as well as with the compilation of the collection as it stands. 'Automne malade' itself appeared for the first time in *Alcools*, as the result of a transformation of an original manuscript dating from 1902.[74] This transformation is one small part of an overall process of preparing *Alcools* as a coherent collection, and in this way it is involved in the movement away from Symbolism, and in the development of an explicitly different modernity that comes to a head in Apollinaire's development in 1908 and again in 1912. An outstanding example of the involvement of the preparation of *Alcools* as a collection with Apollinaire's new initiative and his push towards a new modernity is his suppression of all punctuation from the poems in the collection — a move that he decided on, as is well known, in the final stages of his creation of *Alcools* as an entity, and that may have occurred to him as a result of his contact with Cendrars.[75] 'L'Adieu', through which I embarked on this reading of *Alcools* and to which I now return, is also a text that exemplifies the process of change and of superimposing layers of thought characteristic of the preparation of *Alcools* and of *Méditations esthétiques*.

'L'Adieu' reveals an aspect of Apollinaire's poetic expression that throws light on his attitude towards the relation of painted object to natural object. We have just seen that, in Apollinaire's reading of Picasso's painting, the object on the canvas is the material of a search for the object, and that it does not represent or reveal an object in nature; nor is a space for creative imagination established beyond doubt. The object is not represented, nor does it escape representation. Instead, there is the tracing of an implicit/explicit presentation of the relation of seeing, remembering and painting. Seen in terms of language, this view produces an erosion of dialogue. The tracing of perception in its own displacement produces statements that are not in a position to be clarified by counterstatement. The possibility of a subject, shared by those engaged in dialogue, being articulated in that space between statement and counterstatement is eroded. Artistic expression is thus directed at the unknown. It turns its back on rhetorical structures of difference that articulate the unknown in terms of its suppression, and that define it in terms of a context objectified in dialogue.

(i)

'J'ai cueilli ce brin de bruyère
Mets-le sur ton coeur plus longtemps
Nous ne nous verrons plus sur terre'.
'J'ai mis sur mon coeur la bruyère,'
Et souviens-toi que je t'attends'.

This is the first published version of the poetic artefact entitled 'L'Adieu', and it is itself an alteration of five consecutive lines from the posthumously published early poem 'La Clef'.[76] The differences between this version and the poem that appeared in *Alcools* ten years later are startling, and they reveal a great deal about the knife-edge along which Apollinaire develops and distils his thought. Let us look again at the *Alcools* version:

(ii)

J'ai cueilli ce brin de bruyère
L'automne est morte souviens-t'en
Nous ne nous verrons plus sur terre
Odeur du temps brin de bruyère
Et souviens-toi que je t'attends

In this poem, Apollinaire presents his experience of language in terms of a desire to overcome transience. This desire, and the barriers of 'otherness' that maintain it as a desire, are constructed in the erosion of dialogue that is built up in the changes from first to final versions. The removal of the second and fourth lines of poem (i) not only eliminates the poetic banality of flowers placed on the heart as a memento; it also erodes any suggestion that there is a person addressed in the poem, in the context of whom the narrator, the 'je', is made present and identified.[77] In poem (ii), there is no person who answers, no one seen to respond to a request. There is no one who can be asked to remember, or who performs the gesture of remembering; acts of memory are not defined or addressed towards specific events, as they are in the earlier version, and there is no suggestion of a hope that specific events or sensations may be preserved from erosion in time.

This is emphasised by the changing role of the imperative 'souviens-toi' from one version to the other. In the earlier version, the imperative 'souviens-toi' in the final line is spoken by the fictional person addressed in the first three lines and specified by them, whereas in the *Alcools* poem, in the 'souviens-toi' of the final line and the 'souviens-t'en' of the second, no difference is established between a person addressed and the person writing. The poem, though containing vestiges of dialogue, increasingly forces itself on the reader as an expression of a single fictional person's thought process moving throughout the text. Certainly this process seeks to maintain an image of a person as well as remembered sensations of desire. But in the absence of response in the poem, this objective is not realised. The text questions the power of memory to lay hands on crucial experiences that define identity. The poem in its final version traces dissolving contours around a single writing voice that increasingly encroaches on dialogue, and this ultimately presents voice as continuously unique, as continuously 'other' in relation to remembered experience.[78] And this is not an 'otherness' that creates a difference that can be encompassed and used to identify. The repetitions in the poem erode any power to encompass. As I say, this is particularly true of the imperatives 'souviens-t'en'/'souviens-toi', which collapse the difference between an attempt to appropriate the past (the fictional narrator addresses himself), and an attempt to provide the user of language with an attitude to the present ('he' addresses someone else). Throughout the poem, memory triggers desire, just as the present emerges as a continuous experience of 'otherness'. Even pronouns do not dominate the difference between them; their function of specifying persons and of identifying experience has been withdrawn from them:

Nous ne nous verrons plus sur terre

and made the desired object of a ceaseless wake:

Et souviens-toi que je t'attends

With all this happening in the poem, 'L'Adieu' benefits crucially from the suppression of punctuation in *Alcools*. It obscures distinctions between instances of experience, and the returns in the poem to recurrent emotions are transformed into an obsessional flow that it is impossible to arrest and identify with. The withdrawal of punctuation creates a multidimensional syntax, although this does not mean that lines or words can be read in an indiscriminate order. But what it does mean is that no line is emphasised more than any other, so that reading the poem becomes a search for emphasis and for direction. The simplicity of the syntax within each line contributes to a sophisticated process of effacement within the poem as a whole, within which identity is an image traced out as it unfolds in time. The syntax in the unpunctuated 'L'Adieu' produces a reading in which the past and the present eclipse each other, and in which the effort to represent is the pursuit of an 'I'.

5—'AUTOMNE MALADE' CONTINUED

(i) ISOLATION

In 'Automne malade', the erosion of dialogue, its suppression perhaps, takes the form of undermining the grounds on which readers interpret the poem and come to grips with it. The poem, even more systematically than in 'L'Adieu', undermines the power of its image content to refer to experience outside the reading of textual elements and their relation to each other.

Sur les nixes nicettes aux cheveux verts et naines
Qui n'ont jamais aimé   (1.10)

How do we enter into dialogue with these lines? Apollinaire is verging on tautology as well as coinage. True, 'nicette' is the feminine form of the archaic 'nicet' (without malice) and the suffix ' – ette' makes the nixies playfully diminutive — an impression enhanced by 'naines' at the end of the line. But 'nicette' is phonetically so closely related to 'nixes' that it is hard to see it being chosen with any view other than to emphasise this similarity. 'Nicette' tells us hardly anything more about 'les nixes' than that noun does itself. Furthermore, these lines employ adjectives that seem, on an immediate level, inapplicable: the dwarf-nymphs and the green hair. The unusual position of the adjective at the end of the line — the fact that it is significantly separated from the noun it qualifies — further strains the relation of adjective to noun. 'Naines' is spatially close to 'cheveux', but because of the discrepancy in gender, there is no adjectival chain established between 'naines' and 'verts', and the reader is brought up against a qualifier in an unfamilial context, or comes across a word without remembering where it belongs.

But despite — perhaps even because of — the tortuousness of the reading this line involes us in, we may feel that its impact resides overridingly in its nursery and nonsense rhyme features. The dwarfs remind us of Snow White, and the pathetic loveless sprites are part of fairy-tale folklore. But Apollinaire continually shuffles the cards of the various poetic tonalities that make up the poem. Fruits and fertility mix with melancholy and death. There is no unifying tone in the poem, and the joyful autonomy of verbal fantasy is undermined. 'Automne malade' is essentially a lonely poem, and a reading of it in terms of dialogue made impossible involves us closely with this.

We may begin with the loneliness of the sprites themselves. It was through our reading of the sparrow-hawks of the previous line (p. 11) that we discovered the intransitive quality in the writing, which itself deals in an erosion of dialogue. We saw that the sparrow-hawks move in an indefinable space that, ultimately, is located only in the words 'Sur les nixes nicettes...', a quasi-tautological phrase that keeps itself, and the space of the sparrow-hawks, on the other side of exchange and communication. The space that 'Sur' ironically — playfully, lonesomely — fails to locate is a space stamped out in the words that articulate it and in which it is *read*. Within this 'space', 'nixes' are discovered — water-beings that imply shapeless and constant movement, and that have indeterminate mythological associations. But the loneliness of the sprites and of the rest of the poem is not only expressed in the image content and the relation of images to each other. The erosion of dialogue also takes place in the signifiers that put the nixies on the page. 'Les nixes' engender their own qualifier 'nicettes', and the fact that they have never loved is a reality of the language in which they exist, which defines them and in which they are sequestered.

The playful nixies embody a fantasy that is attempting to escape into reality, into words shared by readers and writers and dreamers. But instead, this fantasy is undermined, buried in and as the language that puts it on the page. This is compounded by the nixies' physical attribute: 'cheveux verts'. To give the secluded, word-bound sprites a physical characteristic at all is, ironically, to intensify the desire to make a fantasy real. The colour 'vert' is a fictional colour, an abstract one; it creates its own perceptual moment and effaces links with other colours. Combining with its playful nonsense and with its appropriateness to Rhenish-Symbolist water-sprites, 'verts' coupled with 'naines' dismantles in reading the power of memory to recognise patterns in experience and to draw them in.

'Les nixes n'ont jamais aimé'. This lyrical expansion with which the second section of the poem ends not only brings nostalgic emotion into play, it is a further erosion of dialogue set in motion by the poem's imagery, in which the signifier tends to dominate, provoking a desire to identify with language and to engage in it. The 'nixes nicettes... et naines' are unique; no perspective on the relations by which they exist is attributed to them. Their isolation is not referred to, it is enacted in the text. The words do not come out of the nixies' mouths; even reading them silences them and emphasises their passivity. The isolation of 'les nixes' expresses an alienation *in* language and *as* image — the images of myth, memory and the present. The richness and diversity of their experience and the reader's are displaced in opaque signifiers, in loneliness and tautology. Like the autumn 'space' itself, 'les nixes' are given no option but to die

en blancheur et en richesse   (l. 6)

(ii) FRAGMENTS

In the final section of his poem, Apollinaire continues with an imagery and a rhetoric of seclusion that express, whether implicitly or explicitly, a sequestration in the very 'feel' of language. Once again, Apollinaire's *Alcools* verse comes to life by puncturing as well as delving into the nostalgic appeal of transience and 'nuance'. We have already seen the way in which the statement 'Et que j'aime ô saison que j'aime tes rumeurs' can be interpreted as expressing a simple enjoyment of transience vague enough not to demand definition ('rumeurs'). Having created this image, Apollinaire systematically fragments it. For the lack of definition itself, responsible for seeming to lull the reader into nostalgia, becomes increasingly problematic, sharp and indivisible. The line

Les fruits tombant sans qu'on les cueille   (1.15)

is pivotal, although in syntactic terms it is self-contained. As in so much of Apollinaire's versification, this line is a pivot in so far as it both creates and erodes the contours that would contextualise the thought process he is tracing. Syntactically, it is both independent and subordinate. We respond to the uniqueness of the image but as we read, we remember that the fruit falls in the poem's orchard, which, as we have already seen, dismantles at the same time as contains all the seasons that pass through the 'automne malade', so that the orchard is indistinguishable from the continuous process of seasonal change and from the indivisible whiteness of snow. Autumn is (dis-)covered in the passage of seasons, just as the passage of seasons erodes autumn as an object or a perception. The 'rumeurs' cannot therefore be exclusively interpreted in terms of fruit that is so abundant that it need not be picked, or in terms of a 'richesse' that demands only a glance to be admired. The single quality Apollinaire attributes to the fruit is that it falls.

The fruit *is* the fact of falling, it *is* movement both demanding and defying identification. The fruit falls in a space not defined in time, but effaced in the reading time-span. The fruits are not picked, they have no audience; they undermine their own engagement with language and the world. The fruit, as it falls, seems to trace out the terms in which it is perceived and creates a perception-in-fiction. As it falls, the fruit incarnates its sequestration. As an image, it confronts the reader with — and engages the writer in — a uniqueness as alienating as it is expressive. The fruit falls in a 'space' that is exclusively a language space, but that is not located in language; a 'space' pressed between two lines or statements, but not specified by them. As an image-signifier, the falling fruit expresses a progressive exclusion not *from* language, but *in* language and *as* language.

(iii) UNIQUENESS DISSOLVED, FAILURE RESISTED

The objects that take form in 'Automne malade' articulate a world that is increasingly expressive, and increasingly impossible. Apollinaire's poem is a world of displaced experience, taken over by its increasing range of associative implication. The objects in the poem move in a language that confronts this expressive superabundance by striving to establish a *unique* intervention in it — an autonomous creativity. Simultaneously, the language of the poem *incarnates* a sense of proliferating, uncontrolled expressiveness, in that its pivotal, non-punctuated syntax erodes differentiation and autonomy. The objects that construct the poem emphasise their fictionality; metaphoric moments are not moulded to a single locatable experience. Through interpretation, the objects in the poem become dimensionless, indistinguishable from the context in which they dissolve. Within the fiction of the poem, they become signs that do not dominate the space they suggest and that they articulate.

The development of this attitude to objects-in-language comes to a head in the final eight lines of the poem. Here, Apollinaire marks a final stage in an exploration of the relation of his controlled flow of poetic language to memory:

> Le vent et la forêt qui pleurent
> Toutes leurs larmes en automne feuille à feuille
> > Les feuilles
> > Qu'on foule
> > Un train
> > Qui roule
> > La vie
> > S'écoule (l. 16)

Nothing could be further from a Verlainian dissolution of barriers than these lines.[79] Just as the fruits of the previous line come to be identifiable exclusively through the condition of falling, perception of the natural world is presented as an invisible focus, both created by language and represented in it. Objects focused on are wrapped up and lost in the process that articulates and specifies them. Once again, the pivotal ambiguity of the non-punctuated syntax that links the lines alternately establishes and fragments the linguistic space in which statements function. 'Le vent et la forêt qui pleurent', on the one hand, is in apposition to the fruit and the previous line: 'les fruits tombant sans qu'on les cueille'. As such, it is responsible for the explicit transformation of 'Les fruits...' from an enjoyment of 'rumeurs' into an aggrieved expression of transience. But equally, on the other hand, 'Le vent et la forêt qui pleurent' is the subject and the verb for which the following line provides an object, emphasising 'pleurer' as a transitive verb. The single statement — or the two consecutive statements — 'Le vent et la forêt qui pleurent/Toutes leurs larmes en automne feuille à feuille' is an articulated chain involving objects, grief and flow, within which each of the three is irreducible to the others. Grief is an object that flows. The object that flows is both the source of grief and its representation; the fact of representation is the source of grief. The flowing 'object' that is grief is both tears and the constricting voiceless-ness of being equated with leaves. The 'object' is also the wind, lost and articulated in the forest by means of which it becomes audible. In the midst of this process, autumn itself is de-located and exploded, to the point of becoming an adverbial phrase within the tautological structure of these lines. It has no independent existence; it is a moving point in a potentially endless flow of associative implication and pivotal syntax.

This flow is a metonymic chain — 'Les fruits tombant/feuille à feuille' — that does not create contours of definition.[80] In the language of Apollinaire's poem, the object exists exclusively in displacement as the object-in-language. This does not simply involve an equivalence between the object and its expression in language. For the structure of the poem – its tone – seems to be one of observation in relation to the process it is tracing. There is an interplay between transience and observation on the one hand, and articulation and the promise of intervention on the other, that is fundamental to the metaphoric as well as the syntactic structure of the poem. And this interplay *is* the object in the poem, and it gives form to the perception of objects as we encounter them. The object-in-language confronts the object-in-perception, the dissolved object, inconceivable without language and created through representation in language, but lacking the terms by which it can be fixed as a communicated perception. The creation of a displaced 'object' within a poem whose dissolving components articulate flow has the same effect in language as the pursuit, in Apollinaire's understanding of Cubism, of a potentially endless enumeration of component elements in the object. For in Cubist representation, the endlessness of enumeration articulates perception, and simultaneously dismantles any focus on perception itself. Equally, in the poem, the 'object' flows insofar as it dissolves in perception, and is repeatedly displaced in the very attitudes and rhetorical postures designed to stabilise it and come to grips with it. To repeat, grief is an object that flows; language is an object that flows; perception is an object that flows. Grief is an endless strangulating lack, it is not *there* in language, but substituted for an object that flows. Grief and its representation do not meet.

How, then, do we read the sudden, anxious rush to a blank space that Apollinaire confronts us with in the last six shortened and urgent lines?

Les feuilles
Qu'on foule
Un train
Qui roule
La vie
S'écoule (l. 18)

It seems as though both reader and writer are here confronted with the rawest structures in the poem, with the poem as an experience of itself and of language at large. Reading the poem so far has confronted us with grief, with a language that displaces the experience it 'represents'. In the last six lines Apollinaire develops this language until it is lost in the page around it and in continual acts of reading. He uses cliché to resist reference, not to simplify it, and expressiveness rushes in rather than fading into triviality. The images are transparent. They create a language that is abstract — not because it abstracts away from experience and the experience of language in the creation of meta-level, but because it presents us with a dissolving, a fragmentation of specificity in expression. In our reading this fragmentation has taken place principally in terms of two image contexts built up throughout the poem: grief and transience. But in the final lines, grief and transcience are compressed in a limiting, excluding and emphatically rhyming structure; a metonymic experience of language. Apollinaire does *not* compare grief to transience, but dissolves one in the other. In relation to the other, each is an inadequate expression of itself, because each is expressed in terms of the dissolving of stabilising terms of reference.

What makes the final lines both a development and a culmination of the process incarnated in the rest of the poem is that they focus our attention on language as such. Transience expresses dissolution on the level of the signified where we interpret images and assume a command of the language we read. But in the last lines, this assumption of command is outmanoeuvred in a creation of transience on the level of the signifier — where rhyme and rhythm structure reading in a way that disrupts the process of signification, the relation of concept to context. Furthermore, the language that Apollinaire steers his reader into, and that erupts on the page in these final lines, is one that even as it incarnates transience in the signifier, remains ensnared within the *attitude of representation* it strikes. This attitude does not discover a perspective or a context in transience; it does not discover a position from which to dominate experience, and from which to wrench memory and history from the hands of the 'other'. It tantalisingly re-emphasises an unmeasurable and estranging gap. The language Apollinaire confronts us with by increasingly emphasising the signifier is one that resists appropriation and undermines any identifying focus on itself. In the reading and writing in which it involves both author and critic, this language *is* transience, neither linear nor chronological; it is the dissolving of identity in a proliferation of the signifier.

But is this dissolving not a failure of language? Does it not preclude the affirmation of a unique language, a unique voice in language, and the affirmation of identity itself? The value of Apollinaire's poem is that, while involving the reader with 'failure' in language, it also presents the terms of a resistance to failure. The dissolving that Apollinaire's language both incarnates and represents is an expression of the way uniqueness is displaced in language itself, and in the relation of language to memory and to time. As we read Apollinaire's poem, we are reminded once again that our experience of language cannot escape a confrontation with failure and with grief. But in confronting this grief, we confront the fact that language not only articulates in traces our world and our experience in it, but it then seduces us into living by its representations of us, of our history and of our desires.

Reading Apollinaire's language involves questioning our own relation to language. His and our language are both something we want to take part in, to delve into, and to explore. At the same time, they are something we want to take apart and dismantle, they are something we want to withdraw from the categories of response and definition that have taken possession of them, suppressed their grief and retold their stories.

6—'LES FIANÇAILLES': CREATIVITY AND LOSS

INTRODUCTION

In this appreciation of *Alcools*, we have seen how apparently diverse elements in Apollinaire's output intermesh in surprising and illuminating ways. Poems as youthful in origin as 'L'Adieu', or 'Automne malade' with its Rhenish overtones, have revealed important connections between themselves and Apollinaire's writing on the visual arts. Within the time-span of the composition of *Alcools*, 1908 is a year in which a crucial concentration in this heterogeneity took place. It is not only the year Apollinaire composed *Les Trois Vertus plastiques*, his notes to the Fauvist exhibition in Le Havre that form the first part of *Méditations esthétiques*. It is also the period of an important involvement with the neo-Symbolist group headed by Jean Royère. Both at the time and in retrospect, Apollinaire emphasised the important influence thinking about Royère's work exercised on him, and indicated the connection between this involvement and some of the major texts of *Alcools*: 'Lul de Faltenin', 'Le Brasier', 'Les Fiançailles', along with 'Onirocritique', which was included in *L'Enchanteur pourrissant* in 1909.[81] I want now to concentrate on one of these major texts: 'Les Fiançailles'.[82]

Before beginning, it is worth drawing attention to two points from the important article Apollinaire devotes to Royère.[83] The first is the continuing enthusiasm he had for 'vers libre', initially developed by the previous generation of Symbolist poets: 'Les symbolistes nous ont encore donné le vers libre, que Vielé-Griffin appelait récemment une conquête morale'.[84] Apollinaire thinks of 'le vers libre' as the surviving element in a radical but decaying artistic initiative, and as providing young writers with the opportunity of continuing the drive towards new modes of expression, new ways of challenging nature and asserting creativity. The other point from this article it is important to bear in mind is Apollinaire's excitement at the notion of 'fausseté', which he describes as 'enchanteresse', and 'une mère féconde'.[85] He seems to herald a new Symbolist abandoning of scientific truth in favour of inventing languages able to mould themselves to sensation and to an uncharted sense of self. These languages will be the beginning of a new and rational creativity.

This approach suggests perhaps a rediscovered poetic heroism, and Apollinaire's poems of the period seem to bear this out. But the new poetic creativity that Apollinaire senses is not an unmediated espousal of potency and vigour, and Apollinaire presents it in terms of a number of oppositions. The 'clarté' that it pursues is necessarily obscure — he quotes Royère as commenting 'ma poésie est obscure comme un lis'.[86] The images produced in the rejuvented lyricism involve blindness ('cécité') as well as creativity. The vision that this lyricism offers is not only anti-naturalistic, but also quotidian: 'les miracles lyriques sont quotidiens'.[87] Apollinaire concludes his account of lyrical ambiguity by giving an explanation of the title of Royère's *Soeur de Narcisse nue*.[88] He refers to Pausanias of Lydia, the second century A.D. geographer and collector of myths, who records an unusual version of the Narcissus story.[89] Narcissus, according to this version, is not attracted to the externalised image of himself that he discovers. He thus ceases to be a mythical realisation of a central Decadent desire — to create at will a new and exclusive sense of self in language and in images, and to relish the failure that this enterprise inevitably produces. In the version Pausanias records, Narcissus, having fallen in love with his twin sister, is fatally attracted to the image of *her* that he discovers after her death as he looks into the pool. Narcissus's image of himself is thus an image of otherness, of a *female* lover as familiar to him as himself, whose presence he senses at the very moment when she is withdrawn from sensual contact and buried deep in memory. In this way, Apollinaire and Royère rescue poetry from the spectre, raised by the notion of 'fausseté' and its Decadent antecedents of an ahistorical, asocial, potentially neurotic trap, consisting of inventing for poetry an illusory power to smother otherness by indulging it. Instead they pursue a poetry that breathes the anxiety of continual otherness; the image of the displaced body that comes from the altered Narcissus myth expresses the immense desire to be one produced continually in the experience of difference: 'Nous sommes tous des rivaux de Narcisse. Elle est si belle et elle est nue...'[90]

Before beginning a reading of 'Les Fiançailles', let us compare these two introductory comments on the poem by different editors of *Alcools*:

(i)

The death of the past and the rebirth in the purifying flames of poetic creation confer on the poet-hero the gift of prophecy.

(ii)

De composition plus complexe que 'Le Brasier', 'Les Fiançailles' est aussi plus déchirant par l'expérience tragique de la solitude et du dénument qu'il exprime.[91]

Neither is intended as a definitive appraisal of the poem, but both derive from interpretations of Apollinaire's article on Royère. The power of the visionary is confronted with the threat of isolation and privacy: 'Et, je veux aussi placer l'ache, tour à tour symbole de la mort et couronne des victorieux, sur la tête de Jean Royère.'[92] Does one prevail over the other?

(i) 'LES FIANCÉS PARJURES'

Le printemps laisse errer les fiancés parjures   (1.1)

An essential link is broken, a promise of contact has led to isolation; a convention has been deprived of its power to signify; the image of spring is overidden by the arbitrariness of circumstance. This is in tension, however, with the mannered stylisation of this first section and its artificially restricted terms of reference. Symbolist lyricism is evident in the verb 'feuilloler' (to make the music of leaves) in the lemon trees of love, and in the image of the madonna at dawn with the eglantines.[93] On the one hand, the tightness of the metaphoric structure involving feathers, birds, plants and trees revels in the sense of difference and autonomy it provides. By the same token, it seduces us into thinking that it absorbs the gap between self and the world, reader and writer, language and its user. But this impression of an encompassing of gap is in tension with the excesses of the language in the section as a whole. For we are reading a language in which image proliferates — not a diversity of heterogeneous images, but image as such. As we shall see, this calls into question the power of image itself to impose contours in time and space; and it is the fact of relation that is presented as a silence and a broken contract.[94]

The second line of the poem presents the reader with a pressure point of this kind:

> Et laisse feuilloler longtemps les plumes bleues   (l. 2)

The subject of the verb 'laisse feuilloler' is 'Le printemps'. The introduction of feathers in a sentence dealing with spring — even a deconstructed spring — does not specify spring or an experience of it, and here the poem begins. The Symbolist associations of the musical blue feather-leaves give them a power to dissolve difference; the musical movement of the leaves might once have acted as a linguistic magic incarnating impulses of desire in the psyche: 'Le printemps laisse errer... et laisse feuilloler longtemps'. But the arena for such a magic is undermined, for the blue feathers are part of a network of images in the stanza in which specificity is eroded. Immediately after the appearance of the blue feathers there follows a movement towards specifying them ('Que secoue le cyprès où niche l'oiseau bleu') that is not fulfilled. The feathers *are* related to a particular bird, and the leaves to a tree, but the significance of this context is not revealed, its expressiveness is almost out of control. The feathers dissolve in the bird, the leaves in the tree, so that the apparent focus created by associating them with each other is in fact a resister in relation to which the reader can discover no perspective, and through which seeps the cypress tree with a bird in it. But where is the audience and how would it interpret this?[95]

The lines seem to ask, how can experience be identified? What is the significance of objects in perception and memory? Can this language — a language that is both improvised and restricted within the structure of the here and now, and that stretches back indeterminately into previous poetic modes — be identified with? Apollinaire intensifies the question by rhyming a word with itself, a device he uses, as we saw in 'L'Adieu', to create a plastic voice, images fixed on objects refusing to yield their import.

> Le printemps...
> ...laisse feuilloler longtemps les plumes bleues
> Que secoue le cyprès où niche l'oiseau bleu   (l. 1)

As an adjective, blue has the function of specifying the bird, its feathers, or the symbolic function of either. But this function is undermined: 'bleu' is vague, it it not a concrete colour that defines; it is abstract, an invasion of memory in the reader's and writer's perception. Rhyming the blue bird with its blue feathers intensifies this, as it undermines the possibility of identifying the bird in relation to something other than itself. The experience that the blueness of birds and feathers refers to on the page, that it refers the page to, is irretrievably metaphorised, located repeatedly for the first time as a word. This is emphasised by the syntax: the bird's dissolving in the cypress tree solidifies the association that acts on them in the feather/leaf verb 'feuilloler'; on the one hand, seamless, associative flow, both at the level of syntax and at the level of imagery; on the other hand, resistance.[96]

Explicit conceptualisation is excluded in Apollinaire's analyses of creativity in *Méditations esthétiques* and in the article on Royère, tracing the relations between sensation, memory and image. But, clearly, the more the reader is astounded by the complex web of efface-ment through which Apollinaire articulates these relations, the more a conceptualisation through which to rise to it may be sought. Con-ceptualisation can be described as a search for context through the endless instances of perception. But the conceptualisation demanded of the reader of 'Les Fiançailles' leads to an eroded distinction between levels of thought and experience, the reader searches for a gap in the destabilising flow of imagery through which to interpret and con-textualise. This desire for difference, as we have begun to discover, is mainly articulated in the way the images are presented syntactically — a chain in which the links dissolve, creating what Jean-Pierre Richard calls 'le lié lyrique' of *Alcools*.[97] It is at work more explicitly in the first section of 'Les Fiançailles' than in any of the others. This 'lié lyrique' dismantles the possibility of inserting a gap in the proliferation of image. Moreover, having failed to identify image, the reader is tempted by the spectre of identifying *with* it. But there is no 'déchirure' in terms of which the reader can discover the dialectical edge between image and experience. This makes conflicting demands on both the reader and Apollinaire himself. He is either seduced into accepting that creativity is the novelty that image provides, or he engages in a search for a context in terms of which to interpret — a context that is in fact indefinitely extended in the language of the poem itself. The conceptualisation the verse demands is undermined in the language that demands it. 'Bleues' or 'bleu', like the 'verts' in 'Automne malade' are *abstract* colours, signifiers with ambiguous expressiveness. On the one hand, they provide a liberation from the notion of a singular, specifiable context, and an involvement in a novel experience of the here and now. On the other hand, they express anxiety: the experience they discover *is* novel — startlingly novel, repeatedly different.

As we shall see, Apollinaire explores the relation of conceptualisation to writing further in the third section of 'Les Fiançailles': 'Qu'ai-je fait aux bêtes théologales de l'intelligence'. Here in the first section, the undermining of concepts in relation to images is developed in terms of familiar myth, and the poem reaches within a few lines a level of poetic expression many readers might think of as quite outside Apollinaire's range. It presents us here with writing that shows that to involve conceptual experience with poetry is *not* to impose on poetry an arid structure of paradox, alien to its privileged power to reach the raw and the private. The self-eroding conceptual dimensions of 'Les Fiançailles' are a metaphoric expression of anxiety in identity, a potential failure to take part in the forms of represenation that culture offers:

> Une Madone à l'aube a pris les églantines
> Elle viendra demain cueillir les giroflées
> Pour mettre aux nids des colombes qu'elle destine
> Au pigeon qui ce soir semblait le Paraclet　　　　　　(l. 4)

The Christian references in these lines represent an allegorical level of thinking that invites us to grant thinking the capacity to encompass circumstance and to dominate it. Initially, we are invited to respond again to the idea that the Virgin gives birth to a son who will be crucified and thereby become assimilable to the Holy Spirit. We are almost seduced into accepting the approach institutionalised by the Madonna, which seeks a spiritual independence from the fact that perception is historical, that interpretation is determined by context, however mobile. But what happens as we read is that reading itself is emphasised, so that the paradoxes suppressed by the mythology are laid bare. The Madonna and the Paraclete, the presence of God, are placed in an image context that suggests that their power to transcend the material world is in fact nothing other than progressive involvement with it. The Madonna picks eglantines at dawn: the image is desymbolised in that the event takes place at a specific time in the cycle of the day and of days. The Paraclete, the figure of the Holy Spirit, is alternately an unspecified pigeon, and a plural set of doves; it has only the appearance of assuming its mythological significance; it only appears to be indistinguishable from its Name:

> [le] pigeon qui ce soir semblait le Paraclet (1. 7)

The mythological context does not assimilate experience; Apollinaire's writing presents it as dissolving in experience; the desire it seeks to realise, the vision of existence it seeks to vindicate, is dismantled in the dialectic of memory and object.

The dissolving of Christian mythology in the 'lié lyrique' of the poem represents a dissolving of meta-level in relation to experience, and to reading. On the one hand, the reader is faced with the fact that the implicit expresses, that images of objects both express and repress the history of dismantled desires. On the other, reader and writer are in search of a context to establish expression as communication, as a social exchange, as the entry of identity into the culture that produces it. But the language in the first section of 'Les Fiançailles' does not dominate (or seek to dominate) the implicit. Apollinaire undermines the Christian image-symbols; they fail in their bid to provide a key context in terms of which to assimilate diversity. The text is not an expression of what is perceived, but a representation of the fact that perception takes the form of what is (not) expressed. The text is displaced in its reading and rereading, in interpretation and memory. This tautological structure represents unbounded expressivness and provides an access for language to the action of memory on perception, to the way things *are* in perception — in perceptual moments and in their indeterminate build-up. Equally, the text locates itself in a potentially alienating 'space', in which expressiveness waylays communication, and in which identity is suspended in image and in time:

> Et parmi les citrons leurs coeurs sont suspendus (1.11)

The language is a structured rejection of a marriage between the spirtual
and the material, the imagined and the contextualised, the experienced
and the dominated. In the aftermath of this broken contract, expressiveness is left uncontrolled ('laisse errer') and taunts the poet with the
appearance of his passivity, the inadequacy of his response:[98]

> Le printemps laisse errer les fiancés parjures (1.1)

(ii) COLLAPSE

Such is the anxiety that Apollinaire expresses in opening his poem. This
anxiety is transformed into despair at the opening of the following
section. It is a moment where Apollinaire is isolated, disengaged from
the imagery that, a moment ago, was weaving memory into appearance. The ambiguous creativity of that imagery turns definitively to
despair at the moment where Apollinaire is named, in the sense of being
given a first person pronoun, a rhetorical identity:

> Mes amis m'ont enfin avoué leur mépris (1.12)

He is named, inevitably, by the others, who do not empathise with his
private states of mind. Apollinaire recognises his existence *in* perspective and, simultaneously, the language of his obsessional enquiry
collapses:[99]

> Je buvais à pleins verres les étoiles
> Un ange a exterminé pendant que je dormais
> Les agneaux les pasteurs les tristes bergeries
> De faux centurions emportaient le vinaigre (1.13)

The figure of an exterminating angel is turned against other elements
in the Christian iconography of angels. The shepherd no longer leads
his flock to a self-sufficient code of truth, the sheep-pens are deserted,
memory is an empty space, and there is no mythology with which to
represent its history. The shepherd and the centurion are pluralised.
De-specified and deprived of their original symbolic context, they no
longer play a part in the birth of a redemptive Christ-figure. The
centurions carry off the vinegar and regard it as their own property. This
transformation from the mythological into the quotidian is effected by
the exterminating angel, who transforms an imagery able to articulate
sensation into a moribund convention, while the author's persona —
the image of self in language — sleeps.

The fact of sleep is significant, not only because it implies the suspension of the power of consciousness, but because it involves the discourse of dream. Dream discourse represents experience in a dimensionless time, and in an imagery that is both a compression and yet still a sequence. Its relation to the fact of language and of social exchange is buried as it is expressed. The 'lié lyrique' so much in evidence in the first section of the poem is analogous to the dream discourse as it is evoked here: an image-space in which the writer-dreamer is suspended from interaction with an audience, and in which his experience of language and of social structures in general is oppressively passive. The possibility is undermined of establishing an attitude *in* language to dispossession in the relation of perception to language itself. The poet's ego dissolves as his capacity to produce a language able to change with change is represented as a series of devalued private images, within which 'le lié lyrique' is a flow of sourness and decay. Light from street-lamps and from the moon flows like urine; people taking off their clothes means only that larger and larger piles of unidentified clothes are amassed, and shadows once rich to the imagination now only abuse it:[100]

> Les becs de gaz pissaient leur flamme au clair de lune (1. 19)
>
> A la clarté des bougies tombaient vaille que vaille
> Des faux cols sur des flots de jupes mal brossées (1. 21)
>
> Les ombres qui passaient n'étaient jamais jolies (1. 27)

(iii) FANTASY

Like the previous section of the poem, the next also begins with the assertion of an 'I'. The self is placed in its relation to the 'other', displaced in the language of others:

> Je n'ai plus même pitié de moi
> Et ne puis exprimer mon tourment de silence (1. 28)

An attempt is engaged in to make a stand against dispossession, and to envisage a language to counter it. The previous section opened in an awareness of privacy as failure. Here, the dynamic of privacy is accepted. The first gestures are made towards accepting privacy as a crucial challenge thrown down to creativity, and towards coming to terms with a potentially creative language that dissolves in the language of dispossession and appearance.[101]

> Je n'ai plus même pitié de moi
> Et ne puis exprimer mon tourment de silence
> Tous les mots que j'avais à dire se sont changés en étoiles
>
> (1. 28)

The lines develop the history of the 'tourment de silence' that the poet persona suffers from — a torment even language cannot cure. The notion of a history or a chronicle is not as paradoxical or as out of place as it might appear in the context of 'Les Fiançailles'. Clearly, Apollinaire is not inventing a fictional autobiographical figure and then proceeding sequentially as though his poem were a third-person narrative; nor is 'Les Fiançailles' a diary in free verse. The 'I' in a written or spoken sentence often fails to name conclusively, and can be an instance of identity assertion, asking (or suppressing) questions about the relation of 'I' to others. The poem consists of a series of epic stages, with the narrator represented in different, self-eroding attitudes in each one. This sequence of stages constructs a search for emphasis along a dissolving dividing line between a struggle with experience and with images, and a passive acceptance of them. The narrative pronoun 'je' is constructed in the memory of this struggle, and the effort to represent it.

Apollinaire appraises a language the power of which is insufficient to have given it possession of the world:

> [Je] ne puis exprimer mon tourment de silence
> Tous les mots que j'avais à dire se sont changés en étoiles
>
> (1. 29)

His words add to appearance (the stars), transforming even memory (the things he had to say) into otherness. This otherness is beauty, in the sense of novelty, or re-creation, of maintaining consciousness unknown to itself; the beauty of the stars shining from nowhere, from within the blackness of a language in which they express, intransitively, without establishing communication and without undermining the threat of privacy. This language is no synthesis of introspection and action, memory and the present. Apollinaire's 'tourment de silence' is one that even language as he has known it cannot cure — a language that fails in its bid to suppress silence in a representation of it ('je ne puis exprimer...'). And yet the rhetorical assertion 'Tous les mots que j'avais à dire se sont changés en étoiles' *is* an attempt to give contours to a stage in a remembered process, and to communicate it. But at the same time, it expresses the anxiety of memory transformed into the

images that present themselves — any image. It is not a lyrical penetration of the ineffable. It is an assertion that invents stages in an open-
ended process, in the history of a desire to discover identity in the
expressiveness that incarnates it and displaces it. I can only recognize
the language I use as changed and changing.[102]

Apollinaire develops further his struggle against fantasies in language:

Qu'ai-je fait aux bêtes théologales de l'intelligence   (1. 33)

'Théologales' describes words tending towards God, these words
are beasts ('bêtes') as well as objects of nostalgia — 'Qu'ai-je fait'.
Apollinaire points out emphatically, as we saw in *Méditations esthétiques* and in the article on Royère, that what he regards as antihuman
is the attempt to transcend the terms of perception (privacy), as opposed
to representing the history, buried in appearance and in language itself,
of the dialectic involving perception and privacy, image and introspection. There is no evidence in appearance or in intellectual tradition
of the dynamic 'inhumanité', the multispecific 'vérité' Apollinaire
envisages in *Méditations esthétiques*, and that he believes Picasso to
be creating. Words that tend towards God — the words of God — are
beasts, inhuman in the sense of bypassing the human condition; they
are objects of nostalgia, in that poets are forced to abandon their most
cherished ambitions and work with a language whose expressiveness
is increasingly impenetrable, and within which creativity is focused
on discovering vestiges of communication. Intelligence is depicted as
a beast, just as the conceptualisation in which the text immerses the
reader is self-eroding and self-undermining. The poet is left confronting
language in language.[103]

Now, in effect, the anguished cry 'Qu'ai-je fait aux bêtes théologales
de l'intelligence', whose autonomy immediately recedes in the absence
of punctuation, stamps a definitive shape, though a retrospective and
receding one, on the diversity of possible interpretations thrown up by
the previous lines.

Un Icare tente de s'élever jusqu'à chacun de mes yeux
Et porteur de soleils je brûle au centre de deux nébuleuses

(1. 31)

If we read this imaged assertion in isolation, we are inclined to react
to it as a realisation of the most ambitious of creative projects. The poet
is equated with the sun and burns with the heat and the brightness he
carries; the scope of his awareness stretches within two nebulae,

and from one to the other; he *is* the source of light, the texture of perception itself that the poet-apprentice Icarus seeks to discover and master.

But to read the lines in this way takes no account of the development in the writing from image flow to rhetorical assertion and the struggle for emphasis. This development links a dismantling of fidelity to appearance and its novelty with a dismantling of the power images hold over us. To deal exclusively in image is the realisation of a poetic desire, but also of a fantasy. It is different from confronting the fact of image, which is an attempt to represent the process in memory that produces an image and its potency. This development in the text is highlighted at the point where two suns, two eyes and two nebulae appear on the page. It is evident, here, that Apollinaire's vision of Picasso's achievement affects his vision of his own projects. By separating the eyes of his narrator one from the other ('chacun de mes yeux' and 'au centre de deux nébuleuses'), Apollinaire *is dismantling perspective*. For perspective is based on the fiction of a horizon, and on establishing two interrelated and independent sources of light and perception: two parallel lines meet on the horizon, and two eyes focus on an object. But here, Apollinaire presents two eyes separately, operating independently of each other: two eyes, two growing blurs of light, 'deux nébuleuses', in search of each other across a dark space. The world moves unpredictably when interpretation and experience itself are related to objects in this way. Within perspective, the relation of the object to the way perception is approached and analysed is *seen*; it is as self-evident as appearance itself. Perspective dominates perception with the fiction of objectivity it imposes, and in bypassing the diversity of contexts.

But without perspective, the world is unhinged and is continuously re-presented as different. As the split Icarus climbs, Apollinaire disrupts perspective by pluralising sources of vision and contexts of perception. The language of 'Les Fiançailles' at this stage does not dominate perception, it does not establish itself as an independent source of light and creativity. Instead, perception is presented as a network of images-in-displacement. This network is a blur. The newfound relation of image to rationality in 'Les Fiançailles' is not designed to produce a simplistically dynamic view of the creative imagination. Neither is the blur or the sameness the language creates passive or inconsequential. It is a deconstruction of certain lyrical, Symbolist image-tokens. Stars and constellations, in a deconstruction of perspective within the 'lié lyrique' of the poem, are not an expression of expansion or synthesis, or the power of artifice to give concrete shape to the ineffable. Instead, they are an expression of a frustrated desire to establish an *attitude*: 'je brûle'. The stars and constellations act on reading like an object in perception, they produce the drama of identity threatening by repeated novelty and continuity itself.

Apollinaire ends the section with a despairing critique of another element in the poet-hero myth:

Jadis les morts sont revenus pour m'adorer (1.34)

Like Orpheus, the poet in Apollinaire's fantasy has the power to breathe and sing in the underworld, to control the beasts and to bring the inanimate to life. Death is the crucial challenge for the poet as hero-creator — not so much his own physical demise as the death of previous languages, the burial of previous powers to express.

Et j'espérais la fin du monde (1.35)

In this line, Apollinaire has nostalgically isolated a moment of fiction, a moment in imagination where the poet dominates, encompassing creation in a thought, and seeing history in an image. But he goes on:

Mais la mienne arrive en sifflant comme un ouragan (1.36)

'La mienne' is the death of the poet projected in the text. Apollinaire is dramatically and definitely excluded from the aspiration to transcend transience and the past. This exclusion is marked as a decision in relation to language, a point of entry in language. At this 'point' of entry, experience sweeps us and Apollinaire into an exploded identity that is the image of death. The hurricane that rushes at Apollinaire is the 'point' of contact with language, an almost impossible recognition that the repossession of language is imaginary.[104]

A fantasy has been recognised. Once again, Apollinaire begins a new section in the poem, a further stage in the process he gives 'conceptual' shape to, by naming himself in a pronoun. In so doing he embarks on another level in his reappraisal of his ambitions and his poetic self-projection:

J'ai eu le courage de regarder en arrière (1.37)

There follows what can be read as a slowed-down exploration of the 'ouragan' that swept through Apollinaire's consciousness in the previous line, the previous 'point' in his thinking and composition.

Les cadavres de mes jours
Marquent ma route et je les pleure (1.38)

Apollinaire not only continues in his effort to assert an attitude, each attitude is also an image and undermines its own power to re-present experience. In these lines and the ones that follow, his language expresses a desire to reappropriate an experience that changes as he watches or turns back, in the slipstream of a dissolved fantasy. Each image-attitude displaces absolutely the objective of the section as a whole and displaces the desired attitude, *in* image and in the language on the page: 'ma route', like the final compressed lines in 'Automne malade', is a word tracing a process *out*, a cliché that has lost its power to refer, and that represents an experience of this 'process' as a resister and a signifier. Equally, as the expressiveness of images can no longer be relied on, experience becomes novel, as novel as it is alienating, an immense growth and transformation that it is the desire of this poet in these lines to present as the pathway of an individual existence and its relation to language...[105] Apollinaire remembers, re-creates, invents the days of his past:

Les uns pourrissent dans les églises italiennes
Ou bien dans de petits bois de citronniers
Qui fleurissent et fructifient (1.40)

These three lines — the section as a whole — move in an unpunctuated, syntactic seamlessness from expressions of failure and lack to presentations of spontaneous expressiveness in the perceptual 'space' between memory and images that change. The section moves from days dying at dawn in bars (1.44) to life improvised in a glance aimed at a sensual horizon (1.46). The section ends with a breath-taking manipulation of image, aimed at filling its reader with the desire to have some of the wealth-in-language it implies and projects. It is an image that re-creates an irreducible, depersonalising novelty, that opens out *again* in the spontaneous, undominated creativity of memory:

Et les roses de l'électricité s'ouvrent encore
Dans le jardin de ma mémoire (1.47)

(iv) CREATIVE EGO

A power to impose a language and to control it has collapsed. An expressive network in which familiarity and invention interplay cannot be fixed. Experience spills over and roams unbounded. There is no language to produce objects on which the ego can fix, either to project and articulate dominant obsessions, or to isolate a sphere of action.[106] An ability to discover identity in the relation of experience to language, perception to image, has disappeared. But in the next three sections of the poem, Apollinaire discovers a poet who fights back against the undermining of the creative ego. Each one begins with a rhetorical assertion of identity, and asserts identity in the face of change and dissolving recognition. Each of these sections, however, expresses a different level of confidence in this project.

The first of these sections claims for itself in the strongest terms a liberated language that establishes its own uniqueness:

> Pardonnez-moi mon ignorance
> Pardonnez-moi de ne plus connaître l'ancien jeu des vers
> Je ne sais plus rien et j'aime uniquement (1.49)

In the gesture of discovering his language as a relation to its masters, the poet whom Apollinaire projects and identifies with forces his own discourse on his absent and unpredictable audience. The imperative realises the impossible desire of creating an equivalence between intended and received signification. Or rather, it would realise such a desire definitively, were it not an imperative demanding forgiveness — a plea for acceptance.

But it is a joyful plea. The assertion that 'Je ne sais plus rien' proclaims a sense of liberation derived from rejecting positivism. In the article on Royère, Apollinaire isolates the anti-creativity of a 'scientific' approach and of the 'vérités' it presupposes, accusing its promulgators of giving the illusion of engaging with nature, while undermining an effective exploration of the relations that bind us to nature and to our own thought.[107] This assertive rejection of knowledge once again opens the window on Apollinaire's Symbolist inheritance, and in particular its interpenetration with Decadence. In *A Rebours*, 'Des Esseintes' nurtures objects, images and situations designed to subvert the dominant notion of objectivity in the organisation of appearances, and to replace it by constructing a world of artifice (or 'faussetté', to borrow Apollinaire's term) that subverts the distinction between perceiver and perceived, production and consumption.[108] But the creativity Apollinaire desires is not an occult, mystical investigation of the senses.[109] The poet, as he stands here on the brink of forgiveness and acceptance, discovers his continuity in the events that unfurl in his perceptual space. His love-affair with the world is undifferentiated:

'j'aime uniquement'; it extends with experience and proliferates with diversity. It is not a Narcissistic suppression of the 'other' and of others, as the image of loving uniquely might imply:

> Et je souris des êtres que je n'ai pas créés   (1.54)

It is a love-affair with existence, articulated *in* the relation to others; it is an ecstatic awareness that the ego survives, that life is possible in the otherness of image, and in a language that describes the experience and the expressiveness it produces. As 'je' in his fictional text, Apollinaire discovers an intransitive identity that neither dominates nor dissolves.

Simultaneously, he reminds himself of the problem. As he discovers assertiveness through poetry and in the 'vers libre', he finds words for the impulse that represents his desires in terms of anxiety and threat:

> Mais si le temps venait où l'ombre enfin solide
> Se multipliait ...
> J'admirerais mon ouvrage   (1.55)

The possibility of independence in the intransitive identity he has discovered rests on a language that he is not as yet in command of, a language that threatens to dissolve in the love-affair it is intended to produce and create, in the structures of the world itself, and in the absorption there of perception and of its source.

As if to respond to the challenge of this threat, Apollinaire puts himself — his identity as the assertive poet fighting back for a place in his history — *in* the concrete world, *in* events as they unfurl:

> J'observe le repos du dimanche   (1.58)

This, then, is the second of the three stanzas opening with an assertion of maintained identity. Apollinaire explores the power of the poet he has invented, and puts him to the test. Though his poet is one who strives for a collapse of perspective, this collapse never emerges as a 'fait accompli':

> Comment comment réduire
> L'infiniment petite science
> Que m'imposent mes sens   (1.60)

The equivalence Apollinaire draws between the senses and science clearly evokes the empirical approach to knowledge, as well as the system of perspective that both supports and vindicates it. But Apollinaire discovers that this system is never definitively refuted ('Comment

comment réduire') and that appearance dominates creativity and threatens to erode it. Moreover, the power of perspective and appearance itself to block creative investigation is intensified by the poetic tradition from which Apollinaire emerges as the poetic 'je' of these lines. For 'l'ancien jeu des vers' that he apologises for not understanding — as an initiation gesture into the reality of language and of appearance — is the Symbolist exploration of the senses. It searches for an interplay of familiarity and inventiveness, the intention of which is to give contours to sense experience, and thus to re-create time in time: 'le sentiment même de la durée', as Nadal puts it. But despite the scope of Symbolist (and Decadent) artifice and its power to subvert the dominance of 'objective' organisation, it fails to distinguish sense experience from the imposition of appearance; it fails to represent the process that produces image, and to confront the displacement of fertile images *in* appearance. The contours that 'l'ancien jeu des vers', and perspective as well, strive to trace around experience collapse in the realisation of the illusion on which they are based, and the fantasy they project.

In the void left in the wake of this collapse, sense experience invades. Once again, Apollinaire's pursuit of the non-objective traces that represent the continuousness of perception, the quasi-autonomous gifts it weaves through time, which are impossible to receive, is met with the central, obsessional danger: the invasion of the perceptual space by objects that compress and bury their expressiveness. The reading space becomes filled with objects that displace identification, and that describe it. Sensual perception itself becomes the 'point' of danger and of death:

> Monstre de mon ouïe tu rugis et tu pleures   (1.69)
>
> Le toucher monstrueux m'a pénétré m'empoisonne
> Mes yeux nagent loin de moi
> Et les astres intacts sont mes maîtres sans épreuve   (1.72)

The senses poison, in that memory floods the present space and dismantles identity. Eyes are not integrated with the other senses, perception proliferates sourcelessly, projected in otherness. Perceptual 'space' is allowed a free investigation liberated from the self-fulfilling prophecy of perspective; but equally, it is not circumscribed in objects, images or time. The text represents it as a signifier, and identity is grasped and lost in the images which describe it. These images (in the lines just quoted) are the *world's* image of time, yet to be identified with; they remain intact:

Mes yeux nagent loin de moi
Et les astres intacts sont mes maîtres sans épreuve

There is an unwieldy monster, beautiful in its ungainliness, that wanders through the reading space of this section.[110] It is the endlessness of experience yet to be expressed, knowledge undermined in an invasion of image and sensation. It is a monster at its most despairing when it is transformed almost mockingly into a poet-hero:

Et le monstre le plus beau
Ayant la saveur du laurier se désole   (1.76)

But for the third time in succession, Apollinaire responds to the spectre of dissolving poetic powers he invokes by opening the following section with a rhetorical strengthening of resolve:

A la fin les mensonges ne me font plus peur   (1.78)

The lies of ignorance are no longer the concern of the ego Apollinaire develops: 'Pardonnez-moi mon ignorance'. The illusion of a transcendent poetic structure has been dispensed with. But lies have been more sharply confronted in the text; they now take the form of Apollinaire's beautiful monster whose despair is itself a confrontation with lies — the ones that reassert objects, take poetry away from the poet, and give it back to the senses:

Monstre de mon ouïe tu rugis et tu pleures   (1.69)

Et tes griffes répètent le chant des oiseaux   (1.71)

Sense experience is represented in a proliferating network of substitutions and images, that re-presents memory and fragments identity ... Having asserted that the lies and displacement no longer frighten him, Apollinaire proceeds to confront his reader and himself once again with an instance of them — this time in the form of a joy at a startling incongruity:[111]

C'est la lune qui cuit comme un oeuf sur le plat   (1.79)

The moon is a deconstructed symbol; it does not create a mythical context in which the interplay of sense experience and memory can be assimilated.[112] It is brought down to earth and dissolved ecstatically in the quotidian.

This dissolving of symbol in image heralds a new influx of image in the text, which now proceeds exclusively in terms of image until the last three lines of the section (1.87–9). The text once again begins to confront reader and writer with the fact of image, but this time it does so by explicitly excluding rhetorical location or assertion of identity: personal pronouns disappear until the last lines of the section. Although a space for this proliferation of image is opened out by an expression of joyful freedom from lies and anxiety, an unproblematic liberation does not unfold. In effect, the autonomy of the images is eroded by the qualifying gestures, the gestures of description that support it: the flowers are an Easter bouquet, the rain in the streets is yesterday's. An experience of self, a desire to identify with events, is projected in images that displace it. Only in describing or qualifying images — which themselves displace the paths through experience that produce them — does Apollinaire relate to his experience or identify it. Thus the gestures qualifying images are integrated with the images themselves; the self-describing images of this section fail to dismantle the fact of image, they (de-)scribe experience and its relation to perception and memory.

Description fades in image, which presents itself increasingly as all-exclusive:

> C'est la lune qui cuit comme un oeuf sur le plat

Clearly, the comparison that articulates the image does not specify any one experience; it intensifies the impenetrability of the image. It cannot be read exclusively as a joyful indulgence in a liberation from an illusory sense of coherence. The disparateness of the elements it integrates is indivisible, and erodes the distinction between difference and sameness. Identity — the desire of the reader and writer of this line to identify with events — is displaced in the identicalness of the elements as they interact in the perceptual space.

The threat to identity of 'identicalness' in the events created in perception is one that must be met. An indistinguishability between non-objective, pure creativity and alienation cannot be left unchallenged. The text implies that the simple *assertion* of an identity able to maintain itself intact and to remain identical with itself *in* the otherness of social and linguistic exchange — 'j'aime uniquement ... Et je souris des êtres que je n'ai pas créés' — is insufficient if it is not *created* in the text. A creative ego that neither dominates nor dissolves cannot be established in the presentation of intransitive perception and of an intransitive identity. Otherness does not dissolve, it demands to be represented in a difference that glows independently, as well as being assimilated. Compare these stages in Apollinaire's construction of a maintained identity and of a strengthened creative ego:

Je ne sais plus rien et j'aime uniquement   (l.51)
Toute la sainte journée j'ai marché en chantant
Une dame penchée à sa fenêtre m'a regardé longtemps
M'éloigner en chantant   (l.87)

The two stages in the poem seem to be involved with the same experience of continuity: a sense of past, present and future available in
a language whose expressiveness is continuously intensified, and is
continuously creative. But equally, in the second piece of writing,
continuity is a network of hinges, a superimposition of postures in time
and space that Apollinaire the writer strives to dominate, but that the
'je' of the text cannot assimilate. The woman continuously watching
is invisible to the man who remembers her watching as he turns his
back and moves away; he asserts what he cannot know about the past
and its relation to his present. The 'je' in the text assumes an audience,
imagines his interaction with others, becomes aware of his love affair
with otherness; he imagines what he cannot dominate, creates what
he cannot create, whereas Apollinaire, the author whom we imagine
and who is not there in the text, is not involved in the unnamed and
unnameable melody ('chantant'). As he composes it in words and as
signifier, it is re-presented to him in terms of an expressive difference
between memory and the page that he strives to dominate and in which
he is sequestered. The author, who discovers a language in which
perception is displaced, meets the character who invents what he
cannot dominate.

As he relates author to character and watches the distinction between them dissolve, the reader discovers a text in which the unique —
an identity that remains active in relation to the unexpressed — is
unlocatable and eludes incarnation. The 'je' in 'j'aime uniquement'
is neither author nor character. In neither case is the desire for a unique
'je' realised, the desire for an identity that remains intact as it develops
in time, *in* its relation to history and to the possession of language by
others. The unique is other; (its) displacement is experience of the
world. But the imagery developed in the poem directs itself more and
more intensely at the desire to transcend the paradox of uniqueness and
continuity, and the tension between them. 'J'aime uniquement' is a
desire satisfied in the *invented* framework in which the woman leans
and watches — a framework that dissolves what is seen and what is
possessed into one another, likewise what passes by and what can be
drawn in, what is remembered and what can be taken; and the glow
of the space that separates them emerges continually.[113]

By directing itself with increasing intensity at these fundamental desires, the language of the poem responds to the challenge of experience itself — the survival of identity in a language it cannot claim as its own. This is emphasised by the fact that the image of the man being watched by the woman whom he cannot see is the culmination of yet another seamless transformation in the text from interpretation, the adoption of an attitude, to the continuity of experience itself:

> Voici mon bouquet de fleurs de la Passion
> Qui offrent tendrement deux couronnes d'épines
> Les rues sont mouillées de la pluie de naguère
> Des anges diligents travaillent pour moi à la maison
> La lune et la tristesse disparaîtront pendant
> Toute la sainte journée
> Toute la sainte journée j'ai marché en chantant
> Une dame penchée à sa fenêtre m'a regardé longtemps
> M'éloigner en chantant (l.81)

Experience seems indistinguishable from the Christian mould that guides it through time into social exchange and assimilation. But paradoxically, the more quotidian the Christian mould is made, the more it becomes the object of nostalgia. Traces of the category to which experience once belonged have less and less power and magnetism. The past is secret, its mysteries are sealed in the displacement in terms of which identity *is*, and the poetry of the last three lines is powerful in that it survives: it represents but also contributes to the potentially threatening network of image and transience that articulates perception.

(v) HEROISM. DIVERSITY. REPRESENTATION

Heroism, diversity and representation constitute the experience of poetry in which Apollinaire seeks irrevocably to involve his readers in the final section of 'Les Fiançailles'. The imaged assertions in these culminating lines seem to preclude any simplistic poetic heroism, any fantasy that, in poetry, the writer is outside time, manipulating chronology at will, and appropriating the images it proliferates. He offers a heroism that rejects the fantasy of transcendence.

Yet a belief in heroism seems firmly embedded in the language, in its reference to Christian warriors and Christian martyrdom. Apollinaire refers to the Templars, to a bird that invites association with the Holy Spirit, and to fire, suggesting both purification and the martyrdom of saints. The poet-hero seems firmly established as he asserts his ability to prophesy, and to reflect his own death and his own humanity:

Templiers flamboyants je brûle parmi vous
Prohétisons ensemble ... (1.98)

Je mire de ma mort la gloire et le malheur (1.104)

The terms of his existence and of his corporality are revealed to the poet as he sees them projected through his own history and through time. Apollinaire seems to assimilate his development at a glance, and present it with perfect freedom and immaculate familiarity in a poetic form in which others see their own destiny reflected, its secrets revealed, its anxieties transformed into joy.

But of course these are words, the lines are words. Assertions of a purifying victory over sequentiality and context, and over the power of appearance to invade privacy and preclude vision of the future, are counterbalanced by still more words, where ecstasy overlaps with artificiality. The fire that purifies ('le désirable feu') precedes a cluster of fireworks ('la girande') twirling endlessly and tracing arcs in the night. They draw and efface the vestiges and the irredeemably private impulses that are the only hope of 'seeing' perception and the history it refuses to yield.[114] The bird/Holy Spirit is transformed into a jousting target: 'l'oiseau de la quintaine'. The objective of the poet-hero comes round and slaps him as he goes past, his virility is emasculated in being directed obsessively at a dummy.[115] Also, the bird/Holy Spirit is a painted bird, suggesting the illusion of flight and transcendence: 'Incertitude oiseau feint peint' (1.106).[116]

The artificiality or 'fausseté' in these presentations is not purely a liberation from positivism and from perspective, or an assertion of creative freedom. For it confronts us with the fact of illusion itself, and of displacement. 'Les mensonges ne me font plus peur', but neither can they prophesy other than at the expense of being exploited as images. Increasingly, Christianity is presented as failing to offer an alternative to transience and alienation. The Christian references are used to express states of being rather than to exploit situations in search of a prophecy able to take the present from the past and re-create the future. 'Templiers flamboyants' — the Templars are not burning in order to symbolise, they burn endlessly. They consume their identity, their martyrdom articulates and re-creates the Fall. The fire that opens out the present into a context of prophecy is the expression of a desire — a desire as unrealisable as circles are endless, and as clear as abstract shapes giving birth to perception in images fixed in no one, for all to see and be seduced by:[117]

> Et la girande tourne ô belle ô belle nuit   (1.101)

The courage the text opens our eyes to is not concerned with trans-cendence or victory, but rather with a survival maintained through improvisation:

> Incertitude oiseau feint peint quand vous tombiez
> Le soleil et l'amour dansaient dans le village
> Et tes enfants galants bien ou mal habillés
> Ont bâti ce bûcher le nid de mon courage   (1.106)

The bird/Holy Spirit falls from grace, from everywhere and nowhere, endlessly. There is no beginning, no birth in time, experience remains watched and not contextualised; there is no exchange, no possibility of intransitive expansion. The bird is a mirage of its symbolic function, it is a (de-)constructed symbol (like 'la lune' earlier), confronting a 'specific' identity with those very images that it fails to appropriate. And yet watching the bird is also an expression of what it would be like to exclude alienation from survival: improvising movement in the air, in the perceptual space, movement that is instantly identified with, and in which identity unfurls intransitively in the world:

> Le soleil et l'amour dansaient dans le village

Equally, the improvisation space is invaded by others — *your* children build the fire in which I live, while I admire the unpredictable diversity of *their* clothing.[118] The courage 'Les Fiançailles' ends by offering is not purification by fire, but erosion in burn*ing*. The diversity of events as they unfurl dismantles my identity and takes it away from me; to survive, I re-present and re-create my identification with images that others seem to control, and with the sense of difference and its continuity.

7—CODA

It becomes increasingly apparent that the crucial experience of this poem and of the reading of *Alcools* I have outlined is focused almost exactly in the centre of 'Les Fiançailles':

> Mais si le temps venait où l'ombre enfin solide
> Se multipliait en réalisant la diversité formelle de mon amour
> J'admirerais mon ouvrage   (1.55)

If darkness were solid, in a language I had invented, then the action of the world on me would glow in a language I could admire and claim as mine.[119] If only the representation I produce of my development through time could be different from repeating it again and again without seeing it. If only the diversity of images, contexts and objects with which I alternately, and exclusively, strive to identify, expressed and re-created the hidden structures that move me. If only. If perception rushes into memory 'comme un ouragan', then re-presentation is what I am.

Alcools — distillation, in the sense of manufacturing signs? Or dissolution, in the sense of invasion? Exchange or privacy? Poetry or death?[120]

NOTES

1 'La Chanson du Mal-aimé', 'Clotilde', 'Marizibill', 'Marie', 'La Tzigane', 'L'Emigrant de Landor Road', 'Cors de chasse'.

2 OP, p. 85.

3 The poem is an octosyllabic pentil, and its layout on the page automatically produces this impact. Octosyllabic pentils are an important feature in Apollinaire's poetry at various stages, and in a letter to Billy later in his career he refers to his work in the metre as one of his important contributions to the traditions of French prosody (OC, VI, p. 778). ('Les Collines' springs to mind.) Also, the eight-syllable line is much in evidence in Symbolism, by which Apollinaire's early poetic experience is so strongly influenced. Maeterlinck uses the metre to open up new possibilities in *Serres chaudes* (Paris, 1889), and Verlaine develops it in 'Un Veuf parle': *Oeuvres poétiques complètes*, ed. Y.-G. Le Dantec, Bibliothèque de la Pléiade (Paris, 1938), p. 295. See also Marie-Jeanne Durry, *Guillaume Apollinaire – 'Alcools'*, 3 vols, (Paris, 1956–64 and 1977), II, pp. 117–20, and III, pp. 71–4.

4 In his first preface to *Les Orientales* (Paris, 1829), Hugo characterises the work as 'ce volume inutile de pure poésie' and claims for it the power to transcend boundaries in experience, and to undermine the values that impose limits on what can be accepted as subject matter appropriate to poetry ('les limites de l'art'). (Victor Hugo, *Oeuvres poétiques*, ed. Albouy, 3 vols, Bibliothèque de la Pléiade, Paris, 1964–74, I, p. 578.)

Rimbaud, in his famous letter to Demeny of 1871, talks of the poet as 'voyant', exploding the limits of the personal and the subjective in an exploration, *via* his projected 'immense et raisonné dérèglement de tous les sens', of a dimensionless universal sensibility — 'JE est un autre'. (Arthur Rimbaud, *Oeuvres*, ed. S. Bernard, Paris, 1960, pp. 345 and 346.)

From 1895, le Blond and de Bouhélier experience an arid idealism in the anti-representational poetic forms initiated by Baudelaire and Mallarmé, and announce that 'l'au-delà ne nous émeut pas, nous croyons en un panthéisme gigantesque et radieux'. (Maurice le Blond, *Essai sur le naturisme*, Paris, 1896, quoted in Marcel Raymond, *De Baudelaire au surréalisme*, nouvelle édition revue et remaniée, Paris, 1940, p. 68.)

5 G. S. Kirk, *The Nature of Greek Myths* (London, 1974), p. 170.

6 In the introductory section to his exploration of Mallarmé's 'Prose pour Des Esseintes', Malcolm Bowie, referring to the illuminating comments of Proust and Valéry on rhyme, points out that the challenge of rhyme emphasised by Mallarmé's verse is the *heterogeneity* of the semantic and phonetic systems. Moreover, the poet is not self-evidently in control of this clash of heterogeneous systems, and knows it. '... et l'accouplement de la variable phonétique avec la variable sémantique engendre des problèmes de prolongement et de convergence que les poètes résolvent *les yeux bandés*' is Valéry's telling formulation of the experience that Bowie quotes. Thus the melodious return of sound in the rhyme scheme of 'L'Adieu' as well as in its phonetic pattern as a whole intensifies the question, raised by rhyme itself, about the relation to each other of the semantic and phonetic forms of memory, the relation of focus to duration, perception to identity. The rhyme scheme of 'Prose pour Des Esseintes' is necessarily infinitely more complex than that of 'L'Adieu', but Bowie's subsequent fascinating discussion of a movement from diversity to unity ('the many to the one') in the rhyme scheme of 'Prose' has something revealing to say about the relation of repetition to diversity and memory in 'L'Adieu'. (Malcolm Bowie, *Mallarmé and the Art of Being Difficult*, Cambridge, 1978, pp. 23–5 and p. 75.)

7 Much later, as a wounded soldier, Apollinaire wrote of the crucial place the sense of time and its passage occupied in his sensibility: 'Rien ne détermine plus de mélancolie chez moi que cette fuite du temps. Elle est en désaccord si formel avec mon sentiment, mon identité, qu'elle est la source même de ma poésie.' (*Lettres à sa marraine*, OC, IV, p. 686.)

8 OP, p. 46, p. 105.

9 OP, p. 81, p. 99.

10 OP, p. 146

11 'L'ombre croît, le jour meurt, tout s'efface et tout fuit!' Alphonse de Lamartine, 'L'immortalité' (in *Méditations poétiques*, Paris, 1820), *Oeuvres poétiques complètes*, ed. M.-F. Guyard, Bibliothèque de la Pléiade (Paris, 1963), p. 15, l. 4.

   'La fuite est verdâtre et rose/Des collines et des rampes,/Dans un demi-jour de lampes/Qui vient brouiller toute chose.' Paul Verlaine, 'Simples fresques (i)' (in *Romances sans paroles*, Paris, 1874), *Oeuvres poétiques complètes*, p. 128, l. 1.

   Francis Carco, 'Berceuse', in *La Bohème et mon coeur* (Paris, 1922), p. 24.

12 An emphasis on artifice is a dominant feature of French poetry since 1870. Striking examples might be Mallarmé's sonnet 'Le vierge, le vivace, le bel aujourd'hui', Stéphane Mallarmé, *Oeuvres complètes*, Mondor and G. Jean-Aubry, Bibliothèque de la Pléiade (Paris, 1945), p. 67; Verlaine's *'Art poétique'*, *Oeuvres poétiques complètes*, p. 207, l. 21, l. 36; and Apollinaire's own 'Merlin et la vieille femme', OP, p. 89. See pp. 51–3 above.

13 Roland Barthes, 'Ecrivains et écrivants', *Essais critiques* (Paris, 1964), pp. 147–54.

14 Barthes, *Essais critiques*, p. 147.
15 Barthes, *Essais critiques*, p. 148. Barthes's italics.
16 Barthes, *Essais critiques*, p. 147. Barthe's italics.
17 Barthes, *Essais critiques*, p. 151. Barthes's quotation marks.
18 Barthes, *Essais critiques*, p. 148. Barthes's italics.
19 I use the notion of 'sense' here with reference to Lyotard's concept of 'sens' and its opposition to 'signification': 'Cette limpidité grâce à laquelle le signifiant, dans l'expérience du langage articulé, s'efface presque complètement derrière le sens, n'est pas aisée à saisir. J'invoque un sens, ce sont des mots qui viennent se former dans ma bouche, et l'interlocuteur entend un sens.' (Jean-François Lyotard, *Discours, Figure*, Paris, 1971, p. 79.)
20 Barthes, *Essais critiques*, p. 149. Barthes's italics.
21 Barthes, *Essais critiques*, p. 149. Barthes's italics.
22 R. H. Stamelman, *The Drama of the Self in Apollinaire's 'Alcools'*, North Carolina Studies in the Romance Languages and Literatures, 178 (University of North Carolina, 1976), pp. 165–66.
23 Michael Décaudin, *La Crise des valeurs symbolistes* (Toulouse, 1960), pp. 180–3.
24 Roger Shattuck, *The Banquet Years*, revised edition (London, 1968), pp. 262–3.
25 I shall follow the example of Philippe Renaud's *Lecture d'Apollinaire* (Lausanne, 1969), and refer to this work as *Méditations esthétiques*. It is clear the decision to front the work with the title *Les Peintres cubistes* was the publisher's, and that Apollinaire felt that such a title did not cover the range of ideas he was dealing with. (OC, IV, p. 927, and also p. 491.)
26 *Les Trois Vertus plastiques* is included in CA, pp. 56–8. For an account of the time span covering the composition of *Alcools* and *Méditatioins esthétques*, see *Les Peintres cubistes*, ed. L. C. Breunig and J. C. Chevalier, Miroirs de l'art (Paris, 1965), pp. 10–11.
27 CAA, p. 242. See pp. 115–19 below.
28 OC, IV, p. 30.
29 OC, IV, p. 30. My underlining.
30 CA, pp. 29–31.
31 '*Les Poèmes saturniens* m'ont sauvé pendant quelques jours de l'ineptie où me tiennent les traces d'une installation et relevé des hontes de la réalité,' writes Mallarmé in response to Verlaine having sent him the work. The passage is quoted by Octave Nadal, *Verlaine* (Paris, 1961), p. 90.
32 Paul Verlaine, *Jadis et naguère* (Paris, 1885), in *Oeuvres poétiques complètes*, p. 250. The first line provided the name for the Decadent group, and the second pre-empted Maurice Barrès's title *Sous l'Oeil des Barbares* (Paris, 1892). See J.-H. Bornècque, *Verlaine par lui-même*, Ecrivains de toujours, 72 (Paris, 1966), p. 151.
33 André Baju, 'Décadents et symbolistes', in *Le Décadent*, quoted in André Barre, *Le Symbolisme* (Paris, 1911), p. 97. More textured and biting expressions of Decadent anti-representation abound in the literature of the period. This attitude is an intensification of Baudelaire's poetic drive, and of Gautier's. Among its targets are Romantic, affective descriptions of nature. The basis of this rejection of natural or objective reality is an exploration

of artifice: 'Au reste, l'artifice paraissait à Des Esseintes la marque distinctive du génie de l'homme... A n'en pas douter, cette sempiternelle radoteuse [i.e. nature] a maintenant usé la débonnaire admiration des vrais artistes, et le moment est venu où il s'agit de la remplacer, autant que faire se pourra, par l'artifice.' (Joris-Karl Huysmans, *A Rebours*, Fins de siècles, Paris, 1975, p. 76.)

34 Verlaine, *Oeuvres poétiques complètes*, p. 206.

35 Des Esseintes's appreciation of colour, for all its anti-quotidian élitism, reveals the kind of interpenetration that exists between Impressionist and Decadent aesthetics: 'En négligeant, en effet, le commun des hommes dont les grossières rétines ne perçoivent ni la cadence propre à chacune des couleurs, ni le charme mystérieux de leurs dégradations et de leurs nuances; en négligeant aussi ces yeux bourgeois, insensibles à la pompe et à la victoire des teintes vibrantes et fortes; en ne conservant plus alors que les gens aux pupilles raffinées, exercées par la littérature et par l'art, il lui semblait certain que l'oeil de celui d'entre eux qui rêve d'idéal, qui réclame des illusions, sollicite des voiles dans le coucher, est généralement caressé par le bleu des dérives, tels que le mauve, le lilas, le gris perle, pourvu toutefois qu'ils demeurent attendris et ne dépassent pas la lisière où ils aliénent leur personnalité et se transforment en de purs violets, en de francs gris.' Huysmans, *A Rebours*, pp. 65–6.

36 Renoir's *La Grenouillère* (1868–9) is included in *Renoir*, introduced by William Gaunt (London, 1952), plate 2. Monet's *La Grenouillère* (1869) is included in *Claude Monet*, presented by William Seitz (London, 1960), p. 85.

37 *Haystack at sunset near Giverny* (1891), *Rouen cathedral: the façade at sunset* (1894), Seitz, *Claude Monet* p. 139, p. 143. I refer to the titles of pictures in the language used in the book in which they are reproduced.

38 'Kaléidoscope', *Oeuvres poétiques complètes*, p. 201, l. 5.

39 *Rue de la Banvolle, Honfleur* (1864), *Boulevard des Capucines* (1873), included in Joel Isaacson, *Claude Monet, Observation and Reflection* (Oxford, 1978), pp. 54–5 and p. 90.

40 'Art poétique', Verlaine, *Oeuvres poétiques complètes*, p. 206, l.13.

41 Octave Nadal, *Verlaine* (Paris, 1961), p. 93, p. 94. Charles Morice explores in the following way the different attractions for the Symbolist of painting and music: 'D'ailleurs, si la Musique nous passionne en effet plus profondément et plus généralement que la Peinture, c'est que celle-là est à la fois plus lointaine et plus intime, plus près de l'origine et de la fin des sentiments et des sensations de celle-ci. La ligne et la couleur se fixent et défient le temps: le son, à peine exhalé, lui cède; il vit de mourir, c'est un grand symbole! Mais il se dépasse lui-même, il force le silence dans ses dernières retraites et y réveille l'écho; c'est toujours un appel vers quelquechose d'inconnu, de mystérieux, une exhalaison, une expansion de l'âme.' Charles Morice, *La Littérature de tout à l'heure* (Paris, 1889), p. 281.

42 Of the four categories of Cubism that Apollinaire designates, 'le cubisme instinctif' is the least appealing to him, and he attributes an Impressionist heritage to it. (OC, IV, p. 25.) A rejection of Impressionism features in the thinking of the Fauvists, with whom Apollinaire associated from 1904. It is common to all avant-garde movements up to the war — so much so that

Apollinaire ultimately regarded it as a simplistic attempt to break with the past. See his letter to André Billy of 29 July 1918, OC, IV, p. 778.

43 OC, IV, p. 18.

44 Nadal, *Verlaine*, p. 93.

45 In effect, Nadal is placing Verlaine and Apollinaire in the same perspective of Symbolist ambition. Robert de Souza expresses the Symbolist enterprise as the establishment of 'l'unification indissoluble des divers aspects de notre pensée et de nos sensations simultanées, soit dans la fugivité d'une plainte ou dans l'éclair d'un cri, soit sous le voile d'un mythe transparent'. (Quoted in Michel Décaudin, *La Crise des valeurs symbolistes*, p. 29.) Nadal describes Verlaine's achievement in this way: 'Replongée aux sources du souffle et du murmure la poésie se trouva avec lui une plasticité et une musicalité appropriées à la rêverie et au sentiment: le langage poétique, instinctivement et décidément restitué à ses rhythmes primitifs, se résuma à son geste nu: plainte, soupir, cri, caresse, chant.' (Nadal, *Verlaine*, p. 88.)

46 Verlaine, *Poèmes saturniens*, in *Oeuvres poétiques complètes*, p. 56, p. 54.

47 'Crépuscule du soir mystique', l. 1, l. 12.

48 Quoting from the poem in this way is clearly to mutilate it — to undermine the immense tautology that structures it and that creates an ironic tension with the drive for interpenetration expressed on the level of the signified. On the other hand, this same circularity mirrors the desired inclusion in nature and in sensation itself — the desired dissolving of reverie in reading, psychic texture in sound, diversity in rhythm. As we shall see, this blurring is quite different from the dissolving of memory and perception as categories that Apollinaire confronts in 'Automne malade' and in his speculation in *Méditations esthétiques*.

49 A similarly revealing paradox informs Huysmans's exploration of artifice. Des Esseintes's objective is not so much to remove nature from the artist's attention and to produce a new interaction with the world, but systematically to invert rhetorical and image patterns to produce images to do the job better than those hitherto gleaned from the 'observation' of nature. 'Il n'est, d'ailleurs, aucune de ses inventions [those of nature] réputée si subtile ou si grandiose que le génie humain ne puisse créer... aucun roc que le carton-pâte ne s'assimile; aucune fleur que de spéciaux taffetas et de délicats papiers peints n'égalent!' (*A Rebours*, p. 76.) Des Esseintes's artifice is not a radical abandoning of representation, but an ironic attempt, both desperate and listless, to galvanise it, to rearrange and re-present objective elements from the world, to externalise sensation and psychic experience in identifiable conglomerations of objects or material qualities. Des Esseintes's artifice is thus paradoxically passive in relation to the fact of the material world and its relation to perception.

50 OC, IV, p. 30.

51 OC, IV, pp. 15–16.

52 OC, IV, p. 30.

53 OC, IV, pp. 30–31.

54 OC, IV, pp. 17–18. In common with much other criticism, Chevalier's sophisticated reading of these terms suggests that 'inhumain' expresses a new poetic heroism: the artist's power to dissociate his language from an

involvement with nature, and to impose his own self-possession, his own creative (and created) identity. 'L'artiste nouveau, maître de soi, est divin, l'artiste humain, "naturel" est inspiré par le démon.... Pour atteindre la réalité, il faut se faire Dieu en exorcisant les monstres.' (Jean-Claude Chevalier, *'Alcools' d'Apollinaire — Essai d'analyse des formes poétiques* (Paris, 1970, p. 185.)

55 The other two 'vertus plastiques' are 'la pureté' and 'l'unité'. (OC, IV, p. 15.)

56 OC, IV, p. 31.

57 A conception of the relation of unconscious to conscious is clearly endemic to Freud's argument at all points. Of particular relevance to my comment here might be Freud's discussion of the relation of perception to memory in the early *Project for a Scientific Psychology* (I, pp. 229–30), and his account of the pre-conscious in his later *Introductory Lectures* (XVI, pp. 295–6). These references are to the *Standard Edition of the Complete Psychological works of Sigmund Freud*, ed. J. Strachey, 24 vols (London, 1953–74).

58 OC, IV, pp. 17–18.

59 OC, IV, p. 18.

60 OP, p. 108.

61 'J'ose à peine regarder la divine mascarade''; 'Le Brasier', OP, p. 110, 1. 47.

62 OC, IV, p. 29.

63 OC, IV, p. 27.

64 OC, IV, p. 29. My italics.

65 OC, IV, p. 29.

66 OC, IV, p. 32.

67 OC, IV, p. 29. My italics. See figure 1, Pablo Picasso, *Still-life with Chair-caning* (1912), and Douglas Cooper and Gary Tinterow, *The Essential Cubism (1902–1920)*, (London, 1983), p. 279.

68 The strength of the metaphoric framework that Apollinaire uses to discuss visual expression, combined with the consistent obscurity of his diction, leads Virginia Spate to the position that Apollinaire understood the 'Orphic' concepts he derived from Cubism in poetic rather than plastic terms. She suggests that Apollinaire may have been influenced by Mallarmé's vision of 'une explication orphique de la Terre, qui est le seul devoir du poète et le jeu littéraire par excellence'. (Virginia Spate, *Orphism, the Evolution of Non-figurative Painting in Paris 1910–14*, Oxford studies in the History of Art and Architecture, Oxford, 1979, p. 65. See also Stéphane Mallarmé, *Correspondance*, ed. Mondor and L. Austin, II, Paris, 1965, p. 301.)

69 OC, IV, p. 30.

70 The conceptual, artistic motion that gives birth to this fiction is also suggested in 'Merlin et la vieille femme': 'Mes tournoiments exprimaient — les béatitudes/Qui toutes ne sont rien qu'un pur effet de l'Art'. (OP, p. 89.)

71 OC, IV, p. 18.

72 OC, IV, p. 30.

73 A phrase such as 'la vérité des objets' highlights the distance separating Apollinaire's thinking at this point from the Symbolist and Decadent aesthetics of artifice. The artificial treatment of objects cannot, for Apollinaire, provide liberated forms of expression open to the diversity of

sensation. If anything, it highlights the elusiveness of objects, concentrates the mind of the artist on the fact of appearance, and thus on the fundamental challenge that 'humanisées' modes of expression seek to rise to.

74 See Michel Décaudin, *Dossier d''Alcools'* (Paris, 1960), pp. 215–16.

75 For a full account of the complex relationship between Apollinaire and Cendrars, and of the debate concerning the paternity of some of the 'modernist' features of Apollinaire's writing, see Marcel Poupon, 'Apollinaire et Cendrars', *Archives des lettres modernes*, 103, Archives Guillaume Apollinaire, 2 (1969).

76 OP, p. 554. The first published version appeared in *Le Festin d'Esope* in December 1903. 'La Clef' appeared posthumously in *Le Guetteur mélancolique*, ed. R. Mallet and B. Poissonnier (Paris, 1952). See Durry, *'Alcools'*, III, pp. 70–71.

77 The posture of poet addressing himself, or natural externalisations of his sensation, or expressions of his aspiration, is a dominant feature of Lamartine's and Hugo's verse: Lamartine's 'Le Soir', and 'Le Vallon'; Hugo's 'Aux Arbres', and 'Aux Anges qui nous voient'. Indeed, rhetorical address and dramatic poetic dialogue are dominant features of Hugo's innovatory control of metre as in 'Intérieur' and 'Le Mendiant'. (Lamartine, *Oeuvres poétiques complètes*, p. 13, p. 19. Hugo, *Oeuvres poétiques*, II, p. 608, p. 760, p. 599, p. 691. Verlaine, *Oeuvres poétiques complètes*, p. 83.) But the eclipse of dialogue from poetry is not one of Apollinaire's own initiatives. It has a precedent in Baudelaire's blurring of attitudes and forms, such as ode and satire. The opening stanza of Verlaine's 'Clair de lune' displays a quite novel use of the second person. Apollinaire's 'L'Adieu' is involved with this trend in French poetry, but changes the emphasis dramatically. This shift is developed in the mobile use of pronouns Apollinaire adopts in later poems such as 'Arbre' (OP, p. 178).

78 On this point, my own interpretation of the poem differs from Garnet Rees's: 'a suggestive discretion hints reflectively at death, time, love and the reincarnating powers of memory'. (Guillaume Apollinaire, *Alcools*, Athlone French Poets, 8, ed. G. Rees, London, 1975, p. 147.)

79 Writing between 1943 and 1944, René-Guy Cadou is one of the many commentators to compare these lines with Verlaine's 'Chanson d'automne', in *Le Testament d'Apollinaire* (Paris, 1980), p. 57.

80 I use the term 'metonymy' here in its opposition to 'metaphor', an opposition developed extensively in linguistics. But I am not using 'metonymy' to indicate descriptive and narrative functions in language. I use it as a way of highlighting an emphasis of the signifier in these lines, and to suggest a sense that uses of language are partial, displacing perception and the cherished experiences that motivate them, and constituting identity as 'other'. For an extensive discussion of the action of metonymy as a rhetorical feature of Apollinaire's verse, see Gilberte Jacaret, *La Dialectique de l'ironie et du lyrisme dans 'Alcools' et 'Calligrammes' de G. Apollinaire* (Paris, 1984).

81 OC, IV, p. 697, p. 495.

82 OP, pp. 128–36.

83 OC, III, pp. 780–3.

84 OC, III, p. 759. Apollinaire makes this comment in his lecture *La Phalanqe nouvelle*: OC, III, pp. 757–68 (p. 759). In the article on Royère, talking of the Symbolist achievements, he writes: 'Le vers libre seul à réussi.' (p. 782.)

85 OC, III, p. 783. For an illuminating interpretation of the way Apollinaire's comment on creative artifice in Royère is integrated with his thinking on the Cubist avant-garde of 1907 and 1908, see Claude Debon, ' ''L'Ecriture cubiste'' d'Apollinaire', *Europe*, 638–39 (1982), 118–27.

86 OC, III, p. 782.

87 OC, III, p. 781.

88 Jean Royère, *Soeur de Narcisse nue* (Paris, 1907).

89 Pausanias, *Guide to Greece*, translated by Peter Levi, 2 vols (London, 1979), I, p. 376.

90 OC, III, p. 783.

91 Rees, *Alcools*, p. 169. OP, p. 1067.

92 OC, III, p. 781.

93 Pilkington points out that Apollinaire may have discovered the verb 'feuilloler' from the medieval *Roman de Durmat*. (Guillaume Apollinaire, *Alcools*, ed. A. E. Pilkington, Oxford, 1979, p. 117.) Apollinaire also uses the verb much earlier in 'La Chanson du mal-aimé', OP, p. 49.

94 Interestingly, Pilkington emphasises the difference in style between this section and those following. He suggests that this section is 'fanciful and idyllic with its flowers, blue bird, Madonna and pigeon like the Holy Ghost', p. 149. In Pilkington's view, the point of the section is to set up a contrast with the reality that Apollinaire wakes up to in the following section of the poem.

95 Anne Hyde Greet, in her edited translation of *Alcools*, suggests that the blue bird has specific connotations in Apollinaire's universe: 'A symbol of happiness, the blue bird is assocaited by Apollinaire with love that is menaced or that has come to an end.' She goes on: 'in this context, cypress-trees also suggest a grave-yard'. (Guillaume Apollinaire, *Alcools*, translated with notes by Anne Hyde Greet, Berkeley and Los Angeles, 1965, p. 267.) Apollinaire also uses the image of the blue bird in 'La Tzigane' (OP, p. 99.) The use of the colour blue has a Symbolist precedent, and this intensifies the overall impression of a decaying mode of expression produced by the section as a whole. (Maurice Maeterlinck, 'Serre d'ennui', in *Serres chaudes*, Brussels, 1890, p. 19.)

96 Pilkington's suggestion (*Alcools*, p. 117) that Apollinaire uses 'feuilloler' to mean 'to flutter like falling leaves' emphasises the compression Apollinaire constructs on a variety of levels in these lines. In effect, the melodic quality of the verb undermines its power to locate its own expressiveness, since it dissolves the semantic levels of the verb in one another. Symbolist melody has created its own problems.

97 Jean-Pierre Richard, 'Etoiles chez Apollinaire', in *De Ronsard à Breton: Hommages à Marcel Raymond* (Paris, 1967), pp. 223–34 (p. 227).

98 Anne Hyde Greet draws attention to the ambiguity in 'errer': to wander and to be mistaken (*Alcools*, p. 267). She suggests that the forsworn lovers' mistake might be to have attempted reconciliation.

99 This point in the text of 'Les Fiançailles' is reached as the result of a

complex process of composition. Much of the material in this section and the following three is taken from a draught that Apollinaire originally entitled *Paroles étoiles*. The development of the sequence 'Mes amis m'ont enfin avoué leur mepris' and 'je buvais à pleins verres les étoiles' is controversial. In *Paroles étoiles*, 'Mes amis ne craignez pas de m'avouer votre mépris' is followed by 'J'ai l'orgueil de me souvenir de mes souhaits glorieux'. Are these glorious projects specific works, or an entire poetic attitude, such as the Symbolist one? Is Apollinaire replacing biographic elements, an obsession with Annie Playden, with a new-found poetic power in the image? Richard, reading the definitive text, believes that Apollinaire is on the verge of discovering an all-conquering poetic power. See Décaudin, *Dossier d''Alcools'*, p. 205; Greet, *Alcools* p. 269; Pilkington, *Alcools*, p. 150; Richard, 'Etoiles chez Apollinaire', p. 228, n. 24.

100 'Faux cols', l. 22, can refer to the head on a glass of beer. On this level, flows of clothes would be matched by a flow of stale beer over them. See Pilkington, *Alcools*, p. 150.

101 Greet emphasises that the moment of awakening is an awareness of bankruptcy. 'Having rejected the past, the poet does not, as in 'Le Brasier', immediately feel liberated, but, at first, bankrupt, incapable of achieving his new poetry.' (*Alcools*, p. 270).

102 A large body of criticism has approached these lines in a way that, according to my reading, is not borne out by the text. Greet suggests that the stars 'symbolise elusive poems' (*Alcools*, p. 270). Richard reads the lines as a point of climax in a developing thematic structure in Apollinaire's universe. Stars no longer represent the otherness of things ('un là-bas stellaire'), or a repeated farewell ('adieu aux choses'). Instead, eyes penetrate the stars: 'Mes yeux nagent loin de moi'; language is elevated to the solar order of the universe: 'le langage lui-même qui s'élève à l'ordre solaire ou stellaire — condamnant dès lors le poète à renoncer aux facilités ordinaires de son expression'. ('Etoiles chez Apollinaire', pp. 227–8.) Burgos suggests that a dialectic victory and disharmony, conquest and conflict evident throughout Apollinaire's work is in the service of a poetic power to substitute space for time. ('Pour une approche de l'univers imaginaire d'Apollinaire', *La Revue des lettres modernes*, 276–9, Guillaume Apollinaire, 10, 1971, pp. 35–67, p. 60.) On the other hand, Pilkington (*Alcools*, p. 151) sees in the transformation of words into stars a recognition that words are beyond the poet's reach, and that he remains powerless to incarnate his visions.

103 Other interpretations of the 'bêtes théologales' include: (1) allegories of the cardinal sins: the leopard/lust, the lion/pride, the wolf/covetousness. Dante meets them in the dark wood and the same three beasts appear in Jeremiah. (Greet, *Alcools*, p. 270). This interpretation suggests 'les vertus théologales', which are faith, hope and charity; (2) signs of the zodiac and their hidden influence in the determination of character. Apollinaire refers to Virgo, his own birth-sign, in line 97; (3) the animals in a bestiary: Apollinaire's own was published three years later in 1911. 'Le Poulpe' is perhaps particularly revealing here: 'Jetant son encre vers le ciel/Suçant le

sang de ce qu'il aime/Et le trouvant délicieux,/Ce monstre inhumain, c'est moi-même'. (OP, p. 22.)

104 Far from reading this section of the poem as a confrontation with danger, Chevalier reads it as the establishment of a 'Je organisateur posé comme une main sur les personnes, sur les choses, sur les essences'. For Chevalier, the 'Je' is free, precisely in that it is exploded in the forms in which it is expressed. Within the 'Je', endless multiplication, and a creative, intervening separation, coincide: 'deux processus complémentaires du même processus de création'. By inverting poetic forms, the 'Je' both multiplies the forms of its existence, and separates them, or itself from them. (Jean-Claude Chevalier, *'Alcools' d'Apollinaire — Essai d'analyse des formes poétiques*, Paris, 1970, p. 223.) Chevalier's formulation of Apollinaire's poetics of 1908 seems unacceptable, however attractive. It is based on the assumption that illusion, both liberating and crucifying, can be equated with rhetorical structures. Whereas illusion, 'une mère féconde' of 'fausseté' (OC, III, p. 783), is not the property of poets or their implement. 'La Réalité' is not, as one half of Chevalier's dialectic suggests, the imposition of the poet's knowledge, his self-possession, his explosion of appearance ('la poésie n'établit pas seulement une communication entre les acteurs humains, elle s'impose comme une réalité, comme une machine, qui fait de la réalité', p. 185). 'La réalité' will never be discovered once and for all (OC, IV, p. 17), it is the fact of illusion itself, the displacement of perception in image, 'la vie même', to borrow Apollinaire's phrase from a different context (CA, p. 297).

105 'Le Brasier', OP, p. 110, 1.58: 'Et voici le spectacle/Et pour toujours je suis assis dans un fauteuil/Ma tête mes genoux mes coudes vain pentacle/Les flammes ont poussé sur moi comme des feuilles'.

106 For this and all further references to the Ego, see Sigmund Freud, *The Ego and the Id*, in *The Standard Edition*, XIX, pp. 13–39.

107 'Sous couleur d'aimer la nature, la science et l'humanité, trop de jeunes gens ont gâté leur art par un enthousiasme écoeurant. . . . Nous n'avons pas besoin de vérités; la nature et la science en ont assez qui nous portent malheur.' (OC, III, p. 783.)

108 See note 33, 35, 41, 49 and 73.

109 The alteration that these lines represent from *Paroles étoiles* is significant: there, Apollinaire had written 'Pardonnez-moi d'avoir reconquis l'ignorance'. By writing 'Pardonnez-moi mon ignorance', Apollinaire precludes the interpretation that he is summoning a Symbolist creativity derived from rejecting nature and logic. See Décaudin, *Dossier d''Alcools'*, p. 205.

110 Such a monstrously ironic poet hero, also with laurels and perplexed by the glory and failure of his senses and of artifice, is evoked in 'Cortège': 'Il me suffit de goûter la saveur du laurier qu'on cultive pour que j'aime ou que je bafoue'. (OP, p. 75, 1.40.)

111 Apollinaire's use of incongruity here is perhaps closest to the one Reverdy develops. Reverdy suggests that the disparate elements in the image emphasise its abstract quality, and its effort to be different from nature while acting on us *like* nature:

L'image est une création pure de l'esprit.

Elle ne peut naître d'une comparaison mais du rapprochement de deux réalités plus ou moins éloignées.

Plus les rapports de deux réalités rapprochées seront lointaines et justes, plus l'image sera forte — plus elle aura de puissance émotive et de réalité poétique.

In André Breton, *Manifestes du surréalisme*, Idées (Paris, 1972), p. 31.

112 'la lune son cou tranché', l. 67.

113 'Je ne vis que passant ainsi que vous passâtes' ('Cortège', OP, p. 76, l. 67.)

114 'Des girandes' or clusters of fireworks were used in the middle ages as Easter and midsummer's day bonfires, and effigies were burnt on them. In 'Les Fiançailles', they suggest artifice, ecstasy and sacrifice. The vision of burning martyrs becoming celestial bodies is displaced in 'la girande', symbol dissolves into surface and the 'girande' makes light itself, a mirage as sourceless as the present.

115 *Le Petit Larousse* gives the following definition of 'une quintaine': 'Mannequin monté sur un pivot et armé d'un bâton, de manière que lorsqu'on le frappait maladroitement avec la lance, il tournait et asenait un coup sur le dos de celui qui l'avait frappé.' It also lists the figurative expression 'servir de quintaine' which it defines as 'être l'objet habituel d'attaques'. 'La quintaine' also carries strong sexual overtones that emphasise the ambiguity of gratification and frustration expressed by the image in the poem. See Pilkington, *Alcools*, p. 154.

116 The undermining of transcendence is built up in the multi-levelled play on words centred on 'feint': faked ('feint'); objective, target or ending ('la fin'); clever ('fin'). See Greet, *Alcools*, p. 275.

117 The power to prophesy associated with the Templars — their leader, Jacques de Molay is said to have prophesied the immanent death of the Pope who had condemned their order — is no longer the power to see the future, but an expression of faith in the present: 'je voudrais éprouver une ardeur infinie' (l. 68), an effort of will to be involved in experience and to represent it.

118 'Puis sur terre il venait mille peuplades blanches/Dont chaque homme tenait une rose à la main/Et le langage qu'ils inventaient en chemin/Je l'appris de leur bouche et je le parle encore/Le cortège passait et j'y cherchais mon corps/Tous ceux qui survenaient et n'étaient pas moi-même/Amenaient un à un les morceaux de moi-même' ('Cortège', OP, p. 75, l. 56.)

119 The grounding for the verb to glow, which has already done so much work in this reading, is provided by Apollinaire himself: 'Rien n'est mort que ce qui n'existe pas encore/Près du passé luisant demain est incolore/Il est informe aussi près de ce qui parfait/Présente tout ensemble et l'effort et l'effet'. ('Cortège', OP, p. 76, l. 70.)

120 For Chevalier, the essential *Alcools* experience is *not* an unanswered question, but the domination of paradox. The poet rejects the procedures of speech, where the hearer constantly strives to appreciate the context, and the speaker constantly needs to add and to qualify, to push back the

frontiers of the obscure. By imposing in its place the closed world of the text, the poet dispels ambiguity from his langauge, even *in* the diversity of his readers' responses, produces the variety of contexts he refers to, made homogenous by the forms he imposes, alters, and reimposes continually. In the controlled illusion of the poem, the poet can be both self and other. (Chevalier, *'Alcools'*, pp. 268–70.) However dialectically Chevalier proceeds in his readings — and nowhere more so than in his analysis of audience control and audience invasion in 'Nuit rhénane' — my own suggestion is that to make such heroic claims for Apollinaire's poetry is to undermine its creativity. *Alcools* does not dominate paradox, but confronts it as a reality of experience, and poetry survives by representing it and incarnating it.

2—POETRY, PAINTING, THEORY

1—WHERE DOES *ALCOOLS* LEAVE US?

To answer the question in this heading, it may be helpful to discuss briefly some of the other writing going on in the period, or in the years leading up to it. I began my comment on *Alcools* with a discussion of two poems, 'L'Adieu' and 'Automne malade', both of which developed over a long period although they were published for the first time in their final form in *Alcools* itself. 'La Clef', from which the lines that were to become 'L'Adieu' are drawn, is reminiscent of Maeterlinck in metre and in its manipulation of allegory; 'Automne malade' is often thought of as 'Verlainian'. A brief look at Verlaine's achievement is useful in an attempt to clarify Apollinaire's, especially as Apollinaire recognises the importance of Verlaine in the formation of his own horizons, particularly as regards the 'vers libre'. I also propose to discuss briefly some verse by Jammes and Laforgue. I choose Laforgue because of Verlaine's influence on Decadence and the part he played in it, and because of the light Decadent writing may throw on subsequent attitudes to artifice, and I have chosen Jammes because both his association with the 'école naturiste' and his emphasis on simplicity and concrete sensation after his return to Catholicism involve him in a new stage in the effort to ensure expressive power for French poetry. Symbolism, 'l'impair', sensation; Decadence, satire, and a combination of the esoteric and the concrete; 'naturisme' and catholicism, morality and anti-idealism — what can such approaches tell us about the unique achievement of *Alcools*, about the directions in which the collection leads us, and about its dramatic opening gesture?[1]

> Les feuilles
> Qu'on foule
> Un train
> Qui roule
> La vie
> S'écoule   ('Automne malade')
>
> Les sanglots longs
> Des violons

> De l'automne
> Blessent mon coeur
> D'une langeur
>   Monotone.   (Paul Verlaine, 'Chanson d'automne')

> — Mon Dieu, sur votre front ceint d'une haie d'épines,
> je chanterai durant toute votre agonie:
> mais lorsque fleurira la couronne terrible
> vous laisserez l'oiseau y construire son nid.
>   (Francis Jammes, 'L'Eglise habillée de feuilles' no. 23)

> Lampes des mers! blancs bizarrants! mots à vertiges!
> Axiomes *in articulo mortis* déduits!
> Ciels vrais! Lune aux échos dont communient les puits!
> Yeux des portraits! Soleil qui, saignant son quadrige,
>   Cabré, s'y crucifige!
>   O Notre-Dame des Soirs,
>   Certes, ils vont haut vos encensoirs!
>   (Jules Laforgue, 'Complainte à Notre-Dame des Soirs')

> Ce sont les Christ inférieurs des obscures espérances
> Adieu 'Adieu
> Soleil cou coupé   ('Zone')

The nostalgia of 'Automne malade' — unaccountable separations, inexplicable memories, irreducible and repeated transience — is not the nostalgia of Verlaine's 'Chanson d'automne'. The final lines of Apollinaire's poem, in relation to the poem as a whole, fragment reference definitively and the language itself undermines the possibility of dominating experience. But Verlaine's poem has some of the features of Apollinaire's. The manipulation of rhetorical forms is dispensed with; points of reference are multiplied. Description of landscape overlaps with the exploration of mood, so that the dialogue between subject and object, psychological and concrete experience, dissolves. 'Chanson d'automne' is a poem of frustration that acquires poetic status because of the melancholia it provokes. The assonantal returns combined with the rhyming ones would be reassuringly circular, were it not for the irregularity of the rhyme scheme and the metre. Each return is a non-coincidence of different experiences, of memory and the present.

But Apollinaire builds on the Verlainian onslaught on French prosodic conventions.[2] 'Automne malade' is a poem with genuine conceptual dimensions, and deals with their erosion and their glow. It deals with the experience of self, of memory and of language, whereas when Verlaine's poem deals in irregularity and non-coincidence, the barrier that emerges is one the language has the effect of *indicating*, in spite of Verlaine's rejection of mimesis in favour of the 'impair', of melody and the exploration of the psyche. This is because his language not only explores the privacy of his experience, but seems to maintain it intact. 'Sanglots', 'langueur', even 'coeur' and particularly 'monotone' are not original uses exclusive to 'Chanson d'automne'.[3] They are *leit motif* words and effects in the lattice-work of Verlaine's poetic vocabulary as a whole and in the framework of recognition it creates. Verlaine's language seems designed to circumscribe the irreducible privacy of his experience, and in this way it *refers* to the frustration it seeks to express. The privacy of his language allows him to dominate language and manipulate his reader's response to it; we cannot but recognise Verlaine's private experience. The sound-patterning that is one of his principal objectives implies a certain 'artisanal' approach to his own language that allows him to take possession of it and to steer it in the direction of encompassing and reference.

What we discovered about the sound-patterning at the end of 'Automne malade' is quite different, although these lines are super-ficially comparable to the effects that Verlaine seeks. At the end, the poem prevents the writer from circumscribing language and thus from possessing or indicating experience. We discovered that the culmi-nation of 'Automne malade' is writing that represents an explosion of plurality from which language, in its relation to memory, fails to distinguish itself and to which it cannot refer.[4] The poem ends with a representation of transience that is paradoxically linear. Trampling feet, departing trains, life draining away — what seems specific cannot be distinguished from the plural; the plural takes specific, singularising form. The language removes itself from us; Apollinaire constructs difference and confronts his reader with it. At the same time, the experience, the 'pre-text' engaging him with language, is displaced as a sourceless involvement with it. As the poem ends, the contours of the private are sequestered in memory and as language, and from this there is no return.

A comparable dichotomy of attitudes is visible in the contrast between the stanzas from 'L'Eglise habillée de feuilles' and 'Com-plainte à Notre-Dame des Soirs', the third and fourth extracts with which I introduced this chapter. In this case, differing attitudes to Christianity and Christian mythology give rise to the expression of conflicting experiences of language in the two texts. Jammes's *Clairières dans le Ciel* refers to the events encompassing the failure, owing to parental interference, of a love affair and James's subsequent conversion or return to Christianity. Jammes kept his immediate acquaintance and readership aware of these events, to the extent of organising a pre-publication reading of 'L'Eglise habillée de feuilles'. Claudel, Jammes's mentor during the conversion period, attended this reading and showed his appreciation of Jammes's development, over which he had presided, and of which the reading was accepted as a culmination. The growth of Jammes's explicit commitment to Christianity structures his language in such a way as to provide it with an audience and a context that relate individual experience to a recognised framework of value.[5] It is a language in which Jammes's own experience is expressed as an involvement with the experience of Christ: Jammes and Christ suffer the same conflict of the spiritual and the physical, and the resolution of this conflict takes place in the renewal of life and creation itself; in Jammes's verse, this renewal is realised before his eyes, continuously, in the texture of his experience. The bird represents birth as well as the omnipresence of the Holy Spirit, and the Christian context of the language allows a free interplay between humanity, redemption and communication.

Laforgue, on the other hand, reacts to language with frustration, as something impenetrable. In 'Complainte à Notre-Dame des Soirs', Laforgue's entry into language is represented by a satirical expression of his exclusion from it: an expression of experience as the impossibility of becoming involved in history — in the dialect of memory and language that produces images of the present. The vocabulary of Romantic aspiration (the moon: the whiteness of unrealised and unrealisable desire, the depths of emotional intensity uncovered by poetry; eyes: the drive towards unmediated communication), the mythology of classical rationality (Apollo's sun-chariot of fire, here dying grotesquely in an apparently cosmic disaster), along with what Laforgue thinks of as a Baudelairean pan-religious mysticism — these are the elements in terms of which Laforgue circumscribes language, locating his moment in cultural history and his alienation from it.[6] For him entry into language is a process by which existence *in* language and *as* history both absorbs and silences individuality and potential creativity. Laforgue presents the poetic language he has inherited as being incapable of expressing exclusion or unwilling to do so. But simultaneously, exclusion from the given language he has inherited allows him to discover a potentially self-defining difference; it creates his access to self-consciousness by confronting him with a barrier between the language of others, and the ineffectual privacy of his experience.

In 'Zone', on the other hand, Apollinaire, though using an image-pattern superficially comparable to Laforgue's image of the sun crucified in its coagulated blood, represents an unavailable distinction between language and experience. In the last lines of 'Zone', Christ is deposed — not only devalued, but lowered from the cross and demoted from his mythological function of resolution, exiled from the space where the axes of present and past cross, the axes of physical and spiritual, language and experience. The rose-chafer that Apollinaire, earlier in the poem, thinks of himself as watching at the centre of a rose is eating the rose, and in this way it represents the centre of a rose; the obscure centre of the rose is experience as it is consumed:

> Tu es dans le jardin d'une auberge aux environs de Prague
> Tu te sens tout heureux une rose est sur la table
> Et tu observes au lieu d'écrire ton conte en prose
> La cétoine qui dort dans le coeur de la rose (1.95)

The sleeping rose-chafer/rose comes into existence as a texture of the poet's self-consciousness, a texture invented, discovered and effaced as he watches.[7] Moreover, the ubiquity of the poet-persona in 'Zone' means, paradoxically, that each new context in the kaleidoscope is *different* from the Apollinaire who writes, who senses his own experience as he composes. Fragmentation, explosion, plurality, displacement — these *are* language in Apollinaire's world. Christ is lowered from a position where experience has access to universal communication. In Apollinaire's world, a being bleeds as the price of seeing ('soleil'); alienation and dispossession *are* experience.

2—TRANSFORMATION AND CHRONOLOGY: FUTURIST SIMULTANEITY

The crucial experience, then, in the reading and the writing of *Alcools* is a rediscovery of language in its relation to memory — of being as the memory of being. Complex and rewarding as this enterprise is for anyone in dialogue with Apollinaire's poetry, it underwent a radical upheaval in the course of Apollinaire's career. Many literary historians and critics have tended to reduce this upheaval emblematically to the space separating *Alcools* from *Calligrammes*. But of course Apollinaire's attraction to a relatively radical and subversive aesthetic expresses itself as early as 1905, with the beginnings of his involvement with the Fauvists and with Picasso. By 1907, his commitment to the work of Derain, Dufy and Matisse had been established, and formed an integral part of his journalistic activity as well as of his thinking about artistic expression generally. Let us remember that *Les Trois Vertus plastiques*, published as part of *Méditations esthétiques* in 1913 as a major statement of Apollinaire's involvement in the new Cubist dynamic of expression, was written in 1908 as the catalogue notes to an exhibition in Le Havre comprising works by, among others, Bonnard, Signac, Vlaminck, Derain, Dufy, Rouault, Matisse, Metzinger and Braque.[8]

Méditations esthétiques juggles with history to the extent of opening its call for radical change with insights first expressed at a time when Apollinaire was as anxious to rejuvenate Symbolism as he was aware of the transformation the visual arts in Paris were beginning to undergo. In the same way, the *Alcools* collection is itself an interpretation of history and of the fact that history does not present itself in terms of moments of immediately recognisable change. In fact, *Alcools* and its composition both encompass and articulate change. Apollinaire's purpose in compiling this anthology of his verse is to bring different aspects of his poetic experience into relation with one another: the Rhenish experience, which it was his original intention to publish as a self-contained entity entitled *Le Vent du Rhin*; the neo-Symbolist reappraisal of Symbolist lyricism represented by 'Lul de Faltenin' (1907), 'Les Fiançailles' and 'Le Brasier' (1908); and the rhetoric of plurality adopted in 'Le Voyageur' as well as in 'Zone' (both published in 1912). The action of 'Zone' as the opening event in *Alcools* at the very least expresses an awareness that experience does not divide itself into watertight, self-contained chapters, that the difference between stages in experience is revealed in terms of a continuously shifting present and of continual re-evaluations of the past.

In keeping with this awareness, I shall not endeavour, in my own account, to adhere to the chronology of the artistic events Apollinaire was influenced by, and influenced, between 1905 and 1914. This is clearly a period of immense artistic activity, and a chronology so complete as to encompass it in its totality is almost inconceivable. Equally, the texture of Apollinaire's intense involvement with this activity would not be encompassed by the chronology of his various interests and enthusiasms, or by neutrally tracking the pattern of their emergence and re-emergence. But I shall not abandon chronology or dismiss the importance of it — indeed, Philippe Renaud's accounts not only of Apollinaire's texts but also of their interaction with the developing cultural activity of their period are invaluably illuminating. I shall point out the context of the events or the aspects of artistic activity I discuss, and try to use this information to discover an overall coherence in the desires Apollinaire articulates in relation to the arts from 1905 to World War I.

In 1914, addressing himself to what he appears to regard as a nïve and unproductive espousal of the external manifestations of a culturally, and perhaps technologically, transforming society, Apollinaire writes:

> Les personnes éduquées dans le vaillant mouvement artistique d'aujourd'hui font une différence très nette entre ces deux adjectifs: 'moderne' et 'nouveau'; et je me hâte de le dire, ce n'est guère que du second que l'on marque l'artiste qui porte dans son oeuvre une audace nouvelle et de la puissance artistique éclatante.[9]

Apollinaire's practice of becoming involved with new artistic initiatives — of seeking the 'nouveau' in every new development of modernity — is seen as early as his involvement with *Vers et Prose*, which was finally launched by Paul Fort in 1905. This review not only had the relatively conservative purpose of revitalising the Symbolist aesthetic by giving it a direction other than the poetic idealism devalued by Decadence and Naturism between 1895 and 1902. It was a manifestation of a desire to give French poetry as a whole the positive direction it was felt to have lacked since the disintegration of the Symbolist initiative.[10] It provided an eclectic focal context in which a variety of ideas and artistic ambitions could be realised. Apollinaire's involvement was not so much a determination to be associated with leading figures or groups of the period ('moderne'), but a will to respond to the urgency of the present and to relate his current poetic activity to the currency of his moment in cultural history ('nouveau'). Simultaneously, Apollinaire was involved with such disparate personalities as the Fauvists living in the Parisian suburb of Le Vésinet, and Alfred Jarry.[11] In the midst of this fermentation, it is clear that, with the dramatic appearance of Picasso's *Les Demoiselles d'Avignon* in 1907, *something has changed* in Parisian as well as European culture. Apollinaire's art criticism and journalistic activity bear witness to his increasing involvement with, and his contribution to, what amounts to a fundamental shift of target in artistic expression.

One of the most striking features of this shift is an increasingly urgent consciousness of modernism as such — the experience, or the illusion, of a moment in history presenting itself as a radical and irreversible break with the past. In a certain sense, Cubism is an expression of this kind of consciousness, for it effects a fundamental break from the dominance of mimesis, and embarks on a radical re-thinking of expression in relation to observed objects. But the nature of its impact was such that it ran the risk of being thought of as a 'school' jostling for aesthetic justification. Moreover, Cubism was regarded by many — and has been up until quite recently by some critics — over-concerned with subverting the rudiments of classical art, and as removed from the vitality of experience because of the conceptualised colourlessness of its approach.[12] Certainly by 1913, the year *Méditations esthétiques* was published, Futurism and the work of Robert Delaunay were making demands on Apollinaire's thinking that were as powerful as those of Cubism.[13] It is for these reasons that I shall be discussing the complex issues confronted in Cubism later on in this account of Apollinaire's pre-war artistic activity. This will allow me to discuss Cubism in relation to Delaunay's Orphism (a term Apollinaire arrived at from thinking about Cubism), which is the other highly conceptualised form of expression with which he became involved.

Futurism, like Cubism, found its initial impetus in the rejection of imitation in art. It combines this rejection with an intense commitment to that sense of a 'break with history' that I mentioned above as characteristic of these years. It offered a colourful, anti-conceptual involvement with the transforming appearance of the world, its new technology, and its new rhythm of industrial innovation. For the Futurists, the proliferation of machinery witnessed by their generation represented a crucial challenge to the individual and the artist: the challenge of existence itself in the present. A defining feature in the Futurist project of rejuvenating art is a focus on speed: 'Nous déclarons que la splendeur du monde s'est enrichie d'une beauté nouvelle: la beauté de la vitesse. Une automobile de course avec son coffre orné de grands tuyaux, tels des serpents à l'haleine explosive ... une automobile rugissante, qui a l'air de courir sur la mitraille, est plus belle que la *Victoire de Samothrace.*' Thus writes Marinetti in the manifesto that launched Futurism in Paris in 1909.[14] He goes on: 'Nous voulons chanter l'homme qui tient le volant, dont la tige idéale traverse la terre, lancée elle-même sur le circuit de son orbite.' The experience of renewed urgency and relevance in artistic activity is produced by the vision of an identity that continuously increases in range and texture. Barriers between individuals and between classes, barriers imposed by social categorisation of experience, are challenged by Futurism. It attempts to overturn them by representing technological objects in particular as an instigation of diversity. The representation of movement and of speed that is a defining feature of Balla's and Boccioni's paintings in particular is conceived of as a *creation* of movement, as a *dynamism* that is visualised as eroding the distinction between appearance and productive forces, between the instant and universality, between consciousness, desire and memory. In Boccioni's *The Forces of a Street* (see figure 2), silhouette is combined with shadow, volume is laid bare by light, stasis is dissolved into movement; a single moment suggests others, depth is involved in surface.[15] This dynamism is the Futurist conception of the individual's power to dominate his experience and his moment: 'The single man, therefore, must communicate with every people on earth. He must feel himself to be the axis, judge, and motor of the explored and unexplored infinite. Vast increase of a sense of humanity and a momentary urgent need to establish relations with all mankind.'[16]

There is no doubt that Futurist notions played a strong part in the development of Apollinaire's thinking on the new art from 1909 to the war.[17] Writing after his return from the war, he describes the conviction he and those around him felt that art should develop and respond to a new world in terms that echo Futurist thinking — speed, diversity, the disintegration of barriers:

> La rapidité et la simplicité avec lesquelles les esprits se sont accoutumés à désigner d'un seul mot des êtres aussi complexes qu'une foule, qu'une nation, que l'univers n'avaient leur pendant moderne dans la poésie. Les poètes comblent cette lacune et leurs poèmes synthétiques créent de nouvelles entités qui ont une valeur plastique aussi composée que des termes collectifs.[18]

There seems a strong connection between the construction of synthetic entities that Apollinaire describes and the Futurist concept of dynamism. Futurist dynamism aims at a dismantling of difference and barrier, and it involves an experience of simultaneity that it is the objective of Futurist expression to represent as well as to create. The Futurist enterprise is to dissociate language (pictorial or verbal) from the praxis of discursive analysis and presentation, and to approach language as a synthesis of experience, in which experience is fragmented and enveloped, both simultaneously and dynamically.

Marinetti extends his vision of simultaneity in writing to an attack on the discursive structures of syntax. In *Destruction of Syntax* —

2 Umberto Boccioni, *The Forces of a Street* (*Kräfte einer Strasse*), 1911 (courtesy Collection Dr P. Hänggi, Kunstmuseum Basel)

Imagination without Strings — Words-in-Freedom,[19] in which he includes and develops some of the ideas thrown out in his telegraphic *Technical Manifesto of Futurist Literature* of 1912, Marinetti expresses the belief that simultaneity in writing, and simultaneity between experience and writing, is achieved by the abolition of tenses, by a condensed proliferation in image and in analogy, and by the suppression of punctuation:[20]

> When I speak of destroying the canals of syntax, I am neither categorical nor systematic. Traces of conventional syntax and even of true logical sentences will be found here and there in the words-in-freedom of my unchained lyricism.   (p. 99)
>
> So the poet's imagination must weave together distant things *with no connecting strings*, by means of essential *free* words.   (p. 98)
>
> By imagination without strings I mean the absolute freedom of images or analogies, expressed with unhampered words and with no connecting strings of syntax and with no punctuation.   (p. 99)
>
> Analogy is nothing more than the deep love that assembles distant, seemingly diverse and hostile things.   (p. 99)
>
> The imagination without strings, and words-in-freedom, will bring us to the essence of material.   (p. 100)

In the same article, Marinetti goes on to advocate the disruption of regular typography: 'My revolution is aimed at the so-called typographical harmony of the page, which is contrary to the flux and re-flux, the leaps and bursts of style that run through the page.'[21] The poet Cangiullo developed the idea into a typographical representation of objects — eliciting much enthusiasm from Marinetti, who complimented him on the lyricism of the drawn analogies he was offering the public.[22]

Many of these techniques and concepts are operating in 'Lettre-Océan', Apollinaire's first lyrical ideogram, which appeared in *Les Soirées de Paris* in June 1914, and was his first text to draw an equivalence between words and the shape of objects.[23] (Futurist typographic practices themselves moved towards the creation of geometric configurations, a trend Apollinaire in turn responded to in his own *Antitradition futuriste*.)[24] As Philippe Renaud points out, the typography of 'Lettre-Océan' is not concerned with the imitation or typographic representation of objects.[25] For him, it consists of a presentation of a Futurist-inspired simultaneity, an emphatic shift away from discursive rhetoric; it effaces the difference between contexts, tenses, moments in time and in perspective; it is a confrontation with the experience of 'simultaneous' perception in relation to the material. I shall be discussing a little later (as well as in the following chapter) the extent to which Apollinaire's approach to simultaneity in 'Lettre-Océan', and to the material in relation to perception, can in fact be understood in terms of the Futurist use of the same concepts. Whatever the answer, 'Lettre-Océan', with its Futurist features, is a climactic expression of Apollinaire's new lyricism and of his vision of quite different artistic possibilities.

3—'DRAMATIST' SIMULTANEITY

In the critical years of avant-garde activity, 1907–1914, Futurism was clearly not the only approach to artistic expression to deal in the concept, or the experience, of a simultaneous synthesis. The aesthetic envisaged by Barzun's 'Dramatisme' is based on a belief in the reality of a universal experience, unifying individuals and overcoming the barriers of class and culture. In *L'Ere du drame — essai de synthèse poétique moderne*, Barzun argues that this experience is to be expressed not only in terms of a disruption within poetic conventions and fictions, but of the assumption itself that poetry is fiction.[26] For Barzun, it is the urgent responsibility of poetry to draw on the diversity of psychological experience, and to bring an extending awareness of that diversity to bear on our experience of the world: 'Conséquence logique de l'évolution poétique, la dramatisation psychologique est essence: elle n'est subordonnée à aucun système, à aucune formule secondaire. C'est une manière de percevoir et de réaliser absolument libre et personnelle, dépendant que du tempérament de chacun.'[27] To emphasise the dramatic dynamism in our experience both of the world and of poetry is regarded by Barzun as the equivalent of an increase in creativity, and this implies discovering an enhanced individuality as well as a sense of collective experience.

The crucial technique that allows this dramatisation to be pursued — and 'l'Individuel', 'le Collectif', 'l'Humain' and 'l'Universel' to be made accessible and operative — is simultaneity.[28] For Barzun, the dynamically, and hence definitively, personal is discovered in explicit confrontation with diversity, in an explosion into diversity of the source of expression: 'Faire retentir le drame universel dans l'oeuvre par la polyphonie des voix simultanées du monde .... Ce retentissement commande naturellement ses moyens de réalisation: d'abord, par l'abandon du lyrisme simple, du *poème à une voix*....'[29] 'L'absolument libre et personnel' is both discovered and pursued in terms of an abandoning, an explosion of singularity in voice and in language: '... ainsi le lyrisme simple est absorbé par un lyrisme multiple, supérieur, qui utilise pareillement tous les modes expressifs connus; ainsi, les ordres psychologiques fondamentaux, à l'état de *voix* et de présences poétiques *simultanées*, dramatisent l'oeuvre'.[30] The 'lyrisme multiple', like the Futurist dynamism, is a protest not only against passive reading and passive response to artistic expression, but also against what Barzun regards as the illusory and self-imposed isolation, the defeatist and self-obsessed nostalgia of the Symbolist poet and his search for transcendence, unification, purity and beauty.[31] It is a protest against the fiction of linear sequentiality in the presentation of experience, and against the assumption that instances of experience can be contained and 'got to the end of' in instances of language, or in units of time circumscribed by language. It is a protest against what the authors of the *Futurist Painting: Technical Manifesto* (1910) refer to as a 'powerless synthesis' aimed at an imitative inclusion of experience in expression, in favour of a simultaneous synthesis and fragmentation of experience.[32] Barzun's objective, like Marinetti's, is to liberate the individual from the restrictions of context and history, and to dominate the present in the creative process.

But Apollinaire's initially enthusiastic response to Barzun's attempt to democratise experience and expression seems to have disintegrated when confronted with Barzun's actual productions, which followed the publication of *L'Ere du drame* and the discussions that took place between Barzun, Apollinaire, Mercereau and Tancrède de Visan among others.[33] Delaunay and Apollinaire alike expressed disappointment that the artefacts Barzun published in his review *Poème et Drame* seemed to reduce the notion of simultaneity to a neutral simultaneous recording of a variety of different voices or participants in a conversation; or, alternatively, to experiments emphasising the auditive effects of language.[34] In 'Simultanisme-librettisme', a serious article in the same issue of *Les Soirées de Paris* that 'Lettre-Océan' appeared in for the first time, an Apollinaire ridicules Barzun's pretentions and his claims on the authorship of the concept of simultaneity. Moreover, he emphasises, in dismissing Barzun's 'theatrical' multi-voice constructions, that the possibility of textual simultaneity was originally perceived by Marinetti.[35]

4— THE PRESENT. SIMULTANEITY AND MEMORY. CUBISM

Are we to believe, then, that the textuality of 'Lettre-Océan' can, after all, be explained exclusively in terms of Futurist thinking and the Futurist ideology? What is the relation between the ideograms and the verse texts of *Calligrammes* and of the 'Ondes' section in particular, and does this relation in turn point to any differences between the Futurists' conception of Simultanist expression and Apollinaire's? Futurism clearly has elements in common with Dramatism, and also with Delaunay's speculation on the nature and objectives of visual expression.[36] Apollinaire himself evokes a sense of common experience in *L'Esprit nouveau et les poètes*, written about five years after 'Lettre-Océan' in 1917, after his war experiences and not long before his death. With an unabated sense of urgency and pleasure, he again refers to the imperative need to discover or invent new forms of poetry to correspond to the experience of a technological boom. But the poetry he calls for is capable of more than this: it must express the explosiveness of living in the present; it must be galvanised by the present and be able both to rise to its diversity and bear witness to its uniqueness. When he wrote *L'Esprit nouveau et les poètes*, the subject of poetry and of the visual arts, their sphere of activity and their objective, was for Apollinaire (just as it was several years before and continued to be for Barzun, Marinetti and Delaunay) 'le monde entier, ses rumeurs et ses apparences, la pensée et le langage humain, le chant, la danse, tous les arts et tous les artifices, plus de mirages encore que ceux que pouvait faire surgir Morgane sur le Mont Gibel pour composer le livre vu et entendu et l'avenir'.[37] Simultaneity is not merely an innovative technique, it *is* the experience it is designed to express: an experience of energetic optimism, a desire for an expression capable not only of providing a vessel for a newly discovered, enlarged sensibility, but also of being a creative intervention in the present and an act of emancipation in relation to inherited language and to history. As Apollinaire realised, such projects are not pursued exclusively within Futurism or among any other single group of practitioners, and we must look at these years more closely to uncover the perceptions behind 'Lettre-Océan'.

One of the issues raised by the energetic optimism of 'simultaneous' art is memory, since it is only in relation to memory that dominance of the present can be established. But memory is not an issue explicitly confronted by Barzun or Marinetti, and it is uncharacteristic as well as revealing that Severini, so much involved with the Futurist obsession with novelty and speed, shculd present the notion of simultaneity in terms of memory: 'Today, in this epoch of dynamism and simultaneity, one cannot separate any event or subject from the memories, the plastic preferences or aversions, which its expansive action calls up *simultaneously* in us, and which are so many abstract realities — *points de repère* for achieving the full effect of the event or the object in question.'[38] To present simultaneity in relation to memory acts as a crucial reminder that Apollinaire's commitment to an aesthetic of novelty, to a radicalisation of the Symbolist tradition, and to a disruption of mimesis in the visual arts takes place initially in the context of Cubism, a movement that explicitly confronted memory in its relation to expression. If we move back at this point from *The Plastic Analogies of Dynamism* (1913) to 1907, we shall be able to see how sophisticated Apollinaire's thinking on these matters already was at the moment when Cubism was launched.

It was in 1907 that *Les Demoiselles d'Avignon* was completed, and 1907–8 is the crucial period in Apollinaire's development that I mentioned in the previous chapter: a period when Apollinaire embarked on a combined involvement with and subversion of Symbolist practices. His writing began to express a desire to discover the fundamentally poetic, the originally, purely, inhumanly poetic ('devenir inhumain'), and to explore his experience of the relation between expression and freedom itself. It is worth reminding ourselves of some of the important dates on which my discussion of Apollinaire's poetics has so far been based. In the twelve months from November 1907 to November 1908, Apollinaire published his significant comments on the work of Jean Royère, which I mentioned in the first chapter. Here he appears to look to Symbolism and a rejuvenation of its objectives for a new impetus and for an urgent response to the present (*La Phalange* no. 15, January 1908). These new objectives begin to find their poetic expression in 'Onirocritique' (*La Phalange* no. 20, February 1908 and included in *L'Enchanteur pourrissant* in 1909), as well as in the *Alcools* texts 'Lul de Faltenin' (November 1907), 'Le Brasier' (May 1908) and 'Les Fiançailles' (November 1908). In June 1908, Apollinaire first published *Les Trois Vertus plastiques*, included in 1913 almost without change in *Méditations esthétiques*, his most sophisticated statement on Cubism and the new aesthetic. I shall now return briefly to this text and show how the ideas Apollinaire works out in it relate more generally to his pursuit of the 'nouveau'.[39]

Long before the doctrines of Futurism and Dramatism, Apollinaire here deals with simultaneity and the abolition of the distinction between time dimensions; neither the observation of nature nor its 'aesthetification' should be the structuring objective of art:

> Mais, le peintre doit avant tout se donner le spectacle de sa propre divinité et les tableaux qu'il offre à l'admiration des hommes leur conféreront la gloire d'exercer aussi et momentanément leur propre divinité.
> Il faut pour cela embrasser d'un coup d'oeil: le passé, le présent et l'avenir.
> La toile doit présenter cette unité essentielle qui seule provoque l'extase. . . .
> Le tableau existera inéluctablement. La vision sera entière, complète et son infini au lieu de marquer une imperfection, fera seulement ressortir le rapport d'une nouvelle créature à un nouveau créateur et rien d'autre.[40]

The essentially individual, the explosion of linearity, unity, repeated and continuous creativity — these motifs are operative both in Apollinaire's statement and in the Futurist initiative. But in June 1908 *Les Trois Vertus plastiques*, let us remember, formed the introduction to the catalogue of an exhibition devoted mainly to Fauvist work. (It included works by Braque, but Braque's first compositions to develop away from Fauvism and to be termed — mockingly — 'cubistes' were exhibited later the same year at Kahnweiler's in Paris.)[41] But what Fauvism and Cubism have in common with Futurism is their explicit opposition to Impressionism. Apollinaire is responding to a moment of difference and a sense of radicalisation in artistic expression when he dismisses Impressionism, in comparison with 'les peintres nouveaux', in his introduction to the Braque exhibition at Kahnweiler's in November 1908: '. . . une furieuse tempête de tempéraments divers, plus ou moins nobles, essayant d'exprimer fièvreusement, hâtivement, déraisonnablement, leur étonnement devant la nature. A ces traits on reconnaît l'impressionnisme.'[42] A glorification of nature and a subservience to it, an obsessive fixation on light and a naive and impotent admiration for it — this is how Apollinaire characterises Impressionism, consistently opposing it to Braque, Picasso, Van Dongen, Matisse, Derain and Metzinger as well as to Delaunay four years later. But the Futurist attempt to transform the praxis of art and the public expectations that surround it seeks to remove any barrier between the experience of a transformed world of mass technology and communication, and the development of a non-mimetic, simultaneous and dynamic art. What Apollinaire perceives as being distinctive in the Cubist and pre-Cubist work of Braque, on the other hand, is the extent to which it discovers experience and creativity in the *independence* of the work of art itself, in competition with the natural world: 'Le tableau existera inéluctablement.'[43] In the same catalogue notes to the exhibition at Kahnweiler's, Apollinaire presents Braque's work as instigating creativity itself, as creating an existence in and as art, as inventing an art that takes place in the world by distinguishing itself from it, by transforming it, and by confronting it with repeated instances of novelty. Apollinaire presents this praxis as indistinguishable from the pursuit of freedom *in* existence and *through* expression; it seeks to dominate the material, and thus discover creativity:

> Puisant en lui-même les éléments des motifs synthétiques qu'il représente, il est devenu un créateur.
> Il ne droit rien à ce qui l'entoure. Son esprit a provoqué volontairement le crépuscule de la realité et voici que s'élabore plastiquement en lui-même et hors de lui-même une renaissance universelle.[44]

5—APOLLINAIRE AND PRE-CUBISM. THE PINK PERIOD, AFRICAN SCULPTURE, PERSPECTIVE

The pursuit of creativity characteristic of Apollinaire's response to Cubism and pre-Cubism cannot be isolated from his earlier exposure to painting and to 'les peintres nouveaux', or in particular from his lasting involvement with Picasso. The relationship began in 1904 soon after Picasso's arrival in Montmartre and approximately at the same time as Apollinaire's involvement with the Fauvists Vlaminck and Derain.[45] Apollinaire rapidly started to publish ecstatic descriptions of Picasso's inventive power. Let us look again at the 1905 *La Plume* article in which, with Picasso's series of works populated with harlequins and acrobats specifically in mind, Apollinaire characterises Picasso's work in the following terms. The passage was later used to open the section on Picasso in *Méditations esthétiques*:

> Si nous savions, tous les dieux s'éveilleraient. Nés de la connaissance profonde que l'humanité retenait d'elle-même, les panthéismes adorés qui lui ressemblaient se sont assoupis. Mais malgré les sommeils éternels, il y a des yeux où se reflètent des humanités semblables à des fantômes divins et joyeux.
> Ces yeux sont attentifs comme des fleurs qui veulent toujours contempler le soleil. O joie féconde, il y a des hommes qui voient avec ces yeux.[46]

The optimistic and rejuvenating creativity Apollinaire conjures up in these short paragraphs seems to be at odds with the contemplative inaction, the continuous and private 'entr'acte' in which Picasso's harlequins and acrobats exist, reduced to residual gestures of their past magical powers.[47] But Apollinaire discovers in Picasso's work a space and a language that oppose the passive recording of the external world with a new access to creativity and to hitherto unexplored configurations of human experience.[48] The clue to this creativity lies in the experience of *memory*: 'Picasso a regardé des images *humaines* qui flottaient dans l'azur de nos mémoires ....'[49] What is remarkable is that Picasso's harlequin cycle is also an instance of that new departure in formal exploration work known as the 'pink period', which comes into evidence in 1904 and ends with the completion in 1907 of *Les Demoiselles d'Avignon*.[50] Picasso's new emphasis in 1904–7 is on the *formal* properties of mass, plane and (as distinct from the Fauvist visual language, incidentally) line. Picasso's formal exploration is articulated in the lines that invent the figures of the period. At the same time, these are lines of expressiveness — lines that trace the spaces in which the harlequins, women and acrobats are secluded by their own postures; gestures that once had poetic powers of suggestion are now merely private.[51] Paradoxically, these gestures carry an undermined power to uncover sensations and desires that have become reduced to their appearance: Apollinaire in turn, at this stage in his art criticism, responds to this as to an indefinite texture of analogy. In response to Picasso, Apollinaire discovers appearance as the articulation of a desire to create that abounds even as creative impulses themselves seep through their burial in memory. Within this interrelation of appearance and analogy, Apollinaire continually weaves references to memory: 'allaités' — unavailable memories of childhood; 'la lune' — with its associations of hidden desires; 'se taisent' and 'confesser' — past defeats, sins, and suffering:

> Vieillis comme les boeufs meurent vers vingt-cinq ans, les jeunes ont mené des nourrissons allaités à la lune.
> Dans un jour pur, des femmes se taisent, leurs corps sont angéliques et leurs regards tremblent.
> A propos du danger leurs sourires sont intérieurs. Elles attendent l'effroi pour confesser des péchés innocents.[52]

The implosion of African tribal sculpture and masks into Picasso's painting in *Les Demoiselles d'Avignon* marks a dramatic transformation in his work. His objectives change and his art can no longer be read in the same way. But there had been a tendency and an event in Picasso's visual language that had suggested that a change was imminent. The tendency is Picasso's increasing emphasis in his figures and portraits on the plastic qualities of painting, an emphasis which begins to stretch the limits of the pink period style towards the end of 1905 and into 1906. It is a shift from the exploitation of plastic expressiveness to an exploration of the plastic elements that make it up: line, in *Enfant nu avec un Cheval* (1905), or in *Tête de Profil* (1906); and volume, in *La Hollandaise* (1905) or in *La Femme assise* (1906).[53] The event that heralds this transformation in Picasso's work is the portrait of Gertrude Stein painted in 1906, during the final composition stages of which Picasso replaced the face with a stylisation reminiscent of a mask. By superimposing a mask on the picture of a face, Picasso explicitly emphasises recognition as a texture of interpretation and memory, and expressiveness as the represented involvement with this potentially draining texture. 'Tout le monde prétend qu'il n'est pas ressemblant, mais ça ne fait rien, elle finira par lui ressembler' — such was Picasso's reaction to criticism of the portrait.[54]

Renaud's interpretation of the explosive influence of African sculpture on Parisian visual art is misleading.[55] It posits a common ground between the neo-primitivism implicit in an enthusiastic exploitation of African and South Sea Island figures, and a quasi-religious mysticism supposedly developed in the final section of 'Les Fiançailles', which was written, let us remember, in 1908 and dedicated to Picasso. For Renaud, Apollinaire's attraction to African figures represents a new element in the impetus to rejuvenate Symbolism, a part of Apollinaire's involvement with Royère and the review *La Phalange*. It is an impetus that can be traced back to the 'naturiste' movement, and is based on a desire that Symbolism should find new, anti-Decadent forms of expression with which to meet concrete sensations. The combination of neo-Symbolism with neo-primitivism gives Apollinaire, according to Renaud, a unique opportunity to develop the will to extent orphically the limits of experience, and to transform appearance creatively.

Clearly, it is typical of Apollinaire the 'brocanteur' and of the unity in eclecticism he pursues, that his involvement with the novelty of Cubism should run concurrently with a new insight into a more conventional poetry. But at the same time, it is misleading to suggest that Apollinaire approached African images as a contact with primary sources of expressiveness. Renaud himself explores another level in 'Les Fiançailles', as well as in 'Le Brasier' and in the involvement with neo-Symbolism as a whole, that discounts any such unmediated contact. Apollinaire's writing creates a tension by which the pursuit in poetry of the domination of experience, of matter and of time, is confronted with the fact that such dominance occurs exclusively within the experience of the poem, its writing and its reading. Even to speak of a 'tension' here is to do scant justice to the radicalisation Apollinaire's discourse undergoes in the composition of 'Les Fiançailles' and to the assertions it strives to make. In effect, the shift in Apollinaire's poetry, as we have discovered, takes the form of presenting identity fragmented in and as language, and of confronting heroic creativity *in* language with the impossibility of dominating appearance in expression, memory in words.[56] Moreover, Apollinaire's radical exploration of the relation between exchange and creative identity develops in part through the influences exerted by African and South Sea Island art:

> ... les Christ inférieurs des obscures espérances

In these words, with which this chapter began, recognition and memory, interpretation and the power to express, engender and displace one another: we scarcely need reminding that these 'objects' of desire *are* memories of an obsession with African figures and masks:

> Tu marches vers Auteuil tu veux aller chez toi à pied
> Dormir parmi tes fétiches d'Océanie et de Guinée
> Ils sont des Christ d'une autre forme et d'une autre croyance
> Ce sont les Christ inférieurs des obscures espérances.[57]

This slow eruption into the text of 'Zone' of an infatuation with Guinean and Oceanic figures, and the allusions to these figures in Picasso's painting from 1907 to early 1909,[58] do not realise the objective of 'retrouver, à l'aide de styles et de croyances très anciens, les sources premières de l'art'.[59] On the contrary, in terms of the visual and poetic texts in which they appear, they represent the process by which language bars access to the 'source' of expressiveness — in fact removes the possibility of such a source. They articulate an irrevocable sense of difference endemic to the reception of events or objects. The 'other' belief(s) ('autre croyance') and especially the 'other' form ('autre forme') — the articulation of 'other' presented by the fetishes of Apollinaire's memory displayed in his bedroom — are instances of 'perception' failing to encompass expressiveness. The figures are alien because of the non-European context from which they have been extracted. They confront the viewer (or reader) with novelty as such, with the experience of 'other'. The figures do not set novelty in motion, so much as articulate an impossibility of encompassing and possessing novelty. Novelty for Apollinaire — as we keep discovering in his responses to Symbolism as well as to Picasso and the new painting — *is* expressiveness itself.[60] The 'fétiches d'Océanie et de Guinée' do not control their novelty; they do not reveal the source of their expressiveness. They are images that articulate memory as the experience of displacement: 'obscures espérances' evoke desires complicated by time, and 'inférieurs' suggests an image or a symbol removed from its place of power.

This 'Oceanic' dynamic of expressiveness and barrier is also the initial impetus in Picasso's development of Cubism. The figures inspired by African masks and faces to the right of *Les Demoiselles d'Avignon* and in some of the studies for it, as well as the portraits and figures that succeed it, such as *The Dancer* (1907–8) and *Tête d'Homme* (1908–9), create an image that Picasso proceeds to develop and represent in terms of the Cubist conceptualisation and the Cubist praxis of divisionism.[61] This process starts to take shape in the images he produces from about 1908–9 to about 1912, for example, from *Head of a Woman* (1908–9) to *Violon* (c. 1912).[62] *The Dancer*, rather than evoking the roots of artistic and imaginative power ('les sources premières de l'art'), attracts the viewer's attention to its formal characteristics. Its visual impact is created in the organisation of its space, which proclaims its independence from the laws of perspective. In the 1908–9 *Head of a Woman*, this questioning of perspective and the fictions it manipulates is developed into a dissolution, in fact a *texturing* of the experience of recognition. We could say that the 'sourires intérieurs' that Apollinaire discerned in the female figures in Picasso's pictures of acrobats, are transformed, re-presented as a barrier to the recognition of interiority.[63] The deconstruction of perspective presents interiority as indistinguishable from a sense of barrier. But this barrier is not an opposition such as presence/absence, available/unavailable. It is a transition, a transition without end in which interiority — the crushingly personal — is textured in observation, in the continuous links drawn out in expression between observation and memory.

6—SIMULTANEITY AND PERSPECTIVE

But how precisely is this kind of transition brought about by the rejection of perspective? The operation of perspective consists in the establishment of a fiction. This fiction allows an object or series of objects to be recognised in an objective totality, and perceived in the totality of their context. Infinity is regarded as indistinguishable from a point on the horizon, by reference to which a particular point of view is presented as all-inclusive. This process in fact disguises the singularity of the context that allows a choice of point of view to be made. Perspective exploits the horizon by presenting it as a series of points in terms of which, potentially, infinity is encompassed. In this way, the observer — painter and viewer — is provided with a focus that opens the world out to visibility, that reveals, or at least implies, the invisible and the secret, and that presents an aspect or an attitude as an all-encompassing perception. The Cubist initiative, on the other hand, consists of striving to make a plastic reality out of the objectives that perspective realises through *fiction*. The Cubist objective *is* in fact to allow the observer/painter to visualise an object or a figure in its totality. But the Cubist artefact realises this objective by creating an entirely different present for the object. It offers it to the viewer from a multiplicity of points of view, a multiplicity of angles in perspective, *simultaneously*. The simultanism of the Cubist approach in fact implicates it in the action of memory in thinking, and this is what distinguishes Cubist art from the implicit idealism of any approach to visual representation that seeks possession of the world in perspective.

But paradoxically, simultaneity is itself a fiction: two points of view or a multiplicity of aspects cannot be perceived simultaneously, but only sequentially — though *not* in the sense that one perception is preserved and received intact in juxtaposition with another. (One) experienced of the world is transformed in time (by the next). (An) experience (immediately in the past) is received and displaced in experience of the present, that is, perceived as transition, the texture of transition, the texture of experience itself. The experience of memory can be seen on the Cubist canvas as a seamless alternation and/or displacement, consisting of an interplay between focus and transition. Such an interplay is incarnated in a Cubist portrait such as Picasso's *Arlésienne* (1911), in his exploration of the relation between line (which in *Arlésienne* can be thought of as focus) and plane (which can be thought of as transition).[64] It is an interplay that presents heterogeneity as effaced, and that re-presents experience in texture on the canvas.

'Abstract' art is in one crucial sense an inaccurate term, since it rejects imitation of the concrete world in favour of its own concrete plastic elements: form, line, paint. The manipulation of these concrete elements on canvas makes possible a simultaneous involvement with experience, *and* a representation of it in its relation to memory and to expression. Apollinaire recognises this crucial concreteness of 'abstract' art as early as his comments on the 'Salon des Indépendants' of 1908, which featured many works in the Fauvist style including pre-Cubist works by Braque which display a Fauvist emphasis on plane (*Le Vallon*, *Paysage*, possibly *Grand Nu*): 'Et qu'on ne parle plus d'abstraction. La peinture est bien l'art le plus concret.'[65] The so-called abstraction involved in Cubism is concrete in that it both represents experience, and is indistinguishable from it; it acts on consciousness in the same way as appearance does. Cubist abstraction rejects the notion of a stable distinction between the process and the product of expression — between appearance and transition on the one hand, observation and focus on the other.

Apollinaire, writing about memory and creative power, both imagines and actually re-creates the workings of this untenable distinction between process and product as he ends 'Cortège':

> Rien n'est mort que ce qui n'existe pas encore
> Près du passé luisant demain est incolore
> Il est informe aussi près de ce qui parfait
> Présente tout ensemble et l'effort et l'effet[66]

Any suggestion of a belief in the creative powers of the past, and a corresponding lack of interest in the future, seems completely inconsistent with the urgent demand we keep witnessing in the period 1909–1914, for an artistic response to a world being transformed by the irruption into it of mass technology and a self-conscious modernity. But the last lines of 'Cortège' are not so much a eulogy of the past as an exploration of the relation between experience and the process of expression. Experience *is* the past ('luisant'); expression creates the past-ness of experience, and presents the future as absent — 'incolore' — and as to-be-constructed. Cubism responds to this matrix by approaching the future in terms of an object-in-construction. For the Cubist painter, his praxis *is* experience, articulated in its appearance on canvas, in the texture produced in painting.

These pronouncements from *Les Trois Vertus plastiques*, by now familiar to us, may help us sum up the development of Apollinaire's thinking in relation to Cubism:[67]

> Il faut pour cela embrasser d'un coup d'oeil: le passé, le présent, l'avenir.... La vision sera entière, complète et son infini au lieu de marquer une imperfection, fera seulement ressortir le rapport d'une nouvelle créature à un nouveau créateur et rien d'autre.[68]

Simultaneity of time and space is not regarded by Apollinaire as an all-inclusive totality. It is as a consequence of this that he raises and dismisses the spectre of a marriage between the 'infini' and 'imperfection'. He rejects illusions of dominance, suggesting that they are irrelevant to the human condition. For Apollinaire, simultaneity is kept alive through repeated beginnings. Not only does simultaneity represent the relation of experience, as well as of memory, to expression itself, it is the framework of a creativity that rejects the possibility of objectifying this relation, of arresting it, or of establishing distance from it: 'le rapport d'une nouvelle créature à un nouveau créateur'. The simultaneity implicit in Cubism — and to some extent in the pre-Cubist, Fauvist-inspired explorations of plane — confronts the viewer, in the object he sees, with the reality of displacement. It produces a texture that *is* the object displaced in the expression as which it exists. Cubist simultaneity offers the viewer an alternation between focus, an uncompleted gesture of establishing an object on canvas, and a creative transition, which *is* the relation of created object to memory, the incompleteness of this relation in the painting and in the present. 'La vision sera entière' because it *is* relation: the movement of eye, and of brush on a surface, effaces the source and the end of relation itself. Cubist painting creates an access of experience to expression by simultaneously maintaining and obscuring the difference between them. Each perception of the object gives birth to a new object, to a new painting, a new articulation of the incomplete (self-incompleting), but *human* relation between the world and experience of it: 'le rapport d'une nouvelle créature à un nouveau créateur et rien d'autre'.

7—CUBISM OR FUTURISM?

All this means that the Cubist praxis of simultaneity, and Apollinaire's response to it, appear more stimulating and more complex than the Futurist approach to simultaneity. The Cubist approach emphasises the artistic object as a conceptual object — an object that inaugurates experience (that *is* experience), as well as a critical self-consciousness in experience. Cubism produces artistic objects that continuously re-present the struggle to establish self-consciousness, to distinguish it in the seamless transition from object to memory that, for the Cubist practioner, constitutes experience. But the Futurists' development of the concepts of simultaneity and of dynamism, and their representations of speed, seek to undermine the action of conceptualisation in expression. It is a desire to incorporate the world and experience of the world within expression itself; a desire simply to abolish barriers in the relation of expression to experience. In 1913 Severini puts it in these terms in his *The Plastic Analogies of Dynamism — Futurist Manifesto*: 'We want to incorporate the universe in the work of art. Individual objects do not exist any more.'[69] The Futurist initiative seems implicitly flawed in that it strives for the liberation of experience — the unfettering of identity from the confines of context, discourse and history — by dissolving, rather than defining, the objects that articulate perception, and that equally articulate the experience of constriction and oppression. The formulations of the Futurist objective given in the manifestos avoid envisaging the possibility of any dynamic of difference within expression itself. Rather, the Futurist objective is presented as a desire to release, through expression, an assumed potential in perception to embrace and dominate the world, to render division and inhibition inoperative through the discovery of an indefinitely extending network of analogy incorporating events and contexts.[70] The Futurist desire is to release consciousness from what it regards as the divisive categorisation imposed by analytical and discursive responses to the world. It would be revealing to speculate about the connections between the Futurist dismissal of analysis equated with the discursive and the Futurist attempt to re-create the world in terms of difference-dissolving images; between these aesthetic notions and the admiration of power and nationalism that makes possible the Futurist passage into Fascism.[71] In any event, it is clear from the expressions of the Futurist aesthetic before the Great War that it does not, as Cubist painting does, regard analysis as in anyway positive, but as resistance to the power of analogy to transform expression into a kind of ludic weapon that explodes disparateness: 'The spiralling shapes, and beautiful contrasts of yellow and blue, that are intuitively felt one evening while *living the movements of a girl dancing* may be found again *later*, through a process of plastic preferences or aversions, or a combination of both, *in the concentric circling of an aeroplane or in the onrush of an express train.*'[72]

On the other hand, it is not difficult to discover reasons for Apollinaire's attraction to the stated Futurist objectives, which seems so much in evidence at the time of the publication of 'Lettre-Océan' in June 1914.[73] The most obvious feature in the avant-garde visual arts in the years from about 1907 to 1914 is their proliferating diversity: in France Cubism and Delaunay, Picabia and Duchamp; Futurism in Italy as well as in France; Kandinski, Marc and Macke in Germany. Having been radicalised by Cubism, it would have been surprising had Apollinaire allowed the Cubist influence on him to become an aesthetic 'school' the single development of which would provide the expansion of expression he constantly envisaged. In fact, it seems that Apollinaire first responded seriously to the development of Futurist expression in the context of his frenzied efforts from 1912 to the autumn of 1913 to publicise the essential solidarity within the diversity in the arts of his period by exploring the term 'Orphism'. He developed his 'Orphic' conception of artistic expression from his contact with Robert Delaunay and endeavoured to launch it as a simultaneously unifying and self-renewing artistic process.[74] In the event, Apollinaire's relationship with the Futurists finally came to an end when Marinetti and Boccioni in particular alleged that the ideas Apollinaire was presenting as Orphic had in fact already been presented to the French public on the occasion of the first Futurist exhibition in France, held in Paris in 1912 at the Galérie Bernheim Jeune, and in its collaboratively written catalogue.[75] Despite this enmity, and despite the variety of stimuli coming to Apollinaire from the visual arts in 1912 and 1913, the fact remains that the notion Severini articulates in his *Plastic Analogies of Dynamism*, of an artistic creativity empowered to transcend a perspective-bound perception of nature and of appearance, is one that would stand as an expression of the objective Apollinaire himself seeks to realise in this period of artistic hyperactivity: 'We must forget exterior reality and our knowledge of it in order to *create* the new dimensions, the order and extent of which will be discovered by our artistic sensibility in relation to the world of plastic creation.'[76]

8—DELAUNAY, CUBISM AND FUTURISM. THE AUTONOMY OF THE ART OBJECT

The autonomy of the artistic artefact is the concept Severini and Apollinaire have in common. But Severini's approach, as he articulates it in *The Plastic Analogies of Dynamism*, is distinct from the approach both of Cubism and of Delaunay's Orphism, to which Apollinaire

111

E

became strongly committed, in that the creative domination of perception and of social exchange that it has in its sights does not take the form of analysis or intervention, but of an act of imaginative will. As I signalled at the outset of this chapter, my comments so far have not been chronologically based, but have endeavoured to reconstruct the conceptual coherence of the issues raised by Apollinaire's writings on art in the period 1905–14: writings that provide a challenging series of viewpoints for the consideration of his poetry. It remains for me to discuss this crucial Orphic period of 1912–13 — crucial in that it is a period when Apollinaire is absorbed in his relationship with Robert Delaunay, whose theories and works involve the reader or the viewer, more explicitly than does Futurism, in the attitudes struck and experiences explored by Apollinaire in his pre-war radical texts in the 'Ondes' section of *Calligrammes*.

Though it has a different overall purpose, the visual-conceptual vocabulary developed by Delaunay on canvas from 1912, as well as retrospectively in words in the 20s, is related to both the major objectives we have considered in the art of the period 1907 to 1914.[77] Delaunay's work is related to the Cubist conceptualisation of the canvas developed by Picasso, Braque, Juan Gris and Metzinger. It is also affected by that sense of an urgent necessity, a once-and-for-all opportunity, to respond to a present expressed in transformational technology. The *Villes* series, or the 1909 *Tour Eiffel aux Arbres*, are artefacts that dissolve what Delaunay regarded as the defunct formalism of persepctive-bound painting.[78] Moreover, they are artefacts that confront the viewer with movement and speed, and the desire to create rather than simply present a transformable and mobile world. This desire is articulated in relation to the urban environment and the urban experience, and to the iconography of the technologised world of mass communication.

This involvement with movement and with the experience of modernity, combined with Delaunay's rejection of perspective, is focused on in the argument that presents Delaunay's Orphism as a reaction against a certain austerity and impersonality in Cubism. It is argued that this reaction forms the initial impetus in Delaunay's desire to develop Cubism more radically, and to extend the scope of art in the post-representational era. Even if Delaunay's approach is taken purely as a reaction against Cubist 'austerity', what becomes increasingly explicit in Delaunay's approach is a concentration on colour — a desire to reverse the Cubist tendency to exclude this plastic element from its productions. But to respond to Delaunay's contribution in terms of a rejection of the Cubist 'analytical' style is to suggest that all original and creative art is fundamentally anti-conceptual. Apollinaire himself, in his comments on and presentations of Cubist work, is careful to pre-empt accusations of obscurity, difficulty or sterility that might be levelled against the art he publicises so enthusiastically. This is how he expresses the Cubist break with Impressionism:

> Cependant, le public, habitué aux taches éclatantes mais presque informes des impressionnistes, n'a voulu comprendre du premier coup la grandeur des conceptions formelles de nos cubistes. Les contrastes des formes sombres et des parties éclairées ont tout d'abord choqué parce qu'on n'était habitué qu'à de la peinture sans ombres. Dans l'apparence monumentale des compositions qui dépassait la frivolité contemporaine, on n'a pas voulu voir ce qui y est réellement: un art noble et mesuré, prêt à aborder les vastes sujets pour lesquels l'impressionnisme n'a préparé aucun peintre. Le cubisme est une réaction nécessaire, de laquelle, qu'on le veuille ou non, il sortira de grandes oeuvres. Car se peut-il, peut-on croire un instant, que les efforts indéniables, je crois, de ces jeunes artistes, demeurent stériles?[79]

But by 1912, it is clear that Delaunay has developed an approach to plastic expression that implies a twofold response to Cubism, a response far more sophisticated than a simple aversion to conceptual-isation and its presumed 'austerity' or sterility. On the one hand, he seems to have regarded Cubist productions as a necessary destruction of the restrictions exercised by perspective. For Delaunay, Cubism provided a definitive rejection of Classical forms. At the same time, he claims that Cubism is restricted precisely by what it sets out to attack, that is, the focal status in perception of the object. Delaunay's interpret-ation is that the Cubist emphasis on attacking perspective entails a dependence on the object, almost an obsession with the object, that reduces the scope of the plastic artefact to a mere sophistication of the perspective system. Writing probably in about 1924, Delaunay makes the point in these terms: 'Ainsi le cubisme croyant apporter un nouveau langage — expressif — ne faisait qu'apporter une modification extérieure dans un système qu'il n'abolissait pas — mais qu'il soutenait: l'introduction de plusieurs points de vue d'un objet sur la toile ressortissait de la même vision sinon complétée.'[80] But for Delaunay, an urgent challenge remained to be responded to: that of creating language, of creating a form of expression capable of establishing its equality and its reciprocity in relation to nature, to reality, and to experience of them in the present. 'Ce grand procès

mystérieux des temps modernes: de la destruction à la construction...'
writes Delaunay in the same text.[81] And in another fragment, also
written or jotted down in about 1924, Delaunay, partly in relation to
Apollinaire, characterises his own plastic objective, his own anti-Cubist
manipulation of colour:

> Cette tendance créatrice de la couleur vers la peinture pure — d'un art
> entièrement nouveau ayant ses lois de création — et paraissant se dégager
> de toute représentation dans le sens objectif, visuel de la nature — allait,
> au contraire — en se perfectionnant dans son sens le plus profond du mot
> — vers une construction objective à l'égal de la nature, avec une lisibilité
> comparable à un spectacle de la nature.[82]

One of the objectives expressed in the metaphor 'la peinture pure'
is the autonomy of the plastic artefact — an autonomy distinct from
the one we saw Severini positing (p. 111). (Severini in fact unilaterally
declares it, rather than analysing it or arguing it through.) Delaunay's
is a purely plastic autonomy, activating the desire it expresses to engage
in the ceaseless movement and transformation that the present articulates. For Delaunay, to engage in the present is to use expression to
reciprocate the present, to become involved in a dynamic process that
prevents experience from being objectified and silenced in perspective
('le sens objectif, visuel de la nature'). In opposition to this objective
in plastic art, Delaunay interprets the Futurist enterprise as a passive
worship of the present, a naïve belief in the power of the imitation —
albeit an undermined and subversive imitation — of speed and movement. For Delaunay, Futurism is an inadequate, post-Impressionist
response to the world, not equal to the present, but vainly attempting
to catch up with it. In a satirical, rhetorical address to an imagined
Futurist, Delaunay makes the point by stressing the Futurist's inability
to create or take command of his existence; he accuses him of an
obsession with appearance and the object, of a refusal to conceptualise,
and thus an inability to re-create in its full complexity the relation of
his own experience to the object:

> Votre art a pour expression la Vitesse et pour moyen le cinéma-
> tographe...Votre futur est déjà passé...Battez-vous, faites des sports,
> des voyages, des guerres mais surtout ne retombez pas dans une
> philosophie que nous connaissons trop: le simulacre du mouvement de
> foules successivement unanimistes. Vos moyens sont dynamiques,
> mécaniques, c'est-à-dire contre-rythmiques...
> Vos personnages ne sont que des signes conventionnels, académiques
> et au fond archaïques. Quand vos constructions simulent le plus la vie,
> c'est l'idéal de l'ingénieur que vous suivez. Vous restez dans l'Objet qui

se meut à la manière de tous les simulacres, qu'il vous faut alors douer
d'une sensibilité.
Vous marchez véritablement à la mort.[83]

9—DELAUNAY: COLOUR, REPRESENTATION, EXPERIENCE

Delaunay's dismissal of Futurism is a thoroughgoing one. He approaches
plastic expression differently, and has a different conception of what
can be achieved with it — so different that it is surprising that he should
feel the need to think of Futurist work in the same context as his own,
or that Apollinaire should. In fact, Delaunay notes down his feelings
about Futurism in response to the increasingly bitter polemic, which
I mentioned in passing on page 111, concerning the authorship of the
concept of simultaneity, and its relation to movement, or, for the
Futurists, to speed.[84] The issue raised by this series of journalistic and
polemical events, which occurred in late 1913 and early 1914, is not
so much that of authorship, but of the ambivalence of Apollinaire's own
attitude. As Francastel emphasises, it is Apollinaire himself who at this
point seems to refuse to recognise the divide separating Futurism from
what he himself terms the Orphism of Delaunay.[85] It is very much as
though Apollinaire refuses to decide which of the two approaches to
art more closely enshrines his own pursuits, and this ambivalence can
be seen at work in the contrast between poems such as 'Arbre' and the
war poem 'Merveille de la guerre'.[86]

We need, then, to be quite clear about what separates Futurist
simultaneity from Delaunay's, and to build a reading of Apollinaire's
pre-war conception of the modern on the basis of it. A concept of
simultaneity is common, as we have seen, to Cubism, Dramatism and
Futurism as well as to Delaunay's work. What distinguishes
Delaunay's use of simultaneity is that it deals primarily and fundamentally with colour. For Delaunay, the handling of colour on canvas
goes beyond the imitation of movement; it creates and initiatives
movement itself by manipulating volume: '... volume réel obtenu par
la couleur, un volume obtenu par la qualité et l'ensemble des couleurs,
même sans éléments de clair-obscur, par l'intervention directe des
rapports simultanés des couleurs...'[87] In dismissing the 'clair-obscur'
in colour, Delaunay is refuting Futurism and what he thinks of as one
of its central features. The articulation of volume as colour ('volume
réel obtenu par la couleur') gives Delaunay the opportunity to construct

independently of the object, to create a *'peinture inobjective'*, to discover an autonomous power in language — *'peinture purement expressive'*. This language is not reducible to style ('en dehors de tout style passé'), or to a conception of language as a repeatable process, or a technique ('ni technique, ni procédé'). Colour is the articulation of light, the experience of *sight* itself:

> La Lumière n'est pas procédé et elle nous vient de la sensibilité.
> Sans la sensibilité (l'oeil) aucun mouvement.[88]

The dynamism of Delaunay's approach to expression and of his conception of the plastic is that, unlike Futurism but as a radicalisation of Cubism, it explicitly confronts expression as such. Paradoxically, this is made clear at a moment when expression seems de-emphasised and de-located — the point where the concrete reality of perception is (re-) created. Delaunay's painting manipulates colour *in order* to bring light on to the canvas. But at the same time, it is painting that can be termed praxis ('métier'), in that colour, though indistinguishable from light — and therefore from a sense of the present — is not the equivalent of light: colour articulates light and displaces it in the process. Delaunay interprets light as being indistinguishable from a sense of the present, only in so far as both are non-arrestable, and in so far as neither can be represented as an object in perspective. For Delaunay, light is effaced in and as a sense of the present — in sight, in the unframable window of the eyes: 'C'est dans nos yeux que *se passe* le présent...' — ('se passe' literally, in the sense of effacing itself, as well as in the sense of happening). Delaunay explicitly focuses on the action of displacement, at the very point where he thinks of expression as being capable of constructing autonomously ('purely'). He emphasises that colour — and the relationship of volume and movement that exists between complementary colours — is itself *representation*: '"La simultanéité des couleurs" par le contraste simultané et toutes les mesures (impaires) issues des couleurs, selon leur expression dans leur mouvement *représentatif* est la seule réalité pour construire en peinture.'[89] Complementary colours evoke and produce one another. But for Delaunay, this movement between colours exists *exclusively* as surfaces on the canvas, and this exclusiveness sets up a relation that involves painter as well as viewer in that endless beginning of representation which is the articulation of consciousness in relation to experience:

> Les moyens réels sont les couleurs dans leurs contrastes, leurs mouvements.

3 Robert Delaunay, *Une Fenêtre (étude pour Les Trois Fenêtres)*, 1912 (photo-graph by courtesy of the Musée National d'Art Moderne, Paris), © ADAGP, Paris 1987

> Leurs mouvements n'existent vraiment que par les fonctions des surfaces simultanées, avec profondeurs (profondeurs de la matière qui est le commencement des moyens) obtenues par le créateur des contrastes simultanés.[90]

We can read Delaunay's 'moyens' as the practice of representation, 'profondeurs' as consciousness and the sense of self, and 'matière' as experience and the sense of 'other'. The coherence behind Delaunay's often opaque and highly-charged notions can be summarised like this. His approach to representation confronts displacement, and this distinguishes him from the Futurist project of abolishing difference, and of giving birth to an explosive expansion of experience. It is an approach that accepts a fragmentation of identity and expresses an impossibility of contextualising it, or of discovering it in terms of a Futurist identification with appearance, multi-contextuality and speed. It is as though, for Delaunay, the canvas *is* experience — of identity, of the present. The reading it demands of the viewer and the painter, its manipulation of the displacement that constitutes the relation of colour to light, efface the contours of the painting itself. Delaunay's painting confronts difference in so far as it gives rise to the effacement of difference on canvas and in (colour) contrast. On the one hand, it is a painting offering the creativity that has produced it as proof of difference — proof of competition with given appearance, of reciprocity with experience, of difference from given language. But on the other hand, each painting *is* experience, it contrasts represent the *pursuit* of contrast and difference, the sensation of light and the 'otherness' of time.

Apollinaire makes the point in these terms, writing in 1913: 'Delaunay croyait que si vraiment une couleur simple conditionne sa couleur complémentaire, elle ne la détermine pas en brisant la lumière, mais en suscitant à la fois toutes les couleurs du prisme. Cette tendance, on peut l'appeler l'orphisme.'[91] Apollinaire responds to the fact that, for Delaunay, there is no gap between colours, that the difference between them is not locatable in visual (or verbal) language, and that light is not built in colours that can be isolated from each other. Delaunay, while dealing in colour contrast, is in fact grappling with transition. He is working with patterned contrasts that represent transitions by which light is perceived. Delaunay thinks of transition in terms of light and the eye, and as the material of perception itself; equally, this 'material' has no form other than continuous and repeated transition ('se passe'). This circularity in which Delaunay's thinking and painting involve us is an indication of a desire — the desire to establish self-consciousness in perception. In Delaunay's work, perception pursues self-conscious perception, and from there an actual construction of experience in the present, a representation of physical and psychic matter. But this representation is a re-presentation, in which the 'matière' of experience — transition, light — is displaced as the 'matière' of expression — the artist's creative handling of contrast.[92] The crucial, dissolving contrast in Delaunay's thinking is between light and intervention in terms of light itself.[93] By using contrast to represent the bright glow that evades it, Delaunay seeks to give expression to 'notre psychique en éveil', a seamless transition from conceptualisation to experience, from vision to invention, intervention to novelty and wonder, back and forth continually.[94] Delaunay's fictional creations of contrast put on display the very experience of thinking and being.[95]

10—UBIQUITY OR DYNAMIC DISPLACEMENT?

In 1913, Apollinaire seems to allow the public controversy as to the authorship of the concept of simultaneity to damage his relationship with Delaunay; the controversy was exacerbated by his own refusal to acknowledge the difference in objective expressed by the Futurists' thinking and Delaunay's. Clearly, this prevents admirers of Apollinaire from responding to the radical texts he produced before the war simply in terms of his involvement with what he himself termed 'Oprhism'. One of the most perplexing questions thrown up by Apollinaire's writing remains whether the emancipation of perception and expression produced in Delaunay's conceptualised and conceptualising 'objects' provides the 'lisibilité' of Apollinaire's post-*Alcools* texts, or whether a Futurist inspired multi-contextuality holds the key to Apollinaire's new literary ambitions. Naïve, explosive, ubiquitous simultaneity, or a dialectic of simultaneity and displacement? But the chronology of Apollinaire's interests and obsessions will not decide this question. Before confronting it again in chapter four, we need to be fully aware of the textuality of displacement created in 'Ondes', the first, pre-war section of *Calligrammes*.

NOTES

1 For an account of Jammes's association with Bouhélier, and of the appeal he commanded after his return to Catholicism, see Décaudin, *La Crise des valeurs symbolistes* pp. 62–4 and pp. 380–5. Apollinaire pays homage to Verlaine as well as to Mallarmé and 'les maîtres aimés du symbolisme' in his lecture *La Phalange nouvelle*, OC, III, p. 759. The verse I am about to discuss is taken from the following poems: 'Automne malade', OP, p. 146, l. 18; Paul Verlaine, 'Chanson d'automne', *Oeuvres poétiques complètes*, p. 56, l. 1; 'L'Eglise habillée de feuilles' no. 23 (in *Clairières dans le Ciel* Paris, 1885), (Paris, 1980), p. 177, l. 21; Jules Laforgue, 'Complainte à Notre-Dame des Soirs' (in *Les Complaintes*, Paris, 1885), *Poésie* (Paris, 1979), p. 44, l. 8; 'Zone'. OP, p. 44, l. 153.

2 In 1905, Apollinaire contributed to the inaugural issue of *Vers et Prose* a review claiming that 'Verlaine fut notre dernier grand poète en date'. *Vers et Prose*, Paris, 1905, quoted in Décaudin, *La Crise des valeurs symbolistes*, p. 181.)

3 'Il pleure dans mon coeur/Comme it pleut sur la ville;/Quelle est cette langueur/Qui pénètre mon coeur?': Verlaine, *Romances sans paroles*, 'Ariettes oubliées', iii, *Oeuvres poétiques complètes*, p. 122, l. 1. 'Bon chevalier masqué qui chevauche en silence/le Malheur a percé mon vieux coeur de sa lance.': *Sagesse*, i, p. 144, l. 1. 'La Chair sanglote sur la croix': *Sagesse*, viii, p. 185, l. 3. 'Triste à peine tant s'effacent/Ces apparences d'automne./Toutes mes langueurs rêvassent/Que berce l'air monotone.': *Romances sans paroles*, 'Simples Fresques', i, p. 129, l. 9. Verlaine satirises his own 'monotone' effect in *Sagesse*, ix: 'Et l'air a l'air d'être un soupir d'automne/Tant il fait doux par ce soir monotone/Où se dorlote un paysage lent.': p. 186, l. 12.

4 This suggests a quite different poetic power from the poetic heroism Chevalier ascribes to Apollinaire, by which the poet is in control of the problematic of exchange, self and other, in that he both proliferates the forms they take, and distances himself from them: 'le Je est par là en même temps multiplicateur et séparateur, deux processus complémentaires du même pouvoir de création'. (Jean-Claude Chevalier, *'Alcools' d'Apollinaire — Essai d'analyse des formes poétiques*, Paris, 1970, p. 223. See chapter one, n. 111.)

5 In his preface to the *Poésie* (1980) edition of *Clairières dans le Ciel*, Décaudin quotes Claudel's response to the first and private reading of 'L'Eglise habillée de feuilles': 'Quel fils vous avez rendu à notre vieille mère l'eglise! J'admirerais, ce que vous ne pouvez peut-être pas bien voir, l'usage que Dieu a commencé à faire de vous et l'art avec lequel il sait se servir de cet artiste. C'est tout l'ancien Jammes qui a pris une grandeur, une vie et une dignité nouvelles parce que désormais derrière lui se trouvent les régions éternelles'. (p. 10). See also Décaudin, *La Crise des valeurs symbolistes*, p. 380, n. 4.

6 Laforgue's implied satirical reference is not to Baudelaire's dandyism, his rejection of semblances of moral salvation, or his self-exhausting, creative 'ennui', all of which are clearly developed in Decadent poetry. Laforgue's satire is directed at the aesthetic resistance to 'ennui' provided by such

poems as 'Correspondances' and 'Harmonie du Soir', and at the promise of communion suggested in 'L'Invitation au Voyage'.

7 Apollinaire's rhyming of 'angoisse' with 'passe' a few lines earlier is revealing: 'Et l'image qui te possède te fait survivre dans l'insomnie et dans l'angoisse/C'est toujours près de toi cette image qui passe' (OP, p. 41, l. 87). These lines suggest that the experience in which Apollinaire identifies expressiveness is obsessively reincarnated, and equally, that it cannot be identified or identified with. It is as expressive as an image, repeatedly 'other' and continuously transient.

8 CA, p. 451.

9 CA, p. 382.

10 'Tout se passait,' writes Décaudin in connection with the *Vers et Prose* group and its thinking 'comme si les événements anti-symbolistes des années 1895–1902 n'avaient pas existé ou pouvaient être négligés.' The opening page of the first number of the revue acts as a kind of manifesto for a Symbolist revival. (Décaudin, *La Crise des valeurs symbolistes*, p. 181 and p. 182.)

11 See Roger Shattuck, *The Banquet Years*, revised edition (London, 1968), p. 262; *Album Apollinaire*, ed. P. M. Adéma and M. Décaudin (Paris, 1971), p. 84, p. 90, p. 100; Guillaume Apollinaire, *Contemporains pittoresques* (Paris, 1929), pp. 19–36.

12. In his comments on Jean Metzinger in *Méditations esthétiques*, Apollinaire is particularly sensitive to the charge of abstraction and over-conceptualisation levelled at the Cubist aesthetic, and counters it subtly and strongly. In a complex discussion covering image and analysis, sterility and colour, ranging from the neo-Impressionists to Picasso and Metzinger himself, Apollinaire characterises Metzinger's art in the following way: 'C'est alors que Jean Metzinger allant à la rencontre de Picasso et de Braque, fonda la ville des cubistes. La discipline y est stricte mais ne risque pas encore de devenir un système et la liberté y est plus grande que partout ailleurs.' (OC, IV, p. 35.)

13 In fact 1912, the year Apollinaire began to compile *Méditations esthétiques*, can be regarded as a climax in his avant-garde activity. He wrote important articles on Robert Delaunay, (CA, pp. 266–70), and it was also the year of the first Futurist exhibition in Paris. At the end of *Méditations esthétiques*, published the following year, Apollinaire lists Marinetti as a supporter of a certain kind of Cubism, albeit one he characterises as Impressionist — 'le cubisme instinctif'. This category includes the work of Boccioni and Severini. (OC, IV, p. 54. See pp. 24–5 for this and other categories in Cubism that Apollinaire perceived, including 'le cubisme orphique'.)

14 *Le Figaro*, Paris, 20 February 1909. The manifesto is included in F.-T. Marinetti, *Le Futurisme* (Paris, 1911), pp. 141–54; in Caroline Tisdall and Angelo Bozzolla, *Futurism* (London, 1977), p. 6; and in *Futurist Manifestos*, ed. U. Apollonio (London, 1973), pp. 19–24 (p. 21). Butor's perception of *The Victory of Samothrace* and of the way it is received is even more jaded and ironic. See Michel Butor, *Les Mots dans la peinture*, Les Sentiers de la création (Geneva, 1969), p. 13

15 See also Umberto Boccioni, *States of Mind: The Farewells* (1911), Gino

Severini, *Nord-Sud* (1912), and Giacomo Balla, *Girl Running on a Balcony* (1912), in Caroline Tisdall and Angelo Bozzolla, *Futurism* (London, 1977), p. 49, p. 54, p. 67.

16 *Futurist Manifestos*, ed. U. Apollonio (London, 1973), p. 97. The passage is taken from Marinetti's *Destruction of Syntax — Imagination without Strings — Words-in-freedom*, pp. 95–106. The original text is partially reprinted in *La cultura italiana del '900 attraverso le riviste, IV: Lacerba, La Voce* (1914–1916), ed. G. Scali (Turin, 1961), pp. 173–9. Henceforth, I shall refer to this volume as *Lacerba*.

17 CAA, pp. 135–8.

18 *L'Esprit nouveau et les poètes*, OC, III, p. 902.

19 *Futurist Manifestos*, pp. 95–106. Further references to this piece are given after quotations in the text.

20 *Futurist Manifestos*, p. 100. *Lacerba*, pp. 176–7.

21 *Futurist Manifestos*, p. 104. *Lacerba*, p. 178.

22 *Futurist Manifestos*, p. 157. *Lacerba*, p. 279.

23 Gabriel Arbouin indicates the Futurist antecedents of 'Lettre-Océan' in 'Devant l'Idéogramme d'Apollinaire', in *Les Soirées de Paris*, 25 (1914). See Guillaume Apollinaire, *Le Guetteur mélancolique*, ed. R. Mallet and B. Poissonnier (Paris, 1952), pp. 142–4 (p. 142).

24 OC, III, p. 876.

25 'Mais l'essentiel à nos yeux est qu'en écrivant son premier idéogramme, "Lettre-Océan", Apollinaire ne cherchait pas d'abord à imiter typographiquement des objects, mais à créer une synthèse simultanée.' Philippe Renaud, *Lecture d'Apollinaire* (Lausanne, 1969), p. 245.

26 Henri-Martin Barzun, *L'Ere du drame — essai de synthèse poétique moderne* (Paris, 1912).

27 *L'Ere du drame*, chapter 4, reprinted in León Somville, *Dévanciers du Surréalisme — les groupes d'avant-garde et le mouvement poétique 1912–1925*, Histoire des idées et critique littéraire, 116 (Geneva, 1971), p. 190.

28 Barzun, *L'Ere du drame*, pp. 34–35. Renaud, p. 235–6.

29 Barzun, *L'Ere du drame*, p. 98. Renaud, p. 237. Barzun's italics.

30 Barzun, *L'Ere du drame*, pp. 35–36. Renaud, p. 237. Barzun's italics.

31 See *Futurist Manifestos*, p. 100. p. 155; *Lacerba*, p. 277.

32 *Futurist Manifestos*, p. 30.

33 See Renaud, *Lecture d'Apollinaire*, pp. 234–5.

34 CAA, p. 112.

35 OC, III, p. 890. For a further discussion of the limitations of Barzun's entreprise, see David Kelley, 'Defeat and Rebirth: the city poetry of Apollinaire', in *Unreal City — urban experience in modern European literature and art*, ed. E. Timms and D. Kelley (Manchester, 1985), pp. 80–96 (pp. 83–4).

36 Marcel Adéma, in *Guillaume Apollinaire le mal-aimé* (Paris, 1952), p. 181, gives an account of the trivial level to which the jostling for positon among the various simultanist groups at times descended. Adéma also points out that Apollinaire's closely-guarded independence was threatened by the diversity of the theories he supported. Later, this led to a more serious

disagreement between Apollinaire and Delaunay: see Marcel Adéma, *Guillaume Apollinaire* (Paris, 1968), p. 241.

37 OC, III, pp. 901–2. It is typical of Apollinaire's thinking that in discussing 'l'esprit nouveau' and the pursuit of new forms of creativity, he should find support in one of his earliest poems. Merlin's creativity is paradoxical. Though he embarks on a love affair with Memory, he declines to use his magical powers to prevent his own death, and the art that ensures the transmission of his powers consists of images of the plants' and seasons' simultaneous wealth and transience. (See 'Merlin et la vieille femme', OP, p. 88, 11. 13–16, 11. 29–32, 11. 57–60.)

38 Gino Severini, *The Plastic Analogies of Dynamism*, in *Futurist Manifestos*, pp. 118–25 (p. 121). Severini's italics.

39 See pp. 26–41 above.

40 OC, IV, p. 16, p. 17. CA, p. 57.

41 OC, IV, p. 23.

42 CA, p. 59.

43 OC, IV, p. 17.

44 CA, p. 60.

45 Roger Shattuck, *The Banquet Years*, p. 262.

46 OC, IV, p. 27. CA, p. 29. My italics. Picasso composed the harlequin series between the winter of 1904 and the summer of 1905.

47 Wilhelm Boeck writes: 'Tel il [l'Arlequin] apparaît, debout, en spectateur, auprès de la femme à sa toilette ou de l'enfant qui prend son bain, ou assis dans leur groupe en compagnie d'un singe au visage empreint d'une noble intelligence. On trouve aussi un chien dans le cercle familial ce qui révèle bien l'amour de la créature pour la créature, la sensibilité profonde de ces oeuvres. Il est rare qu'un rapport d'action de manifeste entre les personnages; ce n'est même pas le cas dans le plus grand tableau des *Saltimbanques*...' (Jaime Sabartés and Wilhelm Boeck, *Picasso*, Paris, 1955, p. 142. See *Les Saltimbanques*, p. 369, and *Famille d'Arlequins*, p. 133.)

48 'Tout l'enchante et son talent incontestable me paraît au sevice d'une fantaisie qui mêle justement le délicieux et l'horrible, l'abjet et le délicat.' CA, p. 28.

49 OC, IV, p. 27. CA, p. 29. My italics.

50 See Sabartés and Boeck, *Picasso*, pp. 141–48: 'Ces saltimbanques n'ont de commun avec les silhouettes décharnées et débilitées de la période bleue que la gracilité, mais seulement celle qu'exigent leur élégance et leur adresse, et cette gravité mélancolique, mais qui est désormais le signe d'une conscience aiguë des dangers et de la futilité de leur tours.' (p. 142). Within this 'pink' exploration of expressiveness running from 1904 to 1907, Picasso embarks on a confrontation with the formal qualities of his language, which leads him to his first Cubist visions.

51 See, for example, *Tête de femme* (1905), *Femme assise* (1906), *Tête de profil* (1906) in, Sabartés and Boeck, *Picasso*, p. 126, p. 127, p. 137 respectively.

52 OC, IV, p. 28. CA, p. 30.

53 Sabartés and Boeck, *Picasso*, p. 370, p. 137, p. 459 and p. 127 respectively.

54 Sabartés and Boeck, *Picasso*, p. 148 and p. 460.

55 Renaud, *Lecture d'Apollinaire*, p. 83.

56 See pp. 71–3.

57 'Zone, OP, p. 44, l. 150.

58 *Self-portrait* (1907), *Three Figures under a Tree* (1907–8), *Head and Shoulder of a Woman* (1908), in Douglas Cooper and Gary Tinterow, *The Essential Cubism 1907–1920* (London, 1983), p. 233, p. 237, p. 239.

59 Renaud, *Lecture d'Apollinaire*, p. 83.

60 Expressiveness, novelty and *surprise* form one inextricable unit in *L'Esprit nouveau et les poètes: 'La surprise est le grand ressort du nouveau.'* OC, III, p. 906. Apollinaire's italics.

61 *The Dancer* (1907–8), in A. H. Barr, jr., *Cubism and Abstract Art*, reprinted edition (New York, 1966), p. 33, fig. 14. *Tête d'Homme* (1908–9), Sabartés and Boeck, *Picasso*, p. 461.

62 *Head of a Woman*, in Barr, *Cubism and Abstract Art*, p. 38, fig. 20. *Violin*, p. 47, fig. 31.

63 OC, IV, p. 28; CA, p. 30.

64 Barr, *Cubism and Abstract Art*, p. 39, fig. 22. See also *Man with a Mandolin* (1911) and *Man with a Violin* (1912), Cooper and Tinterow, *The Essential Cubism 1907–1920*, p. 269, p. 275.

65 CA, p. 51 and note, p. 450.

66 OP, p. 74.

67 See p. 101.

68 OC, IV, p. 16 and p. 17. CA, p. 57.

69 *Futurist Manifestos*, p. 118.

70 Marinetti gives the following definition of analogy and its power within expression: 'Analogy is nothing more than the deep love that assembles distant, seemingly diverse and hostile things. An orchestral style, at once polychromatic, polyphonic, and polymorphous, can embrace the life of matter only by means of the most extensive analogies.' *Destruction of Syntax — Imagination without Strings — Words-in-freedom*, in *Futurist Manifestos*, p. 99.

71 See James Joll, 'Futurism and Fascism' in *Intellectuals in Politics* (London, 1960), pp. 133–78 and Christiana Taylor, *Futurism: Politics, Painting and Performance*, University Studies in the Fine Arts: The Avant-garde, 8 (Michigan, 1974).

72 Gino Severini, *The Plastic Analogies of Dynamism — Futurist Manifesto 1913*, in *Futurist Manifestos*, p. 121. Severini's italics.

73 See n. 23.

74 'Le caractère du mot orphique employé par G. Apollinaire était dans le sens de rallier au cubisme toute manifestation d'art de l'époque, dans le sens plutôt de faire un groupe homogène pour rallier la jeunesse artistique en faisant une seule force.' (CAA, p. 169.)

75 Boccioni argues that Apollinaire's conception of 'Orphic' simultaneity is merely a reworking of dominant Futurist objectives: 'Even if, according to Guillaume Apollinaire's poetic definition, dynamism is to be called *Orphism*, even if Fernand Léger is always renewing his noble striving towards linear and planar dynamism, we the Futurists, from the beginning bearers of the universal Italian genius, have always proclaimed the indissoluble simultaneity of colour and form.' (*Futurist Dynamism and French*

Painting, in *Futurist Manifestos*, pp. 107–10.) Apollinaire joined Delaunay in dismissing Futurism for its Impressionist, mimetic approach: 'Les mots en liberté de Marinetti amènent un renouvellement de la description et à ce titre ils ont de l'importance, ils amènent également un retour offensif de la description et ainsi ils sont didactiques et anti-lyriques.' (OC, III, p. 884.) But a rift between Apollinaire and Delaunay was caused by the ambivalence of the former's attitude to Futurists whom Delaunay dismisses as impure and passive: 'A cet orphisme appartiennent également les futuristes italiens qui, issus du fauvisme et du cubisme, estimaient injuste d'abolir toutes les conventions perspectivistes du psychologiques.' (CA, p. 274.)

76 *Futurist Manifestos*, p. 118.
77 CAA, pp. 12–13.
78 *La Tour Eiffel aux arbres* (1909), CAA, p. 112; *La Ville no. 2*, in Virginia Spate, *Orphism* (Oxford, 1979), p. 177, figs. 130, 131. See also *La Tour Eiffel — Champs de Mars* (1911), p. 175, fig. 129.
79 CA, p. 199.
80 CAA, p. 57.
81 CAA, p. 55.
82 CAA, p. 169–70 n. Delaunay's italics.
83 CAA, p. 142. Interestingly, Apollinaire, after showing an initial interest, is equally dismissive of the Unanimists. (Renaud, *Lecture d'Apollinaire*, p. 85.)
84 See notes 17, 36, 75.
85 Francastel regards the episode as 'bien davantage une querelle Delaunay–Apollinaire, qu'une querelle Delaunay–futuristes'. CAA, p. 137.
86 See section four of chapter three, and section six of chapter four.
87 CAA, p. 58.
88 CAA, p. 159. Delaunay gave this text — *Note sur la construction de la réalité de la peinture pure* — to Apollinaire for editing and the latter submitted it as an article entitled 'Réalité, peinture pure', to *Der Sturm* in December 1912. CAA, pp. 154–7.
89 CAA, p. 159 (and for the previous quotation). Delaunay's quotation marks, my italics. See figure 3, and Robert Delaunay, *Les Fenêtres simultanées* (1912), in Spate, *Orphism*, p. 22.
90 CAA, p. 115.
91 CA, p. 274. See Robert Delaunay, *1re Représentation. Les Fenêtres simultanées. Ville. 2e motif 1re partie* (1912), in Spate, *Orphism*, p. 197, fig. 144.
92 See n. 90: 'profondeurs de la matière qui est le commencement des moyens'.
93 'Tout par contraste a une valeur; il n'y a pas de couleur fixe, tout est couleur par contraste, tout est couleur en mouvement, tout est profondeur.' CAA, p. 115.
94 CAA, p. 118.
95 'Cette simultanéité est la vie même.' CAA, p. 157. See also CA, p. 269.

3—'ONDES'

1—FROM PICTURES TO WORDS

My discussion of some of the complexities in the avant-garde art that Apollinaire committed himself to has inevitably left to one side the more frenzied and 'enchanted' aspects of his activity: all-night parties and discussions in the Paris suburb of Le Vésinet with the young Fauvists Vlaminck and Derain; meeting and talking with Picasso, Braque, Matisse, as well as Jacob and Salmon, in Picasso's 'Bateau Lavoir' studio in the Rue de Ravignan; attending Rousseau's soirées among his pictures and his bemused and admiring friends.[1] This was the first stage in Apollinaire's exposure to what was happening in the arts when he arrived in Paris. It was followed by his taking part in the earnest discussions and statements of purpose within the little group that built up around Barzun, by a somewhat ambiguous involvement with Futurism, and by an intense enjoyment of Picabia's ludic machine-pictures, his abstract pictures of dancers and towns, and his fast cars.[2] Before the war, and particularly on his return, Apollinaire began to include de Chirico in his critical writings, and this marks a period in his thinking that, with hindsight, has been called pre-Surrealist: along with the war poems, it is certainly the stage in his work that attracted the most attention among the Surrealists.[3] It includes *Les Mamelles de Tirésias* and the vision of a new direction, a new rationality and optimism in *L'Esprit nouveau et les poètes*.[4] Even by confining myself to Apollinaire's pre-war development, it has only been possible to sketch in the most selective outlines of his activities.

But some sort of account, however sketchy, is required to give direction to my close readings of individual poems. Without considering Apollinaire's fascination with the visual arts, it is impossible to come to terms with the gap that separates *Alcools* from *Calligrammes* — a gap well known to readers of Apollinaire. The obsession in his work with the threat of decay, the textures of legend and symbol is firmly challenged.[5] Such textures seem to lose their power to explore the particular sense of the poetic informing Apollinaire's work.

Apollinaire's critical writing from 1908 on incarnates his desire to bring poetry into the twentieth century, in the wake of painting. By 1912 Apollinaire radicalises his muse, forcing it into a confrontation with the present and its ceaseless diversity.[6] As I have shown, the material of *Alcools* is not only the past, but the experience of identity in reading and writing. It deals with the tension between poetic creativity, and the history of poetry that undermines it; between the autonomy of the creative process, and memory, which the creative process displaces and fails to appropriate. In 'Automne malade', or in 'L'Emigrant de Landor Road', the diversity coming at us from the world and from memory defies the power of writer or reader to dominate it, and thus presents itself in terms of an increasing flow of sameness — and an increasingly anxious one: 'Parmi le bruit des flots et des derniers serments'.[7] On the other hand, in 'Nuit rhénane', 'La Maison des morts' or 'Cortège', the text is fragmented, it withdraws from flux and pure transition; diversity acquires angular contours and abrupt shifts of emphasis that are unmeasured and undominated.

But in 1912, the year of the first Futurist exhibition in Paris, the year in which Apollinaire's involvement with Delaunay is established, and the year before the publication of *Alcools*, Apollinaire's attitude to survival in poetry undergoes a radical and remarkable change. A vast poetic spontaneity opens out; an immense capacity to adapt through poetry to variety and to circumstance is discovered — a capacity that is both explored and catastrophically abused in the experience of war.[8] But in the pre-war poems of *Calligrammes* as well, which I shall discuss in this chapter, Apollinaire's writing makes quite new and challenging demands on the reader. The desire to establish an aesthetic autonomy for poetry gives way to a desire to open the text out to any and every circumstance, image or linguistic 'trouvaille' thrown up by the present. In the 'poèmes-conversation' ('Les Fenêtres', 'Lundi Rue Christine', and to a lesser extent 'Arbre') the quasi-authorial voice that reads the poem in our head and that the writer strives to incarnate on the page is diffracted. The 'idéogrammes lyriques' invite the reader to abandon 'analytico-discursive' reading, and to adopt a 'simultaniste-idéogrammatique' approach to words and images.[9] Of course this is not to say that Apollinaire's aesthetic had remained static until his contact with the 'simultaneity' of the Futurists and of Delaunay. When Braque's *Nu* appeared in 1906, and Picasso's *Les Demoiselles d'Avignon* in 1907 — each work a watershed in the development of modern painting — Apollinaire as art critic had already been in the avant-garde of aesthetic thinking.[10] By 1908 his public defence of Cubism, in conjunction with a major reassessment of his poetic past, had already produced a radical shift of poetic emphasis, manifesting itself in 'Lul de Faltenin', 'Les Fiançailles', 'Onirocritique' and 'Le Brasier'. But through contact with Robert Delaunay, Apollinaire's writing takes another dramatic turn, to which the poems of 'Ondes' — the first, pre-war section of *Calligrammes* — bear witness. It is as if listening to Delaunay talk and watching his pictures take shape produce a sudden crystallisation in Apollinaire's mind of the crucial concept of simultaneity that informed his thinking with increasing intensity from Cubism, through his flirtations with Unanimism,[11] and later with Dramatism, his involvement with Futurism and finally with Delaunay's 'perceptual' Orphism itself.[12]

The influence exerted on Apollinaire by Delaunay's conception of simultaneity in terms of light and colour, and particularly by the brightness of his paintings, is a key to Apollinaire's decision to include 'Zone' in *Alcools* and to withhold 'Les Fenêtres', although the two were composed within months of each other during the period when *Alcools* took its final form.[13] 'Les Fenêtres' carries the same title as one of Delaunay's series of canvasses and it provided the introduction to Delaunay's exhibition in Berlin in 1913. It highlights a sense of collaboration between the two artists. But there are some similarities betwen 'Zone' and 'Les Fenêtres', despite their having pride of place in such radically different collections as *Alcools* a nd *Calligrammes*, and these similarities need to be confronted if a naïve image of Apollinaire simply abandoning en entire poetic experience of self is to be avoided.[14]

We can assume that, in some way, Apollinaire intended 'Zone' and its position at the head of *Alcools* to express the culmination of one poetic era, and 'Les Fenêtres' to mark the opening out of the next. But where exactly *is* the difference between the two poems? Both are self-conscious expressions of the 'modern' world and both seek to incarnate diversity in a simultaneous presentation of events and a fiction of ubiquity:

> Te voilà à Marseille au milieu des pastèques
> Te voilà à Coblence à l'hôtel du Géant
> Te voilà à Rome assis sous un néflier du Japon
> Te voilà à Amsterdam avec une fille que tu trouves belle et qui est laide
> ('Zone', l. 106)

> Du rouge au vert tout le jaune se meurt
> Paris Vancouver Hyères Maintenon New-York et les Antilles
> La fenêtre s'ouvre comme une orange
> Le beau fruit de la lumière   ('Les Fenêtres', l. 34)

In chapter two I suggested that there is a clear intellectual link between simultaneity in the Cubist presentation of objects, and simultaneity in the Orphic presentation of light, colour and memory. But the difference between the poetic, as distinct from plastic, experience of simultaneity expressed in the two fragments I have quoted seems so great that it is tempting to think of it as embodying the beginning of Apollinaire's new aesthetic. There is a strand in Apollinaire criticism that believes Apollinaire's attachment to Cubism to have been more a symptom of his constant desire to be involved with innovation in the arts than a sign of any spontaneous affinity. It is argued that Cubism is at once too intellectual and too subdued and colourless to suggest any deep-seated correspondence with Apollinaire's creative temperament. L. C. Breunig invokes the authority of Gaëtan Picon to make the point:

> La poésie d'Apollinaire, comme dit Gaëtan Picon, est 'une poésie dynamique, emportée par la parole, cédant au vertige d'une accélération continue'. Quel rapport peut-il y avoir entre un tel style et une peinture qui présente à l'oeil à un moment donné un effet d'équilibre?
>
> Ensuite [vouloir déduire qu'Apollinaire faisait de la poésie cubiste], c'est oublier — et voilà l'essentiel — qu'en fin de compte le *style* cubiste, en dépit de toute la bonne volonté d'Apollinaire, lui resta toujours étranger. C'est un style austère, presque puritain, aux couleurs terreuses, qui veut réaliser une composition rigoureuse et logique.[15]

Without suggesting that it is useful to term 'Zone' a specifically Cubist poem, Breunig sees Delaunay's art as providing Apollinaire with a more decisive impetus in his drive towards creativity than thinking about Cubism ever could. With this view in mind, 'Zone' certainly does appear more insecure in its modernity, for it is concerned not only with the poetry and prose to be created through posters and newspapers, but also with the vacuum left by lost modes of expression. In 'Les Fenêtres', on the other hand, the 'obscures espérances' of 'Zone' are articulated by the diversity of the present itself. 'Les Fenêtres' discovers a poetic present that opens out to the variety of circumstance and experience, while rising to the fact that such variety cannot be contained in any one present moment. In 'Les Fenêtres', diversity in the present is both engulfed and engulfing. It is attractive to see in this a significant step forward in the development of Apollinaire's creativity: ubiquity, heroism, improvisation.

In a sense, 'Les Fenêtres' can be read as a fulfilment, an enactment of what Apollinaire envisaged in the 'Poème lu au marriage d'André

Salmon' (1909) through the combination of assertion and sensation that is one of the most masterful achievements of *Alcools*:[16]

> L'amour qui emplit ainsi que *la lumière*
> Tout le *solide* espace entre les étoiles et les planètes   (1. 40)

Light, solidity, controlled creative stimuli, the freedom of time and space — these are the project of 'Les Fenêtres', one that gives the appearance of being achieved in a syntax endlessly open to sensation and image, removing the need on which much of *Alcools* is based for a poetry about poetry — a poetic statement about poetic desires. On this level of reading, the textualities of 'Zone' and 'Les Fenêtres' become increasingly sharply divided. In 'Les Fenêtres', poems can be sent out over the telephone wires:

> Nous l'enverrons en message téléphonique
> Traumatisme géant
> Il fait couler les yeux
> Voilà une jolie jeune fille parmi les jeunes Turinaises
> Le pauvre jeune homme se mouchait dans sa cravate blanche
> Tu soulèveras le rideau
> Et maintenant voilà que s'ouvre la fenêtre
> Araignées quand les mains tissaient la lumière   (1. 5)

'Les Fenêtres' sustains the 'traumatisme géant' of speed, novelty and surprise; sustains it as a source of poetic energy. The 'traumatisme' appears not to disintegrate into a sense of invasion, or of melting poetic vision and resolve. The flowing eyes, while not achieving the impossibility of infinite vision (in 'Le Larron', Apollinaire aimed at 'une vue oblongue' as an act of resistance against the relativity imposed by the senses), are tears but also extending rays of light.[17] The anguish of the young man suffering exclusion from women and plurality melts jocularly along the white line of his tie, with which he blows his nose. Anguish melts in the gestures of lifting the curtain and of the window opening — *arbitrary* gestures that reveal the inclusion of the young man and the reader in the language of the present, its multiplying diversity, and in the light uniting the structural webs of the world ('Araignées ... tissaient la lumière'). In 'Zone', the creative expression to be found in posters, newspapers and aeroplanes needs, to sustain it, an explicit reference to the power to develop images — and the text itself is the arena for such a power and also, in effect, for its undermining.[18] But 'Les Fenêtres' seems even to deny the need for a self-conscious poetic arena. It creates the appearance by which the power to create images

130

is indistinguishable from a spontaneous interaction with the world, anosmosis of pen and context on which the fiction of the 'poème-conversation' is based. In 'Zone', the aeroplane that replaces Christ spans equally substantial gaps, and yet it does so precisely because it engenders a host of images from a vacuum of broken symbols whose expressiveness roams like feathers falling from birds:

> Et tous aigle phénix et pihis de la Chine
> Fraternisent avec la volante machine   (l. 69)

From this fraternisation between modernity and a space carved out within traditional poetic invention, the poem traces a disintegration into failed contact, diffused desire, and the failure of light. Compare the young man in 'Les Fenêtres' and the 'jolie jeune fille parmi les Turinaises', with

> Ses mains que je n'avais pas vues sont dures et gercées
> J'ai une pitié immense pour les coutures de son ventre
> J'humilie maintenant à une pauvre fille au rire horrible ma bouche
>   (l. 141)

And compare 'Le beau fruit de la lumière' with 'Soleil cou coupé'.

Does this textual contrast explain the decision to withhold 'Les Fenêtres' from *Alcools* and reveal the kind of impetus Apollinaire derived from his contact with Delaunay? Does it give us an indication that Apollinaire is discovering the synthesis he wants of different 'simultanist' modes of expression? Apollinaire himself seems to assign this sort of importance to the poem: 'Puis j'aime beaucoup mes vers depuis *Alcools*, il y en a pour un volume au moins et j'aime beaucoup beaucoup "Les Fenêtres" qui a paru en tête d'un catalogue du peintre Delaunay. Ils ressortissent à une esthétique toute neuve dont je n'ai plus depuis retrouvé les ressorts ....'[19] The contrast between 'Zone' and 'Les Fenêtres' is, on one level, so stark that at first sight the problem of their inclusion in different collections seems solved. But numerous paradoxes emerge — obstacles to reading 'Les Fenêtres' and Delaunay's painting in terms of an unrestricted, engulfing and *concrete* simultaneity. As I have suggested, there is a view that the difference between 'Zone' (or 'Automne malade' and 'Les Fiançailles') and 'Les Fenêtres' is that the former are poetry about poetry, and that the latter is a poem about the concrete world of events. But this is *not* the difference between Cubism and Orphism. Delaunay's colour may seem more immediate in its impact than the dull colours of the Cubist canvas and the aesthetic issues of perspective and composition with which Cubism is concerned. But the fact remains that Delaunay's painting is *more*, not less, abstract than Cubism: we simply cannot assume that complex presentations of colour are less 'intellectual' than disruptions of perspective. Cubism is populated with objects, albeit vestiges or memories of objects, whereas in Delaunay's painting after the series of exploding Eiffel Towers, objects are increasingly replaced with colour contrasts. Moreover, Delaunay's colour spectrum and the range of perceptual impulses that his paintings encompass are an effect of *appearance*, a pictorially constructed fiction. The aspirations of the painting are fulfilled to the exact extent that it confronts itself as fiction. Delaunay creates the *appearance* of infinity.

An affinity exists between such an emphasis on appearance and the concept of 'fausseté' that Apollinaire developed in his appraisal of Royère's work, in 'Les Fiançailles' and in the other poems of the period: 'Lul de Faltenin' and 'Le Brasier'. While not taking away from the novelty of the impetus Apollinaire draws from Delaunay's art, and without taking away from the difference in the writing he begins to produce in 'Ondes', the clear link betwen the concepts of 'fausseté' and of Orphic appearance challenges any naïve assumption that Apollinaire's new aesthetic makes him abandon the questioning of poetry in poetry, of language in language, and the question of poetic identity in relation to the poetic product. Any examination of the radical shift that occurs in Apollinaire's writing has to take into account its continued exploration of this kind of question. One of the ways of locating this shift more precisely is to consider one of the distinctive newcomers to Apollinaire's writing: the 'poème-conversation'.

2—'LES FENÊTRES'

(i) 'LE POÈME-CONVERSATION': WHERE IS THE WRITER?

Apollinaire had already constructed a poem around a conversation and the rhythm of its development in the Rhenish text 'Les Femmes'.[20] But what distinguishes 'Les Femmes' from 'Lundi Rue Christine', for example, is that in the latter, while the reader rapidly becomes aware that lines or groups of lines are representations of conversational exchanges, there is no sense at all that the writer had restricted himself to overhearing a single real or imaginary conversation. On the contrary, the project in 'Lundi Rue Christine' seems to be to create an overlap between contexts — a proliferation of different contexts within the poem. In 'Les Fenêtres', the desire to include elements from disparate contexts affects the poem's composition itself — and the controversy it has generated.

According to André Billy, the poem has no single author. In *Apollinaire vivant*, he recreates a situation in which he himself, René Dalize and Apollinaire sit in the Crucifix bar and discuss the fact that Apollinaire's introduction to Delaunay's exhibition needs to be sent to Berlin that night.[21] They decide that this is the occasion for a poem, which they can send 'en message téléphonique', and begin to improvise it between them, Apollinaire holding the pen, writing lines from his head or from the mouths of the other two. (Apollinaire thinking of) Delaunay's colour combines with tropical birds remembered from (Dalize's) distant voyages and with (Billy's) projected telephone messages.

Robert and Sonia Delaunay, on the other hand, remembered Apollinaire writing the poem in their studio, and produced the manuscript to prove it.[22] As Décaudin and Renaud after him suggest, the only way of reconciling these visions of the truth is to combine them: Apollinaire obtained a rough draft of the poem in collaboration with his friends at the bar, and later reworked and took control of it.[23] In effect, the publicity surrounding this 'poème célèbre' and its composition assists in focusing the reader's attention on one of its distinctive projects: to combine within a single poem the most diverse experiences, to embrace within a single text the disparate stimuli that structure perception at any moment.[24] Breton admires in Apollinaire a talent for creating a 'poème-événement' — for persuading his readers that a poem can be a radical rethinking of a poet's own poetic methods, and an equally radical challenge to cherished poetic achievements.[25] The controversy the poem's composition produced gave Apollinaire a unique opportunity to transform concrete events, the arbitrariness of circumstance, into that sense of uniqueness that is the first and perhaps most intense indication of the poetic. The paradox of the 'poème-conversation' as event is its aspiration to present circumstance as the incarnation of desire, to re-present casual dialogue as a poetic reconstruction, to encompass the manifold of perception while responding at first hand to its diversity and its lack of dimension.

Apollinaire is in control of this paradox in so far as he undermines the presence of authorial voice in the text. This undermining is immediately made self-evident because of the poem's controversial authorship. But the undermining of authorial presence is also textually created in the effaced difference between the voices populating and structuring the poem. The poem is a controlled construction of absence. The aesthetic that allows Apollinaire to claim that 'je chante toutes les possibilités de moi-même' creates a ubiquity of absence.[26] The syntax of 'Les Fenêtres' allows Apollinaire the liberty of indefinite selection, and of a potentially — or *apparently* — indefinite expansion of the poetic arena.[27] The links binding him to the specificity of a past that refuses to be specified fall away in their rejuvenation as elements in the present itself:

écoute tomber les liens qui te retiennent en haut et en bas[28]

But although the links fall away, they do so in the unifying colours and effaced diversity of a rainy day; moreover, they hold even as they fall away ('retenir' is in the present tense), just as the rails that unite peoples also bind them:

Rails qui ligotez les nations[29]

Furthermore, although Apollinaire imagines in 'Liens' that the combined vision of two or three individuals will open out a new creative space of the present ('Cordes et Concorde'), these people, Apollinaire himself and his friends, are *not* a dominating presence when it comes to texts, in either 'Liens' or 'Les Fenêtres', whose very title evokes Dalaunay, one of the two or three great 'modernists' in question.[30] His presence in the poem is reduced to a neutral and impersonal descriptive quality:

Une vieille paire de chaussures jaunes devant la fenêtre[31]

which only literary historians and the controversy surrounding the 'poème-événement' identify as Delaunay's.[32] Apollinaire himself, in another text, is similarly reduced to a neutral impersonality, to bold type and a new pair of shoes:

Les chaussures neuves du poète[33]

But such complex textual jokes are not at the expense of Apollinaire's own poetic ambitions: they are directed at the delusion of poetic grandeur. The enterprise of 'Ondes' is not to achieve the impossible; it is not to promote the writer or calligrapher to a superhuman ugiquity transcending fiction, appearance, and the spatio-temporal moment, any more than the Cubist aretfact is an unmediated liberation of the object from perspective.

The indefinite power of selection Apollinaire creates with the help of the syntax in 'Les Fenêtres' is one that obscures and fragments his creative identity — this remains 'une ombre', one that is still not 'solide'.[34] The 'objects' that are selected or invented remain open-ended, nobody's possession and mastered by nobody, on the tantalising borderline of the irretrievably obscure:

> Bigorneaux Lotte multiples Soleils et l'Oursin du couchant   (l. 17)

Philippe Renaud thinks of this line as a microcosm of the poem as a whole and of its operation on the reader, and his reading of it suggests many ways of appreciating the complexity of Apollinaire's poetic enterprise.[35] 'Bigorneaux', 'lotte', 'soleils' and 'oursin' are all types of fish, shellfish or crustacea. The line thus suggests a fishmonger's — the one around the corner from Delaunay's studio, or any other — passing through the eye of Apollinaire's recent memory.[36] We discover once again that Apollinaire, in the poems of his 'esthétique toute neuve', creates the appearance of an increasingly extensive and potent intertextuality, the poles of which are the textual artefact itself and the hidden limits of the perceptual field.

Simultaneity approached in this way seems to involve an interplay of opposites. It depends on recognition with regard to specific moments in perception, and aims to undermine the specifying, familiarising frameworks on which recognition depends. In fact, any sense of recognition is attacked by Apollinaire in this line. His list of myterious fish species, because of its obscurity, lies buried in an area of pre-recognition. The capital letters Apollinaire uses to designate each species in fact designàte nothing other than an expansive glow that eludes efforts to grasp it and to identify with it.[37]

Moreover, the internal structure of the sequence of fish-signifiers precludes a unifying build-up of context. 'Soleils' is a semantic pivot, a context-fragmenting pun: it is not only a group of shellfish, but the source of light. Renaud points out that 'soleil' as source of light is developed into 'couchant' by way of the link between the spikes on the sea-urchin and the horizontal rays of the sun. At the same time, this metonymic development is *not* reconcilable with the 'soleils' and the 'oursin' as sea-fruits, with the 'bigorneaux' and the 'lotte', or with a textually re-perceived fishmonger.

The play of unity and difference in this 'microcosm-line' of the poem is still more expressive than the conclusion Renaud draws from it, which is that the line absolutely resists any single interpretation.[38]

For this is not so much a high point in Apollinaire's development of simultaneity as the inception of a struggle with obscurity; it inaugurates a process of deciphering that, because of its involvement with memory, places the notion of simultaneity in a fundamentally challenging light.[39] The line beginning 'Bigorneaux' raises the curtain on an abstract reading and writing, in which objects are not designated and signifiers are increasingly resistant. Supported by the text as a whole, the line is able to re-present, to incarnate the dynamic by which expression seeks to meet a repeated sense of novelty in experience. The fishmonger's in the real world is blurred in plural levels of memory and perception, and the fish themselves appear in a moment of difference that removes them irretrievably from the fishmonger's slab.[40]

But this abstraction of the real world is not a stage in the realisation of a more general aesthetic purpose. The rejection of mimesis is not simply an instrument in the creation of an expanded perception in a plural, a 'simultaneous' moment. The abstraction of the real world is not a framework that allows Apollinaire to make his statement, it *is* the experience he is representing. The tension created by the opposing directions in which the line is pulled by the ambiguity of 'Soleils' (appropriately enough in the plural), triggers a sudden exposure to a non-pictorial materiality of language: the signifier, the specificity of words and phonemes on which our sense of language depends. Within this heightened awareness of the signifier, the distinction between metaphor and metonymy dissolves. 'Bigorneaux Lotte multiples Soleils et l'Oursin du couchant' carries its reader along the invisible borderline between perception and consciousness, memory and expression, the seeing 'I' and the identifying 'I'. It represents a state of pre-recognition, which is *not* an experience outside language. It is an incarnation of perception within language, and at the same time it strives to represent perception independently of its displacement in language and recognition. 'Bigorneaux Lotte multiples Soleils et l'Oursin du couchant' is a chain of 'perception-signifiers'.[41] It represents a crucial experience of language — perception within language at the same time as perception directed at language. It traces an interface between memory, the unavailable history of identity, and word-signs that articulate recognition and the sense of 'I' through obscurity and novelty.

(ii) MULTI-CONTEXTUALITY, RESISTANCE

The simultaneity of 'Les Fenêtres' tempers the idea that it can ever be the stuff of an ecstatic, mobile overview of life and the world. The associations that link the images and statements cannot be traced; recognition within perception is destabilised by the text, along with the author's presence, our sense of his identity, and our ability to control stimuli. Once again in Apollinaire's most rewarding poems, perception is not reducible to itself, it is not a category in experience. We become aware of it as perceived, or as expressed, and the two do not coincide.

Reading the lines either side of 'Bigorneaux Lotte multiples Soleils et l'Oursin du couchant', we discover the consistency with which simultaneity operates throughout 'Les Fenêtres':

Quand on a le temps on a la liberté   (l. 16)

Almost before we read, we are reminded once again that Apollinaire knows what he is doing. The newspapers *Le Temps* and *La Liberté* are copper coinage in the daily life of pre-war Paris, but simply to refer to them within a poem runs the risk of collapsing into the anecdotal, of sequestrating the writer within private experience or a private joke. But here, the circumstantial is not hermetically sealed in a privileged and highly personal moment, preserved by Apollinaire for the consumption of 'gens de la même race' and of literary history.[42] The newspaper titles are transformed in the text from being a shared reference point or talisman into a talisman closed in on itself: 'un médaillon toujours fermé' as Apollinaire was to write later.[43]

As Anne Hyde Greet and Ian Lockerbie eloquently point out, Apollinaire's use of the newspaper titles is a pun that opens the line out to a variety of reverberative and challenging concepts. So let us read the line again; it has no capital letters and invites us to read it 'literally':

Quand on a le temps on a la liberté

Freedom might be time in which to create, Greet and Lockerbie suggest.[44] Better still, if time were of no consequence, then we really would be free, and only then could we see that we had changed the world and our existence in it. We could grasp change and claim it as ours within our own perceptual life. And our perception would be opened out to the exhilarating diversity of the present. This meeting of an emancipated perception and the vastness of the present might give us access to what Delaynay thought of as 'notre psychique toujours en éveil' — a dynamic and *impersonal* state of awareness and creativity.[45] It is a state of being produced in 'pure' abstract expression, in which procedure ('les moyens'), the perceptual process and the concrete world express each other completely. But an unarrested expansion of perception is not Delaunay's idea of pure abstraction, and Apollinaire's text does not fulfil the desire for it. The statement 'Quand on a le temps on a la liberté' is enclosed in the illusory specificity of the everyday, in the glowing talisman of the concrete, tangible, interchangeable images that the everyday offers for sale.

Moreover, the ironic intention in the formula 'Quand on a le temps on a la liberté' is emphasised in the next two lines. Multi-contextual, non-objective 'purity' in expression makes reading not only tantalising but also impenetrable. 'Bigorneaux Lotte multiples Soleils et l'Oursin du couchant', the following line, represents perception as indecipherable — as we saw; it deals in a discontinuity that does not stabalise difference or make identification possible. The next line, 'Une vieille paire de chaussures jaunes devant la fenêtre', continues along the same invisible dividing-line between recognition and the thwarting of recognition. The controversy over the poem's coming to being suggests that the old yellow shoes are Delaunay's and belong in his studio. But even if we defuse obscurity in this way, the text itself eludes our capturing of its individual lines and images. The gesture of anecdotal reference is dismantled. The specificity of an object rich in association is magnified into an intransitive and unknown glow indistinguishable from the present itself — Apollinaire's and ours. As we read we are confronted with a hidden or displaced 'other'. The text does not dominate the object; instead, the reality of the object invades the present.

This is one of the levels on which Apollinaire's stated goal of simplifying poetic syntax through 'Les Fenêtres' becomes significant. Let us remind ourselves of the well-known passage from his letter to Madeleine Pagès: 'J'ai fait mon possible pour simplifier la syntaxe poétique et j'ai réussi en certains cas, notamment un poème: "Les Fenêtres" ....'[46] A crucial element in this simplification is the poem's structure of juxtaposition, which Apollinaire uses to have disparate statements and disparate perceptions succeed one another in a syntactically coherent way. Clearly, the syntax Apollinaire adopts is not aimed at creating a uniformity of context allowing a 'message' to be read and understood in terms of a stble framework of reference. Equally, it is unproductive to argue that Apollinaire chooses the order of the lines/statements/images arbitrarily. In effect, his text exploits an appearance of arbitrariness in the order of the lines and in their relation one to another, and in this way it creates a 'difficult' language. The disavowal of language as a transmitter of messages puts Apollinaire in accord with the would-be atemporal multiplicity of Dramatism, the 'aesthetification' of the modern world practised by Futurism, and the 'defunctionalisation' of objects created in Duchamp's Dadaist 'ready-mades'. But we saw in chapter two that the Dramatist and Futurist promises to reject instrumentality in language remain essentially unfulfilled. For both groups do in fact regard expression — whether linguistic or pictorial — as the place where an immediate transmission occurs: the transmission of an emancipated consciousness, and of an expanding perception.

The question that arises is a familiar one. Is this inconsistency in the Dramatist and Futurist approaches, this broken promise, the source of Apollinaire's attraction to Delaunay's art, and of his desire to become involved with Orphism? But more specifically, is there anything in the syntax of 'Les Fenêtres' that suggests an Orphic impulse in Apollinaire's modernism?

Implicit in Delaunay's approach as well as in Apollinaire's formulation of it is the view that perceptual expansiveness and all-inclusiveness ('notre sensibilité et notre psychique toujours en éveil') are both experience and praxis. But this transmission of an experience liberated from perspective and representation into 'pure' expression is the result of a *tension* between vision and the materials used to articulate it. For the artistic construct involves resistance and displacement. As we saw, it is this tension in Delaunay's manipulation of colour that Apollinaire terms Orphic, and it is a tension present in the syntax of 'Les Fenêtres'. The juxtaposition of the lines and the almost complete absence of conjunctions mean that the statement made in each line is not in a relationship of instrumentality to the next.[47] This disruption involves a creation of resistance in the poem, and in our experience of language. This in turn takes the form of indecipherability, the coherence of which is established in the regularity of the demands made on the reader, as opposed to a regularity in the relation of located 'messages' one to another. By making this choice in relation to syntax and to his manipulation of image in language, Apollinaire is representing an experience of language; for the duration of the poem, the poem *is* this experience. It is the consistency with which Apollinaire represents language as a resister in which perception is both articulated and displaced that constitutes the Orphic originality of 'Les Fenêtres'.

(iii) 'TU SOULÈVERAS LE RIDEAU': DISPLACEMENT

Coherence of this kind prevents the poem from presenting itself as a complete entity in reading. It is uncovered repeatedly in the reading of any group of images chosen from the text, and any such choice is inevitably arbitrary. The syntactic consistency of 'Les Fenêtres' frustrates any attempt to take it in and specify our own experience through it. The syntax carries the reader along a line. On one side, there is the possibility of encompassing the variety of stimuli through which the sense of self unfurls. On the other, there is the spectre of merely passive consumption of stimuli, and of this turning out to be exactly what experience in the present is all about.

This tension is apparent in the following fives lines from the poem:

> Tu soulèveras le rideau
> Et maintenant voilà que s'ouvre la fenêtre
> Araignées quand les mains tissaient la lumière
> Beauté pâleur insondables voilets
> Nous tenterons en vain de prendre du repos   (l.10)

In choosing these lines and reproducing them here, I have in effect made them into a self-contained entity, even though this runs the risk of misrepresenting the operation of this and any other unpunctuated text. But to quote in this way raises more problems here than in the case of poems from *Alcools*, because in 'Les Fenêtres' any line or any series of lines abdicates any role whatever in the build-up of a 'message' or a circumscribed experience. In fact, as an amusing experiment of Renaud's reveals, these lines and any others from the poem can be read in the reverse order, without the 'meaning' being quantifiably altered.[48] Each line emphasises the fact that it is an element in a progression. Not only does reading occlude a sense of the world being restructured and experience specified (the absence of such a sense had been familiar in French poetry since Mallarmé and Rimbaud), but also thinking is itself articulated as *sequence*. Each line, each self-under-mining 'statement' represents a moment in thinking that is both developed and completely displaced by the one that succeeds it; each line represents the fact that it *is* succeeded. This is not just a general feature of the poem as a whole but one of its crucial objectives.

This emphasis on progression is apparent in the first of our five lines. 'Tu soulèveras le rideau' contains one of the many changes of tense in the text (the previous line is in the imperfect). This power the text displays to slip in and out of the time dimensions suggests a transparent, liberating mobility in the perceiving or writing consciousness.[49] But the reality of the text, its interplay of the quotidian and the indecipherable, means that the shifts in tense have implications that are more difficult to come to terms with. The eruption into the text of these tense changes does not only represent acts of imagination and imaginative decisions, it incarnates the process that links them, it re-presents the displacement in this process, so that images are perceived as unlocated in time and lacking a vessel in which to capture their expressiveness. The future tense in 'Tu soulèveras le rideau' seems to claim on behalf of reader and writer a power to break up a logical sequence imposed from without, and thus to transform the concrete world into the forum of their own creativity. But equally, the future tense roams in a disconnected way, it shatters the sense of prophecy that it momentarily evokes. 'To soulèveras le rideau' represents an event in perception — any event — and as such it is bound within perception as process. The creativity it offers is not present in the text, it is articulated in the events, the images, the 'statements', *as* sequence, to the extent that reading does not control this 'creativity'. Instead, thinking is overrun by the events in perception that set thinking in motion.

The emergence of the following line reinforces this experience.

> Et maintenant voilà que s'ouvre la fenêtre

It seems natural for a window opening to follow the act of lifting a curtain. But the text does not exploit this semblance of logical progression. Instead, the unit

> Tu soulèveras le rideau
> Et maintenant voilà que s'ouvre la fenêtre

dissolves the appearance of association in the fact of sequentiality. The reader is not in a position to establish whether the line follows on from the previous one, or whether it can be looked on as a further stage in the formulation of an idea or a vision. 'Et maintenant voilà que s'ouvre la fenêtre' *replaces* 'Tu soulèveras le rideau'; it is a new meeting of interpretation and perception, at a place absent from the text. Not only is would-be complete interpretation thwarted, interpretation is *within* perception, it does not uncouple itself from experience, and it is this that Apollinaire's poem rises to. It gives the reader a direct involvement with interpretation as continuum, a continuum in which interpretation itself is both lost and all-exclusive. The moment of writing effaces access to the structures that prompt it, and this moment is itself fragmented in reading through the poem as sequence.

141

The simplicity of the syntax, then, is a deception Apollinaire practises on the reader, and so is the apparent arbitrariness of the order in which the lines are presented. This has an important effect on our understanding of the poem's 'simultaneity'. It highlights an ambiguity that is on one level a familiar one: transparency is in tension with indecipherability, mobility with an expressiveness whose significance and direction remain unknown. But this ambiguity also takes a more complex form. The 'simplicity' of the syntax not only evokes a power to encompass the diverse stimuli that populate perception, it also suggests that this 'encompassing' is an illusion, and that it fails to distinguish itself from a passive consumption, a passive acceptance of the way things are and the way they appear in perception. The syntactic 'simplicity' of 'Les Fenêtres', which in fact is a studied disguise of rhetorical structuring, means that authorial control is purposefully undermined, and stimuli seem to belong to the world and not to the person seeking to identify with them, to the context which gives them birth and whose 'otherness' defies the poetic enterprise — even though it is incarnated in the sequence of *this* text.

The controversial circumstances of the poem's composition bear this out. On the one hand, the multiple authorship seems to establish a clarity in the writing that supports a fiction of endless, transparent readability — the fiction that any image can be understood and added to by any reader or writer in the present. But on the other hand, this kind of authorship emphasises the absence of authorial control, and not simply with a view to emancipating perception and giving it wider access to creative writing. Apollinaire takes control of his poem at the moment of tension between the fiction of clarity and the anxiety of authorship. (Whose poem is it?) It is a moment when clarity becomes the desire for clarity, a desire to encompass perceptually an involvement with the world, a desire pursued through language and in tension with it.

The text resists, then, and it is on this level that 'Et maintenant voilà que s'ouvre la fenêtre' asks to be read and comes to life as fiction. The fact that the window opens independently of an act of will is, here, more than idiom. It is a moment in perception, it takes the place of a perceptual process that fails to be embraced in attitudes struck to the world and to objects. Equally, 'Et maintenant voilà que s'ouvre la fenêtre', as an image, as a statement and as a moment in writing, aspires to creating an access *in* language to a representation of a relation *to* language. In spite of this aspiration, the beginning and the end of interpretation are effaced, and the line acts exclusively as something that is read. The reader's attention is focused on language proceeding between the eye and the printed page. The poem presents language as language-in-reading; and this language, stripped of the certainty of transmission, *is* 'pure' displacement.

The notion of a desire to represent a relation to language is a complex one. Reading 'Les Fenêtres' we discover that a 'point' or an attitude of representation is not isolated in the text but extends over it; it is impressed in the text in the form of 'objects' and images. The poem seems to stamp out the creativity it strives for as it unfurls, and the lyrical appeal itself of the following line in our series contributes to this process:

Araignées quand les mains tissaient la lumière

The lyrical appeal is an immediate one. The line expresses in words the silent eroticism of touch, and uses a reference to light, which has no beginning and no end, to express the memory of touch, the pathetic impossibility that memory of touch should be as intense as touch itself. The surprise created by the eruption of the spider-light image into the poem emphasises this lyrical appeal and produces a sense of release from the resister of language and of circumstance.

This sense of a surprise eruption is both enhanced and undermined by the poem as sequence. On the one hand 'Araignées' can be read as being in apposition to 'le rideau' and 'la fenêtre' of the previous lines, creating a dramatic shift in the appreciation of those two events in perception. On the other hand, this notional apposition seems designed to defy our expectations, so that 'Araignées quand les mains tissaient la lumière' emerges as being in apposition to an absent referent — or at least one that is potentially so multiple that it is not specified in the text: the 'araignées' could be in apposition to the whole poem. This absence of hierarchy in the events of 'Les Fenêtres' is the result of Apollinaire's consistent manipulation of apposition throughout the poem, and it gradually emphasises a barrier between the levels of signified and signifier structuring any use of language. The signified remains unlocated here, and Apollinaire seems to relish the failure of his signifiers to circumscribe one. 'Araignées quand les mains tissaient la lumière' emerges as being not only in apposition to the poem as a whole and the events within it, but equally to an irreducible 'otherness'. Moreover, the possibility of specifying the context of 'Araignées ...' is dissolved by the image itself — the signified undermines itself.

143

F

The spiders weave endlessly; their weaving does not produce an image representing their or our experience, it becomes indistinguishable from light itself and moves away from the power to give contours to image and to perception.[50]

It is clear, however, that although 'Araignées' does not specify the associations it engenders, the word 'spiders' or 'araignées' preserves the double structure of any linguistic sign, operating the interplay of signifier and signified that produces the reference to the eight-legged animal we all know. But in 'Les Fenêtres' reference is elaborately out-manoeuvred. This is not a simplistic unfettering of a latent, highly linguistic creativity. Compare these 'araignées' with those in 'Liens':

> Violente pluie qui peigne les fumées
> Cordes
> Cordes tissées
> Câbles sous-marins
> Tours de Babel changées en ponts
> Araignées-Pontifes
> Tous les amoureux qu'un seul lien a liés   (l. 8)

Here, the spiders take part in a magnificent structure of chaos and vision, originality and pretension, spanning the diversity of ideas and images, and the aspirations they put on offer. But in 'Les Fenêtres' such a power is razed, streamlined into the past, and taunted along the unspecified lines that move from past to present, investing the moment with the expressiveness of memory. With 'tissaient' in the imperfect, the source of this expressiveness is buried, not only in time, but in the very image that seeks to give it life in the poem. We cannot be free with the spontaneous creativity suggested and imprinted *within* 'Araignées quand les mains tissaient la lumière'; it fails to give contours to the relation binding language to its user. As a word, 'Araignées' *is* that relation, and it undermines our domination of it. The spideriness of the spiders and of the feelers they extend around us is taken away from the familiar animal and used to make a completely different kind of image. 'Araignées' is an image of a word — an image re-presenting *novelty* in the experience of a word, as well as the endless *given* with which language confronts its user. At this point in the poem, reading represents reading.

This explains the urgency of the following line:

> Beauté pâleur insondables violets

Here, reference to time is suppressed. The poem seems to assert a power to exploit the creative potential of image and light suggested by the previous line, and to assert it *now*, in a galvanised experience of perception and the materials at its disposal. The urgent rhythm of the line, with its lack of articles, intensifies the dramatic assertion of creativity and vision that this line establishes in relation to the spiders, the light, and the intense sensuous/abstract sense of self-in-the-world they put before us.

Equally, by an interplay that is becoming familiar, the line need not be read in apposition to the previous one; it could be in apposition to the poem as a whole, it could be an apposition without referent or anchor. As we have seen before, the weaving of this possibility into the text emphasises a barrier between signifier and signified. Here, read as a self-isolating statement, the nouns and the noun phrase are each a signifier displacing other signifiers. This takes place initially in terms of their semantic context. 'Beauté' and 'pâleur' are as abstract as light itself, and they invade our awareness with unbounded potential. Moreover, however unfathomable, 'insondables violets' is one colour, it does not involve others; it is a single colour that is also a plural colour ('violets'). Its singularity remains paramount, nuanced and unlocated all at the same time.

This brings the poem close to Delaunay's work and his use of colour. Delaunay exploits *contrast* between complementary colours to express the *infinity* of colour and light — or to create the appearance of infinity. Delaunay's pictorial fiction deals in displacement, since he manipulates an opposition between simultaneity and contrast; in doing so, he causes his fiction to construct creativity itself, and its materials and method represent the experience of thinking and the pursuit of clarity. Apollinaire deals in displacement and creativity in relation to language rather than to colour, even though at this point in 'Les Fenêtres' his language presents itself to him in terms of colours. The poem offers a reading space as mobile and anti-figurative as Delaunay's painting, although the two approaches meet and part within the violet of this line, and highlight different experiences of the signifier. 'Violets' is not, as it would be in Delaunay's painting, a visible colour representing others by both exploiting and obliterating the distinction between them. But like the 'colour' produced in Delaunay's handling of contrast, 'violets' is a word displacing a colour — a colour the reader cannot see. It is a textualised colour, indistinguishable from the letters v-i-o-l-e-t-s, in which the crucial letter is 's', for it prevents the reader from linking 'violets' to a coloured crayon at home. Apollinaire's text is using colour in a way that presents a relation to language meto- nymically, *as reading,* and that presents words as w-o-r-d-s, as being continually deciphered in a process where the signifier imposes and the signified recedes. The creativity offered by 'Les Fenêtres' is one that is able to meet the continuously different terms of existence in language and in the present. By steering the reader into an increasing dominance of the signifier, 'Les Fenêtres' confronts the desire to intervene actively in perception, with an obscure, fully experienced, ecstatic and menacing present:

> Nous tenterons en vain de prendre du repos

(iv) 'DU ROUGE AU VERT TOUT LE JAUNE SE MEURT': INVENTIVENESS UNDOMINATED

Much of the experience I have been characterising in 'Les Fenêtres' is heralded in the first three lines of the poem:

> Du rouge au vert tout le jaune se meurt
> Quand chantent les aras dans les forêts natales
> Abatis de pihis

These lines, as I mentioned at the beginning of this reading of the poem, are a source of hard-fought controversy as to the poem's authorship. Is it a collective one, the first three lines being shared by Apollinaire and Dalize, with Billy adding the fourth? On this, with respect to the 'événement' of the controversy as well as in the text that unfurls from his pen, Apollinaire remains silent. There is an equal silence on the origins of the objects, events and colours that construct the poem and these three lines in particular. The red, the green and the yellow seem unattached. 'Les aras' might strike their reader as irretrievably obscure, were it nor for the fact that Apollinaire's obscurity and allusiveness has accustomed us to shocks to our desire to understand. The 'pihis' are equally impenetrable and allusive, their specificity borders on that of the coinage — a direction in the text that gathers more weight in 'Abatis'. This last word is rarely seen in this form outside this text; it seems highly specific and correspondingly difficult to decipher; although, given alterations of spelling, it sends out feelers of meaning like the spiders' legs weaving light.

And yet, once again, it might seem perverse not to make use of the machinery that reintegrates Apollinaire's text with well-known events in his life — a life that has been thoroughly and illuminatingly documented.[51] The colours can be related clearly to Delaunay's painting and Apollinaire's experience of it; the 'aras' and 'forêts natales' supposedly provided by Dalize refer perhaps to the tropical parrots and the tropical forests of his travels. The 'pihis', following on from the colourful birds flying through colourful forests, have flown from a zone through which Apollinaire passes; they help draw the *Alcools* experience to a close and they land in a new phase in his poetry.[52]

But is explaining away the poem's obscurity the same as reading it? Was Apollinaire hoping that the details, the arbitrary sequence in the events of his life and that of his friends, would be remembered and reincarnated in every reading, and preserved in every reading? Surely not — the complexities we have discovered at work elsewhere in the poem preclude such an assumption. By insisting on specific responsibility for the authorship of individual lines, it is Billy who reveals that he is outmanoeuvred by the text. For Apollinaire takes control of it. It is not the arbitrariness of individual existences that Apollinaire seeks to encapsulate and preserve for those involved.[53] It is arbitrariness itself that he seeks both to enact and represent in his language, along with the arbitrary relation that links his poem to his existence, and that links his writing to the images that flow through perception ceaselessly and from limitless perspectives.

As so often in Apollinaire's poems from the earliest to the latest, limitless perspective is articulated in terms of resistance:

> Du rouge au vert tout le jaune se meurt

The three colours could be any lights shining simultaneously or successively in the city at night, or in the city bursting into Apollinaire's memory as he writes. The colours could be particular colours, but Apollinaire takes possession of them; they gain their obscure specificity from the relationship that locks them together. The 'jaune' in the three-colour process is like the 'violets' that appears later in the poem: 'insondable', unnameable, irretrievable in the letters that allow it to be read. The colours create one anothers' brightness in the relations that bind them — both in perception and in expression; but perception is expressed only in so far as the brightness of colour is the brightness of displacement: 'tout le jaune se meurt'. For Delaunay as well, no colour survives uniquely: 'il n'y a pas de couleur fixe, tout est couleur par contraste, tout est couleur en mouvement, tout est profondeur'.[54] Apollinaire, though, responds in words. A single colour, just like the infinite range of colour, is the existence of colour as transformation;

it is the *removal* of a single colour from the perception, and its absence in expression: '*tout* le jaune se meurt'. As it glows, the colour articulates its disappearance and its death. As signified, 'tout le jaune' represents the unavailability of the colour yellow *in* perception. As signifier ('j-a-u-n-e'), it expresses the unavailability of the colour yellow in language; it presents perception as *textuality*, and incarnates it in the experience of language itself.[55]

Quand chantent les aras dans les forêts natales

'Les aras' continue the movement of colours and carry them through the air: they trail colour through the air along their immensely long tails. The intensity of their song is not part of a specific event in time and place, or an interpenetration with others. On the contrary, the brightness of the birds' song produces a band of absence within which the birds are secluded and roam uncontrolled. The colours of the birds in motion are the song of a fertile expressiveness eluding the grasp of anyone. They emerge from an area of uncharted richness and diversity, and of obscure birth: 'forêts natales'.

The build-up of expressiveness into indecipherability reaches a climax in the following line:

Abatis de pihis

'Abatis' is not a noun in all French dictionaries; it is an alternative spelling of 'abattis'. But 'abattis' has more than one meaning. It is the giblets of poultry; it is also the slaughter of poultry and of game generally. In addition to this, 'abattis' is also a military defence consisting of felled trees or branches laid in the way of the enemy. So that 'Abatis' is something that provides resolute defence as well as something defenceless, slaughtered and consumed. And what of 'pihis'? Its link with decipherability is still more tenuous; it hovers between appealing to the reader's memory and being a purely private Apollinairian experience. For it is Apollinaire's own 'Zone' that initiates the unstable passage of the word from collapsed Chinese iconography into a current usage:

De Chine sont venus les pihis longs et souples
Qui n'ont qu'une seule aile et qui volent par couples   (l. 61)

In 'Zone', the 'pihis' appear as a series of quasi-hallucinatory birds, explosive with unstated mythical significance, which, in the lushness of their potential symbolism, sweep aside the singular, falsely unifying

symbol of Jesus Christ and the Holy Spirit. Once again, the lushness
of this symbolic flight through the material and the spiritual eludes
reference; it floods through the grid of reference. The attribute of these
'birds' is that they are one-winged, and yet fly together with their
mirror-image, reminiscent of Narcissus and his image or his sister.[56]
But the significance of this attribute remains the object of interpretative
speculation and reading. Its expressiveness remains unbounded. 'Pihis'
emerges as a kind of word-bound Holy Spirit, a symbol deconstructed
as a word. In 'Les Fenêtres', the process is carried a stage further; for
in the later poem, the 'pihis' are slaughtered. 'Abatis de pihis' is a literal
dismantling of the 'pihis longs et souples'; their symbolic power
collapses and lies in tatters. 'Pihis' in the later poem is 'pure' signifier,
it marks language without demarcating communication; it is incar-
cerated in language and as language — within the only fortress that
might protect and reveal its expressive power. The destroyed bird and
the fallen myth are a demise of poetic freedom. 'Abatis' is a space of
signifying mobility that at once constructs its expressiveness and bars
it from being received. 'Abatis de pihis' represents dispossession in
language, and it expresses the efforts to keep up with perceptual life
in language. It is the fragmentation *in words* of expressive reference,
and it leaves the poet with the whole creative task before him: 'Il y a
un poème à faire sur l'oiseau qui n'a qu'une aile'.[57]

The 'pihi pasty', or pâté perhaps, that Greet and Lockerbie visualise
in 'Abatis de pihis' is not a self-evidently edible one.[58] While it brings
(Chinese) myth made unavailable in history down to human and consumable proportions, the concentrated paste that is produced is obviously not digestible. But collapse, barred access and a momentous
task for poets — these are not an expression of failure, but the promise
of creative freedom. The tension in 'Les Fenêtres' is this: the desire to
take part in the indefinite novelty of the present is faced with perception
rushing in and overrunning language; the eruptive and radical novelty
that metaphor has the power to uncover produces an increasingly lush
displacement of its beginning and of its source; experience and memory
merge in an ecstatic brightness, which is also an intense sense of
otherness at the heart of objects, of the sensuality and the images
coming from the present and allowing the expansion at the end of the
poem:

> La fenêtre s'ouvre comme une orange
> Le beau fruit de la lumière

'The lyrical invocation of the poem ... opening out onto life' is achieved in so far as the poem is opened out to everything that undermines our access to life and our engagement with the present.[59] The exotic, mixed race 'Chabins' sing beguiling songs about death in love, the 'Etincelant diamant' is not a concentration of anything other than the arbitrariness of existence itself, and could not be fixed to any ring. The indecipherable, confronted head on at the crux of the poem, is ultimately embraced in an immense act of poetic faith, and in a radical setting aside of the self.

3—'ET LEUR ESPOIR N'EST PAS MOINS FORT QUE LE MIEN': THE 'PRESENT'

The response to the present articulated in 'Les Fenêtres' makes certain critical assumptions about the pre-war *Calligrammes* poems seem like inadequate responses to the texts. Despite Claude Debon's work, *Calligrammes* as a whole is still often regarded as a shift away from the nostalgic struggles with the past perceived in *Alcools*, in favour of a kind of euphoric espousal of the present. According to such an interpretation, as we saw in chapter two, many of the ideographic texts, and 'Lettre-Océan' in particular, are, in effect, interpreted as a development of the Futurist belief in the power of simultaneity and immediate transmission. Equally, the 'poème-conversation' — 'Lundi Rue Christine' as well as 'Les Fenêtres' — would be seen as taking a Futurist-simultanist practice for its model, as aiming to move on from what Barzun thought of as the 'poème à une voix' and offering the reader a multiplicity of contexts, of points in time and space, with unproblematic access one to another. The approach to modernism that supports this view of the poems and pictures is a simplistic one, as I pointed out in chapter two. Moreover, it is incompatible with Apollinaire's approach to the present in 'Les Fenêtres' and other texts of 'Ondes', an approach that relishes the inscrutability of the present, and treads the borderline between the joyful and the indecipherable, the structured and the directionless. Apollinaire's present is more anxious than the Futurist one, or more lyrical, as Greet and Lockerbie suggest, and it is this quality that brings the uniqueness of his poems into the open.[60]

The opening line of 'Le Musicien de Saint-Merry' might be seen as a place where Apollinaire consummates his love affair with the present:[61]

> J'ai enfin le droit de saluer des êtres que je ne connais pas

It is tempting to read this line as an expression of a power to respond to the present in its endless unpredictability. But the following lines go on to express the present — if present it is — in terms of a continuous inaccessibility, formulated in terms of a *desire* to penetrate the present itself:

> Ils passent devant moi et s'accumulent au loin
> Tandis que tout ce que j'en vois m'est inconnu
> Et leur espoir n'est pas moins fort que le mien

The present here is a multiplicity of different persons and images, and the hope of internalising the world is flooded in a crowd of unreciprocated gestures passing by, re-emphasising the desire to find a place in the language of the present. But the present is not there to be espoused and reapproached as a simultaneous, endlessly available modernity. Increasingly in the texts of 'Ondes', the present emerges as a process that produces images — of itself, in the present. This is not just a tautology, or a familiar experience of reflexivity, and it makes the present difficult to confront and to delve into. To do so, we need to manufacture a distinction, however minimal, between present and 'present'. The 'present' is about looking for names and fitting images with moments. It produces images that are perceived as *expressed*, that is, as barring access to their expressiveness and their context. The 'present' derives from the fragmentation of experience as language is used, the endless given discovered through confrontation with words — in reading, in writing or in silence ('Abatis de pihis').

Some lines from 'Liens' help to bring the 'present' into a sharp relief:

> Cordes faites de cris
> . . .
> D'autres liens plus ténus
> Blancs rayons de lumière
> Cordes et Concorde
>
> J'écris seulement pour vous exalter
> O sens ô sens chéris
> Enemis du souvenir
> Ennemis du désir   (l. 1, l. 15)

The present, however, is a texture weaving remembered experience *out* rather than in — 'blancs' — and weaving the 'present'. The links and 'cordes' are a texture, a visual and tactile experience, both self-transforming and continuously the same, hiding the past and past transformations from view. Links are a framework in which the present is inaccessible, both affirmed and replaced as the 'present'. The 'present' emerges from a present that is not there, and that is indistinguishable from an image. The senses are in the present, the enemies of memory, and within them we seek to feel *through* to the present. But the senses here are textualised, there is nothing for them to touch, they glow and come to life in reading and in rereading. What they are the enemies of is the desire to be there, to meet with existence, diversity and change — they outmanoeuvre this desire, which cries out its 'espoir' with increasing urgency. Links, feelers into the present, are not only sensuous but tenuous, vast and uninformative, as white as light, weaving a texture of contourless, abstract images — the 'present'. Our sense of the here and now hovers and withdraws in the 'space' between past and present ('au loin'), and creative desire delves in the loss of identity in the 'present'. The ropes binding us to others and to other is a network of screams; the links they evoke between objects, people and events in the present are broken, they *are* image. The desire to express is diamond-hard and common to all, and remains unexplained, uncoupled from specific moments. The 'cordes faites de cris' forge a desire to confront the unknown of objects and the present, to set free an expressiveness in the 'present' that continuously withdraws and whose intensity constantly increases. The 'present' is what remains after the neutralising effect of perspective is abolished. But the immediate sense of the present which then emerges — 'Cordes et Concorde', 'ô sens chéris' — is not there but 'there', in the 'present'; 'there' in an unquantified enmeshing of the sense of 'I', an abandoned identification of mobility and change, and *words*.

Our reading of *Alcools* texts brought us face to face with memory represented in terms of a dynamic in which writing poetry substitutes itself for the past, rather than taking possession of it and exorcising it. This process of substitution, as we saw, dissolves a specifiable 'other'. The first two poems of 'Ondes', 'Liens' and 'Les Fenêtres', announce that Apollinaire's new enterprise is not a headstrong rejection of the experience encountered in *Alcools*. His new enterprise is to transform this experience radically and to involve a career in poetry with an awareness of a changed world and the changing demands it makes. 'Liens' and 'Les Fenêtres', in common with many texts in *Alcools*, steer us into a perception of time in time, of history within sequentiality, but they do so by asserting a space where the recent development of poetry exerts quite a different power. The explosion of the familiar is not sensed in terms of decaying modes of expression, and it is not dealt with in terms of a pursuit of a creative attitude. Instead, the challenge to the poet is thrown down by a non-subjugated here and now, and by a proliferation of imagery and sensation passing endlessly by. The belief that Apollinaire's idea of poetic novelty consists in overcoming an obsession with the past in favour of an enthusiastic espousal of the present needs to be re-evaluated in the light of Apollinaire's account in 'Liens' and 'Les Fenêtres' of the present as inscrutable and removed from the writer from whose pen it unfurls.

4—'LUNDI RUE CHRISTINE', 'CONTEXT'; 'ARBRE', 'IMAGE'

I want to go on with this re-evaluation by reading two other 'poèmes-conversation': 'Arbre' and 'Lundi Rue Christine'.[62] Reasons of space dictate a compressed approach to these two poems, each of which is as complex and diverse as 'Les Fenêtres' and could take a limitless number of sentences to appreciate fully. But the richness of each of these texts is not the only reason for imposing restrictions on the spontaneous enthusiasm the poems elicit. To be taken over by the poems in this way would be to slide past their awkward uniqueness and one of their essential challenges. To delve into the minutiae of each image and to get lost in the obscure associativeness of the links that bind them can easily lead to losing contact with the differences between each text as a whole. And it is this difference that we need to come to terms with fully, for it recedes; the poems are pushed apart by as many differences as there are feelers binding them together.

This happens not only between 'Arbre' and 'Lundi Rue Christine', which appear in that order in 'Ondes', but also between these poems and 'Les Fenêtres'. They share an approach to composition that undermines any sharply delineated authorial presence, and they allow stimuli from diverse sources to invade the page in an artificial, purposeful lack of direction. The fiction of 'conversation' is also exploited by both poems. In 'Lundi Rue Christine' it takes the form of an artificially direct recording of casual remarks or items of intense exchange taken out of context, whereas in 'Arbre' it is more discreet, and is restricted to the interplay of the pronouns 'je' and 'tu'. This can be read as one of the elements that separates the two poems. 'Lundi Rue Christine' adopts a fiction of a mobile perceptual awareness, by which events are being observed and events-in-perception recorded. While 'Arbre' takes us onto the level of events-in-memory, and delves into 'the nature of the remembering mind,' as Greet and Lockerbie put it, 'Lundi Rue Christine' allows the eye of perception to be pointed outwards, and directed at objects or events in perception.[63] In 'Arbre', the fiction is of a language pointed at the inner eye, the unpossessed voice through which experience unfurls and leaves its trace. On the other hand, the two poems come together again because of the pockets of indecipherability they both put on display, such as 'Engoulevent Blaireau' and 'la quinte major'.[64]

This interplay of readability and resistance is known to us from 'Les Fenêtres', but it works in a different way in 'Lundi Rue Christine'; the relation of recording to construction is not the same in the two poems. This is in spite of the fact that the composition of 'Lundi Rue Christine' is as notorious as that of 'Les Fenêtres', although for a different reason. The image of Apollinaire sitting in a bar in the Rue Christine recording events as they pass through his ears and eyes is a carefully nurtured one.[65] The fiction of a kind of linguistic photography is equally strongly maintained in the text. Here are some items that can be read as having been drawn from one or more conversations:

Si tu es un homme tu m'accompagneras ce soir	(l. 2)
Quand tu viendras à Tunis je te ferai fumer du kief	(l. 9)
Je dois fiche près de 300 francs à ma probloque Je préférerais me couper le parfaitement que de les lui donner	(l. 13)
Je partirai à 20h. 27	(l. 15)
Un journaliste que je connais d'ailleurs très vaguement	(l. 34)
Ecoute Jacques c'est très sérieux ce que je vais te dire	(l. 35)

Here are some items that can be read as random events or observations:

Des piles de soucoupes des fleurs un calendrier Pim pam pim	(l. 11)
Le Danois fume sa cigarette en consultant l'horaire Le chat noir traverse la brasserie	(l. 23)
Ces crêpes étaient exquises La fontaine coule	(l. 25)
Le sol est semé de sciure	(l. 31)
Une fois là il me présente un gros bonhomme Qui me dit Ecoutez c'est charmant	(l. 40)

The idea of a linguistic photography is of course a paradoxical one, as photographs are often used as illustration, and in such cases they offer the viewer a pre-interpreted view of the events being illustrated. But in this poem the crucial question is that of the context in which such pre-interpretations are possible. The items in the poem lack such a context; they are not a step on the way to formulating information or an experience that can be identified and exchanged. Each statement is therefore open-ended; it does not specify its purpose or the context it seeks to establish, and its expressiveness leaks through to the next statement, equally unbounded in reading.

One of the results of this is that items supposedly from conversation dissolve into those from perception, and this is aided, once again, by Apollinaire's acute sense of successful juxtaposition:

> Je partirai à 20h. 27
> Six glaces s'y dévisagent toujours
> Je crois que nous allons nous embrouiller encore davantage   (1. 15)

A departure, its mystery disguised and intensified in the columns of a timetable, is followed by endless reflexions, without a face, pre-empting Magritte.[66] We then move back into a conversation, this time about misunderstanding and further confusion. Here is another example of this kind of overspill:

> Ces crêpes étaient exquises
> La fontaine coule
> Robe noire comme ses ongles
> C'est complètement impossible   (1. 25)

In this case, the elements are these: a remark of satisfaction after a long and varied meal; the calm of the water's unpredictable movement, its varied sound, both of which give form to unnamed thoguhts; a woman in black with matching nails passes by, desires seem alive, and difference and novelty are there before our eyes. What is 'impossible' is that an entire network of desire, a highly personal, unlocated sense of attractiveness, should be intensely *there* as well as hidden in a heightened, intoxicated sense of self. It is almost like a joke: 'Alors c'est vrai/La serveuse rousse a été enlevée par un libraire' (1. 32).

Not the least remarkable feature of the poem is Apollinaire's ability to sustain this intermeshing of different contexts and different registers of expression. Not only does any one line elude definitive interpretation, but any group can also be read in terms of any number of different tones and intents. What Apollinaire sustains is the sense of creative intervention that his text produces, in spite of the studied absence of any unifying authorial presence, and despite the neighbouring in the text of active construction and passive recording. Nowhere is this ability to sustain an intervention in unmastered stimuli more apparent that in Apolliniare's jocular control of the signifier:

> Des piles de soucoupes des fleurs un calendrier
> Pim pam pim   (l. 11)

Familiar items in a bar hover close to an uncontrolled diversity, produced by the presence of these items in *any* bar. 'Pim pam pim', the clash of cups or glasses on saucers, constitutes the very real and very abstract sense that a person is where she or he belongs, making the comments that fit with the sensations of the moment and of life. It is the challenge and the ecstasy of diversity that Apollinaire meets, or that rushes headlong at Apollinaire himself. Once again, but in quite a different way from 'Les Fenêtres', the creativity that Apollinaire seeks and displays is not only threatened by passivity, but positively heads into it, for only at the risk of passivity, the text suggests, can the endless, depersonalised, voiceless, simultaneous poetry of the present and the *now* be glimpsed, and the world democratised. This is the perception Apollinaire arrives at in 'Le Palais de tonnerre':[67]

> ...on voit que ce qu'il y a de plus simple et de plus neuf est ce qui est
> (l. 54)

This simplicity is something we come to look forward to in Apollinaire after any reading of 'Les Fenêtres'. It is a simplicity that allows highly complex poetic ambitions to be acted upon. 'Lundi Rue Christine' develops a fiction that presents language as continuous with consciousness itself. Apollinaire has discovered a diction that seems to overcome the effort to find words for sensations, and that breaks down the barrier separating words from experience. Paradoxically, this poetic freedom is achieved on the shoulders of the absent author, an overriding feature in the fiction of the 'poème-conversation'. The apparently immediate recording of events produces an erosion of interpretation, and interpretation becomes indistinguishable from the experience it strives to define. The possibility of identifying experience is fragmented in the obscure transitions and unbreachable gaps of the poem. For the reader, reading *is* the context specifying and de-specifying experience in the poem.

A perception of 'context' emerges. 'Lundi Rue Christine' re-presents the sense of self incarnated in the barrier between experience and words, identity and images; the poem re-presents this sense of self as the lushness of displacement, the directionless expressiveness of the here and now and its multi-angled perspectives. 'Context' liberates us from the notional singularity of objects and sensation in time and space. It also brings us face to face with appearance, and locks us into the way things *are*, the way they are presented in the mobility of the moment. 'Context' is itself a word-image that seeks to express both the reader's and the writer's absorption in the poem and its intangible enaction of the present, a present 'moment' galvanised by its refusal to yield its history or ours.

'Context' highlights a dissolution of the distinction between perception and images in memory, and this dissolution binds 'Lundi Rue Christine' and 'Arbre' to each other. But in 'Arbre', Apollinaire, in the drive to exploit 'context' and sustain creative intervention, strikes a less consistently confident tone. As he drifts among surfacing memories of friends and events, the mobile relation of language to perception and the present Apollinaire delves into does not only give rise to a poetic ubiquity,[68]

> J'entends déjà le son aigre de cette voix à venir
> Du camarade qui se promènera avec toi en Europe
> Tout en restant en Amérique   (l. 8)

but also to a texture of mirage:

> Ispahan s'est fait un ciel de carreaux émaillés de bleu   (l. 5)

The ancient capital of Persia presents itself in a way that competes with light as well as with time: 'un ciel'. But it also presents itself as a series of small blue mosaic stones that reflect light — that reflect individually, without uncovering different sources of reflection. They construct displacement, they create perception in the 'present' — the reality of experience. The historical context of Isfahan and its associations exist in 'Arbre' as a lack, an absence represented by constructions of sky colour. The shining enamel creates a sheen of reflection that is not the colour on any one blue square any more than it is the colour of the sky. It is the memory of sky colour constructing itself in experience and the consciousness of experience; it is memory displaced in, or as, the 'present'; it is an image — the image-signifier 'carreaux émaillés de bleu'. In Apollinaire's poem, displacement, like light itself, *is* perception, and this '*is*' marks the action of the signifier — the acontextual anteriority of the words we use, the images we see and the words that create them. The words seem to discharge our very sense of the involvement of the cultural and the personal in memory.

This poetic freedom aimed at in 'Arbre' is resolutely double-edged. On the one hand, images resist being interpreted as a series of isolated events; the sequence of the text *is* image. And the light cast by image is indistinguishable from blindness *in* language:

> Où sont les aveugles où s'en sont-ils allés (1.2)

Equally, the images in 'Arbre' can be read and accepted as a mirage, an illustion that Apollinaire exploits. This illusion might be described as the transformation of images from perception into words, of perception into identification with it, of experience into communication.[69]

Where is the identity of the writer in the images he produces? What attitude does the reader take to them? Where is the experience of identity that can be identified with? Like 'Zone' and 'Voyage', 'Arbre' raises the question through its use of personal pronouns. The 'Tu' and the 'je' of the first six lines fragment the space where an independent identity could be established and replace it with themselves as pronouns. The opening 'Tu' can be read as referring to a person the author-persona is addressing. Alternatively, 'Tu' can be read as an abandoning of anecdotal literalness and rhetorical address, and as initiating a representation of internal monologue: representations of thought in thought, of thought leaving traces of itself. 'Tu' wipes out any distance between self and self-expression; it faces us with an impossibility of locating identity in language. Identity is expressed in terms of fragmentation and 'context'.

The text articulates identity in terms of a build-up of image:

> Entre les pierres
> Entre les vêtements multicolores de la vitrine
> Entre les charbons ardents du marchand de marrons
> Entre deux vaisseaux norvégiens amarrés à Rouen
> Il y a ton image (1.29)

This build-up is itself an articulation of lack.[70] The statements that produce 'ton image' do not operate an interplay that would uncover a writer as he writes, or a reader as he interprets. 'Ton image' is articulated as 'context' — a dismantling *in* writing of an access *to* writing: 'ton image'. The repetitions of 'entre' involve the reader in an ironic unifying process that erodes the diversity of information contained in the statements.[71] The reader becomes involved in an all-exclusive in-between, a climactic expression in the poem of language invading experience and failing to take possession of it. Moreover, the lack of a verb in each of the 'entre' statements contributes to an erosion of distinction between observed and imagined, present and remembered experience. Here again, 'Arbre' meets with 'Lundi Rue Christine'. The reader is confronted with an 'immediacy' that undermines the myth of immediacy in experience. The myth of an indefinite power to take possession of stimuli is tautologically recast as indefiniteness itself apparently made visible at any and every moment. This recasting, this 'immediacy' *is* the reading of each of the statements and the sequence they create. And the indistinguishability of statement and image confronts us, once again, with the production of 'image'. It sharpens an awareness of the involvement of 'image' with a structure of identity in language. 'Image' is its own proliferation in writing. As such, it is a repeated fragmentation of identity — in language and because of language. This applies not only to the writer but to the reader addressed by the poem: 'ton image'.

'Arbre' leaves us with a paradox: a dismantled identity, at once searching for a power to distance itself from and to manipulate the images that structure it, and yet spurning such power as restrictive. The knowledge that makes up the new human beings that emerge at the end of the poem to take over the world heralds the emancipation of thought and creativity:

> Et des êtres nouveaux surgissent
> Trois par trois   (l. 43)

But this emancipation is traced along an invisible dividing line between the freedom to create images of identity, and the impossibility of identifying with images and their passage:

> Tout est plus triste qu'autrefois
> Tous les dieux terrestres vieillissent
> L'univers se plaint par ta voix   (l. 40)

And here again, 'Arbre' meets 'Lundi Rue Christine'. In the midst of a directionless 'conversation' between unspecifiable participants, in the midst of the openness that 'Lundi Rue Christine' directs at the diversity of image and experience, the poem ends with:

> L'Honneur tient souvent à l'heure que marque la pendule
> La quinte major   (l. 46)

Honour is as fickle as fame, independent creativity is as easily undermined as the expressiveness of a cliché. But more than this, in the next
line the poem ends with a phrase that is potentially unreadable,
seeming to make a mockery of the entire entreprise. As Greet and
Lockerbie say, 'La quinte major' at root refers to a strong hand in piquet
(five cards in the same suit), evoking an event in keeping with a
moment of excitement in a café. Equally, implicit in any decoding is
the sense that the material before us is made imponderable — and it
might remain so — because of the lack of definitive context accruing
to it. 'La quinte major' as signifier, like the sudden coming together
of cards in a hand, seems to arrive from nowhere, as might the un-
expected chiming of a clock, enhancing the representation of arbitrariness, and of involvement in it, sustained by the poem as a whole.
The pun that Greet and Lockerbie isolate — 'une quinte' is a musical
interval — carries this further, but rather than making a mobile signifier
pliable and multifaceted, it overloads it and threatens to make it
redundant: where could there by any message, and what is the nature
of the diversity we could participate in? The final line sees the gamble
of the poem through: 'Honneur', heroism, the ubiquity of the modern
Orpheus, are brought up against the transience in a thrill or a laugh,
the appeal of a repeated ritual, a mechanistic respone to the present and
to images.[72]

5—IDEOGRAMMATIC TEXT. THE PAGE

What 'Les Fenêtres', 'Arbre' and 'Lundi Rue Christine' have in common
and what makes them unique, tantalisingly indecipherable texts is that
they all represent and incarnate the dynamic of displacement in which
users of language are involved. The difficulty of these texts suggests
that the experience of the present they invite us to share is not so much
an unproblematic love affair, as a self-emptying of the writer. In reading
these poems, I have tried to develop a terminology that distinguishes
itself from certain conventional critical assumptions about the shift
of emphasis that differentiates *Alcools* from *Calligrammes*, and about
the poetics of 'Ondes' in particular. 'Ondes' is not purely the product
of a desire to incorporate and exploit the variety of artistic innovations
developed by modernism in France from the completion of *Les
Demoiselles d'Avignon* in 1907 to the outbreak of war in 1914. In fact,
these 'innovations' are not static, self-contained achievements that a

writer can put to use as an instrument or a technique. They change as they are interpreted and used in the continuing effort to appropriate a historical and cultural moment. 'Ondes' is not an exploitation of a particular experience, but an involvement in experience, and it contributes to *our* understanding of the moment in history in terms of which it is produced.

Clearly, 'Ondes' *is* different from *Alcools*; it makes different demands on the reader and has a different thematic structure. But on the other hand, both are concerned with the experience of memory and loss, the fragmentation of perception, the dispossession of identity in relation to displacement in language. *Calligrammes*, and 'Ondes' in particular, is not an abandoning of the concerns expressed in *Alcools*; it is a development of them in terms of the galvanising experience of the city and of the technology of speed and war, on the one hand, and in terms of the image, and of the image as signifier, on the other. I shall now embark on a reading of the ideograms in 'Ondes' and discover whether the terminology that has been developed in the reading of the other texts continues to be useful: displacement (reading/perception), 'image', the signifier, the 'present'. To do so, I hope, will not only suggest ways of taking the ideograms seriously and reading them pleasurably, it will also provide a new kind of purchase on Apollinaire's struggle with the present, his desire to resist death and to replace the images of history with his own poetry.

Any reading of the ideograms is made more difficult by the lack of critical interest they have attracted. 'Quant aux calligrammes proprement dits, *Idéogrammes lyriques* ou poèmes idéogrammatiques, ils n'ont jamais suscité grand enthousiasme' writes André Billy himself — a friend and an untiring populariser and apologist of Apollinaire.[73] Even Renaud does no good to his case for approaching 'Ondes' as a series of sophisticated texts, including the ideograms, by suggesting that Apollinaire began composing calligraphic texts as a kind of hobby, through a desire to satisfy painterly aspirations, or by way of a 'divertissement': 'Le calligramme, colorié ou non, offrait une amusante synthèse de la typographie et du dessin: quoi de plus distrayant, pour un poète, que de dessiner avec des phrases, des mots, des lettres? . . . La plupart du temps le calligramme est pour Apollinaire un jeu, une expérience gracieuse avec un côté Concours Lépine de la poésie.'[74] What is unfortunate about this is that a serious insight is followed by a dismissive comment. Clearly, the relation of drawing to writing is a fruitful one to explore, since it involves attitudes to improvisation, representation, and memory. But Renaud seems to pay lip service to the traditional dismissal of the ideograms among critics by talking about exploring this relation of drawing to writing as though it were a witty or boisterous game. Moreover, Renaud allows a collaboration with this dismissive attitude to Apollinaire's developing interest in calligraphy and typography to detract from his own insights. Renaud seems to suggest that one impetus that prompted Apollinaire to compose ideograms was a desire to combine Picasso's pre-Cubist drawing ('dessin') with the geometric word shapes developed by Futurist writers in their attack on the discursive deployment of words ('typographie'). Renaud describes this 'synthèse' as 'amusante', and the purpose of such a description — untypical of Renaud — would seem to be to keep the image of Apollinaire's creativity within the confines of the spontaneous and the jovial.

The low esteem in which the ideograms have been held is illustrated by the insensitivity with which they have been reprinted in recent editions. S. Themerson gives a sharp and irrefutable portrait of this insensitivity in his book, simply entitled *Apollinaire's Lyrical Ideograms*, and, more significantly, Greet and Lockerbie's sensitive display of the poems all but rectifies the situation.[75] But let us glance at some of the ways in which the poems have been disseminated.

The poem 'A Linda' is part of the group *Quelconqueries*, which appeared for the first time in the Futurist organ *Lacerba*. It is one of Apollinaire's earliest poetic games, and not particularly significant in itself.[76] But it does rely crucially on the impact of the word/letter 'A', and on a variety of orderings of the letters/word 'Linda'. Apollinaire, as so often, has updated a text kept from an earlier stage, this time for experimental purposes, transforming it into a contribution to a geometric 'aesthetification' of the letter in the manner of the Futurists' anti-discursive calligraphy. It is obviously vital, therefore, to reproduce the updated piece as it was originally presented in *Lacerba*.[77] But in the *Oeuvres poétiques* it is given a completely different typeface — the standard 'Pléiade' one. Moreover, Adéma and Décaudin, the otherwise informative editors, do not see fit to comment on this. In the *Poèmes retrouvés* Décaudin attaches to the Gallimard (Poésie) edition of *Le Guetteur mélancolique*, 'A Linda' is not even given a page to itself.[78] The result is that the reader's attention is drawn away from the typographic experimentation in the 'poem', away from its visual specificity, and from the novelty of the demands it makes — for the sake, presumably, of saving space.

More alarmingly, the printing of 'Voyage' in the edition of *Calli-grammes* that has appeared in the same series makes it even more difficult for the reader to come to terms with the specific textuality of that poem, although this is not the case either in the *Oeuvres poétiques* or in the *Oeuvres complètes editions*. When the reader comes across 'Voyage' in this volume, it is actually necessary for him to turn the page over and then turn it back again to see/read the work in its entirety, even though two of its structural/syntactic units consist of continuous elements that stretch across/throughout the poem. For example, the train/image-statement/calligraphic right-angle:

OU VA DONC CE TRAIN QUI MEURT AU LOIN DANS LES
VALS ET LES BEAUX BOIS FRAIS DU TENDRE ÉTÉ SI PALE?

Or the sky/image-statement/calligraphic improvisation:[79]

la douce nuit luenaire et pleine d'étoiles
C'est ton visage que je ne vois plus

In each of these instances, the reader of the 'Poésie' volume is forced to turn the page over and back three times to read the image-statements in their entirety, which destroys not only the 'immediacy' of the way they present themselves to the eye, but the 'immediacy' of the relations they set up visually with the other word formations in the text.

'Lettre-Océan', a text I shall discuss in a moment, also suffers from editorial insensitivity. In its original version in *Les Soirées de Paris* in 1914, the two designs of the poem appear side by side, with the letters 'T S F' acting as a complex binding between the two. No edition has repeated this, not even, strangely, the original edition of *Calligrammes* in 1918. On the other hand, in the case of 'La Petite auto', as with many others, Greet and Lockerbie's presentation of *Calligrammes* shows the benefit of following the original 1918 edition. In both cases, the word-design in the poem, which explores spatially the memory of the shape car lights cast in the night and the associations they harbour, is given a page to itself, involving holding the book horizontally in order to read the words. In the *Oeuvres poétiques* edition, however, this design is concentrated within the lineated verse of the rest of the text on a page held and read conventionally, and this arbitrarily curtails the action of Apollinaire's text on our imagination.

An initial indication of the complexity of these texts is the fact that they are both read and seen. In a sense, this quality is self-evident, though it is a self-evidence often used as a pretext for refusing to take these poems seriously. But it is a crucially distinctive feature of the calligraphic texts, and it demands a complex response: a reading in which letters are identified, independently of sentences or words, and in which a mode of seeing is specified that does not see objects but letter-lines, is a reading occupied by an open-ended process of deciphering. The ideograms are distinctive, and dramatically so, because they include the shapes and the vestigial outlines of objects. But the poems are not seen to the exclusion of being read, and their reading undermines their immediate visual impact.[80] It is a uniquely expressive form of reading, non-linear, but accompanied by the sense of linearity produced by continuity itself; it has no contours, but it has the 'form' of the words themselves and their visual presence. Reading the poems dismantles the identification of the objects that the word shapes seem to suggest. The apparent identity of word and shape, signifier and image, is split, and this asks questions about the 'identity' of the reader, the perceiver, or the writer. It also opens out images and the fact of image for exploration; indeed image is automatically explored because of the process of deciphering that the picture-poem involves us in. The visual impact of the words is a paradoxical one. Its immediacy recedes while the anteriority of image itself emerges; the hold of images on us is represented and explored in the mobility with which they appear on the page.

I shall discuss these questions with reference to the six ideograms or calligraphic texts of 'Ondes', and I shall explore some of them in detail. As is well-known, five of these texts were to have appeared as a small self-contained volume entitled *Et moi aussi je suis peintre*, the publication of which was cancelled at the outbreak of war (they had already appeared in *Les Soirées de Paris* in June and July/August 1914): 'Paysage', 'Lettre-Océan', 'La Cravate et la montre', 'Coeur couronne et miroir' and 'Voyage'. They reappeared with 'Il Pleut' in *Calligrammes, poèmes de la paix et de la guerre (1913–1916)*, which was first published by Mercure de France in 1918. 'Il Pleut', composed in 1914, did not appear in print until the December 1916 issue of the review *SIC (Son Idée Couleur)*.

I focus on these six calligraphic texts, although I shall not comment on all of them, for the following reasons. Since they form a group, Apollinaire, as Willard Bohn shows in his *The Aesthetics of Visual Poetry*, is implicitly inviting us to read them as such, rather than purely as isolated events.[81] Equally, however, I shall be examining these texts in relation to what we have discovered about 'Ondes' as a whole.

My attempt is not to develop a general theory of literary/visual poetics, such as Alain-Marie Bassy and Jean-Pierre Goldenstein have done, as well as, more recently, Willard Bohn in his pursuit of a 'calligrammar' based on the interplay of metaphor and metonymy.[82] My own concern is, once again, to involve us in the process of reading these texts, in the mobile dynamic of 'anticipation and retrospection' it engages us in, and to see this process through.[83] In doing so, I shall attempt to come to grips with the involvement of reading with consciousness itself — consciousness of self, consciousness of the world — and to delve into what Bohn might call 'the articulation of the Image': the involvement of perception with circumstance, memory with the material world, anteriority with the present.[84]

My final reason for concentrating on the calligraphic texts of 'Ondes' is that they are all pre-war texts. Apollinaire's apparent enthusiasm for war and butchery ('Ah! Dieu que la guerre est jolie') is not something that can be conveniently isolated from his other attitudes.[85] Equally, the entire thrust of his modernism cannot be reduced to his reactions to the war: this relationship with the war needs a different level of interpretation before it can be integrated with the rest of his work, and I shall be returning to it in my concluding chapter.

6—'SIMULTANÉITÉ', READING. 'LETTRE-OCÉAN'

I stated previously that a text that demands to be seen as well as to be read engages the reader in a different kind of 'reading' than does a text which has a lineated verse form. 'Lettre-Océan', the first of Apollinaire's ideograms to be published, was assured a dramatic impact on those exposed to it. It took the form of a kind of living manifesto embodying 'modern' art and exemplifying the response it demanded. In the context of the previous two years' animated debate and experimentation centred around 'le nouveau' and its principal support, 'la simultanéité', Apollinaire sought to present 'Lettre-Océan' as a tangible proof that the new artistic enterprise was launched, and that its various constituent concepts were operating at once. The poem was published on 15 June 1914 in *Les Soirées de Paris*, and in the same issue, Apollinaire published his article 'Simultanisme-Librettisme', in which he offered a kind of retrospective overview of the new, simultanist art that had been developing over the previous two years. Referring to the publication in 1912 of Cendrars's *Prose du Transsibérien*, illustrated

Lettre-Océan

Je traverse la ville nez en avant et je la coupe en **2**

J'étais au bord du Rhin quand tu partis pour le Mexique
Ta voix me parvient malgré l'énorme distance
Gens de mauvaise mine sur le quai à la Vera Cruz

Les voyageurs de *l'Espagne* devant faire
le voyage de Coatzacoalcos pour s'embarquer
je t'envoie cette carte aujourd'hui au lieu

Juan Aldama

Correos
Mexico
4 centavos

YPIRANGA

REPUBLICA MEXICANA

TARJETA POSTAL

11 45
29 - 5
14
Rue des Bâtignno

de profiter du courrier de Vera Cruz qui n'est pas
U. S. Postage
2 cents 2

Tout est calme ici et nous sommes dans l'att
des événeménts.

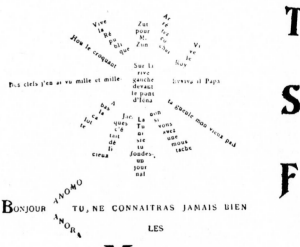

Vive la Ré pu bli que

Hou le croquant

Zut pour M. Zun

Ar rê tez co cher

Vi ve le Roy

Des clefs j'en ai vu mille et mille

Sur la rive gauche devant le pont d'Iéna

Revive il Papa

tu n'ucale mon vieux pad

bas à la ca lot te

Jac ques c'é tait dé li cieux

La Tu as sie tu fondes un jour nal

oun si vous avez une mous tache

T

S

F

ANOMO ANOR

BONJOUR TU, NE CONNAITRAS JAMAIS BIEN

LES

Mayas

Te souviens-tu du tremblement de terre entre 1885 et 1890
on coucha plus d'un mois sous la tente

BONJOUR MON FRÈRE ALBERT à Mexico

Jeunes filles à Chapultepec

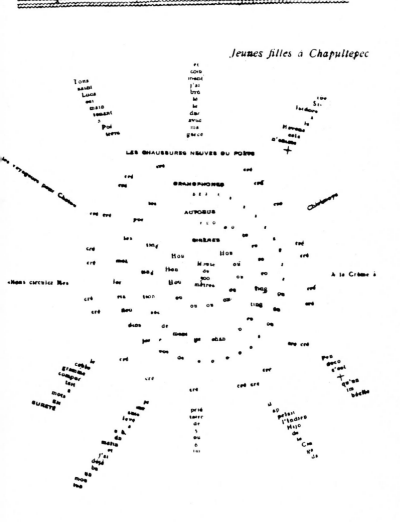

by Sonia Delaunay — an event he seems to place at the onset of a developing simultanist poetry — Apollinaire writes:

> C'est ainsi qu'on a tenté (*L'Enchanteur pourrissant*, 'Vendémiaire', 'Les Fenêtres' etc.) d'habituer l'esprit à concevoir un poème simultanément comme une scène de la vie. Blaise Cendrars et Mme. Sonia Delaunay Terck ont fait une première tentative de simultanéité écrite où des contrastes de couleurs habituaient l'oeil à lire d'un seul regard l'ensemble d'un poème, comme un chef d'orchestre lit d'un seul coup les notes superposées de la partition, comme on voit d'un seul coup les éléments plastiques et imprimés d'une affiche.[86]

Renaud reads or sees 'Lettre-Océan' in the same spirit of simultaneous synthesis, and regards the poem as a climax in the striving for 'le nouveau': Des six idéogrammes lyriques d'"Ondes", le plus ambitieux est le premier en date: "Lettre-Océan". C'est le seul qui soit vraiment "simultané" et "synthétique", le seul *moderne* par son sujet et ses motifs.'[87] Reworking some of Apollinaire's own earlier ideas on the relation of painting to writing, Renaud goes on to present this climax of 'le nouveau' in terms of an ultimate development in the 'poème-conversation', a liberation of the reading process and the perceptual one:

> Ces deux ensembles [the two word forms of which 'Lettre-Océan' consists] constituent très précisément *un poème-conversation simultané* dont la lecture n'est pas, comme dans 'Lundi Rue Christine', soumise à un ordre quelconque. Ici, contrairement à ce qui se passe dans un poème proprement dit, 'l'oeil peut errer sur le tableau...d'abord de bas en haut ou faire le contraire...revenir sur tel mot, sur tel son au hasard'. Cette comparaison fait mieux apprécier tout ce qui sépare les autres *poèmes-conversations* du 'simultanisme' véritable.[88]

Renaud develops Arbouin's notion of an ideogrammatic synthesis.[89] He regards 'Lettre-Océan' as a text that creates simultaneity by dismantling, in a textual immediacy, the dependence of subject and subject matter on the contexts used to locate them and communicate them.

'Lettre-Océan' is clearly involved in the working-out of various contemporary simultanist modes of expression and is perhaps a product of them. Not only is it a dramatic development of the 'poème-conversation', it builds on the Futurist anti-discursive treatment of the page, on Futurist use of onomatopoeia and Futurist exploitation of typography. It also takes part in the disc designs of Robert and Sonia Delaunay, and the aspirations attached to them. It is indebted to the

Cubist practice of collage.[90] But to approach the text of 'Lettre-Océan' exclusively in terms of what it has in common with other modes of expression would fail to take into account certain equally revealing differences between the poem and other simultanist practices. For example, the notion of immediate simultaneity and transmission that informs the Futurist attitude to expression is, as we have seen, inconsistent with the experience of language Apollinaire involves us in in the lineated texts of 'Ondes'. It is also inconsistent, as I argued in chapter two, with Cubist and Orphic practices, and with the differing processes of displacement through which they each come to terms with the material and with the modern. These complexities within simultanist aspirations are not surmounted by looking, as some critics have, to an ultimate mental picture of the artefacts, a conceptualisation of their action on us, to give shape to simultaneous reading or to establish their effect.[91] 'Lettre-Océan' undermines such shape continuously, be it visual or symbolic. Equally, the lineated verse texts of 'Ondes' do *not* offer the reader a simultaneity that involves him in an immediate 'wireless communication'. The simultaneity of these poems is based on an unavailable, mobile distinction between contexts in language, in reading, in perception; not on an interpenetration of an open-ended series of individually recognisable contexts. It is not the sequentiality of 'Lundi Rue Christine' that prevents it from realising a quasi-Futurist experience of simultaneity, or from allowing the reader's eye to move at will in and out of the text, and around it. The creativity of 'Lundi Rue Christine' does not depend on an illusion of a heroic ubiquity in poetry — the illusion that response to images coming from the world can be encompassed and taken in onto the page. The simultaneity we experienced in reading 'Lundi Rue Christine' and 'Arbre' does not offer the reader an image of continuous diversity that can be immediately perceived, controlled and exploited. It is a simultaneity in which context extends indefinitely into memory, involving us with the 'present', and re-presenting perception as continuously different.

The distinction is an important one because it highlights a tension between a broad emphasis on synthesis in the simultanist expression going on between 1912 and 1914, and Apollinaire's own approach to simultaneity. Renaud's quotation about mobile reading is a conscious reworking of Apollinaire's own writing. Here is the original passage: '...dans la peinture tout se présente à la fois, l'oeil peut errer sur le tableau, revenir sur telle couleur, regarder d'abord de haut en bas, ou faire le contraire; dans la littérature, dans la musique tout se succède et l'on ne peut revenir sur tel mot, sur tel son au hasard.'[92] It is Renaud's contention, of course, that Apollinaire achieved in 'Lettre-Océan' what he had previously thought impossible. But the consequence of accepting this view of the overall purpose behind Apollinaire's simultanist writing is that any response to the simultaneity of 'Lettre-Océan' is restricted to the effects it has on the poetic signified of the poem — at the expense of taking full account of the way the action of the text as signifier is also transformed. While opening his reader's eyes to the development of 'non-objective' expression in Apollinaire's writing, Renaud, in one crucial sense, misrepresents it. His approach invites us to assume that a word or a statement, as text or not, has unmediated access to a recognisable situation and its indefinite association with others. In fact, Renaud's notion of a 'poème-conversation simultané' minimises the difference between a word and a letter shape.

If we examine our reactions to 'Lettre-Océan', it is clear that the immediate perception of object-images and their interpenetration is not, initially, the guiding feature of these reactions. If I write the words 'La Tour Eiffel', they are a decipherable sign in so far as they transform a signifier into a relation of a signifier to a signified. The lack of meaning that accrues to the phonetic or graphic qualities of 'La Tour Eiffel' is effaced in the relation of those qualities to a chain of further differentiated and differentiating phonetic and graphic signifiers. This chain itself operates in relation to an equivalently structured semantic chain of differentiation to produce the signification that results in the referent, the denotation of an object or a concept. *This* is the process by which, if I write 'La Tour Eiffel', we all have the same mental construction in mind.[93] It is a process that operates in terms of the *difference* between the signifier and the referent, and in terms of the fact that the signified is *not* reducible to its production in and as the signifier. This refutes any suggestion that communication is either eased or radicalised by making the signifier the equivalent of the referent, which is what happens in the word outlines of the 'Ondes' ideograms.[94] It undermines the view that using words to initiate shapes on the page means that the Eiffel Tower in the world is the same as the one on the page.

Such a view is further undermined by the text of 'Lettre-Océan' itself. The eye *cannot* move freely within 'Lettre-Océan' at the same time as perceiving images, recognising objects or establishing simultaneous links. Moreover, in *Prose du Transsibérien*, the eye weaves its way in and out of Cendrar's images and Sonia Delaunay's discs across the *difference* between them. As I said before, if I write the words 'La Tour Eiffel', we have the same metal construction in mind. But what of the words 'Sur la rive gauche devant le pont d'Iéna', or 'Haute de 300 mètres', arranged vertically, with spokes, or spokes and concentric circles of further words arranged around each phrase? Do we still have the same mental representation of a metal construction, or of a postcard with a picture of the Eiffel Tower? To a certain extent, the answer is in fact still *yes*. The letters 'T S F' — included as Apollinaire reworked his design — suggest a transmitter, and remind us of the Eiffel Tower; in this context, the words arranged as spokes or as concentric circles fall into focus as visual representations of airwaves.[95]

But the same question applies: does a representation of airwaves using the positioning of words carry a message that is recognisable in the same way as the linguistic signs 'airwaves' or 'transmission' are recognisable? The fact that these so-called representations of airwaves are not only seen but read (e.g. 'ta gueule mon vieux pad') prevents them from being in any sense mimetic, from stabilising an object in a definition or a single perception.[96] Apollinaire's visual representations using words do *not* suggest the impossible, namely, that objects are read just like words, but they do emphasise that objects do not present themselves immediately, independently of memory. So in a different sense, the ideograms *do* suggest that objects are read — whether in space or on the page — and that we come to terms with their expressiveness in a process of reading and deciphering. Apollinaire's visual representations using words replace recognisable objects with objects-as-image. This emerges in the continuous reading that the text inevitably produces, and that re-presents our perception of objects. In fact, the 'object' in the poem sets up an equivalence between word and image that prevents the word from being an image of something, if not an image of a word. The visual representations using words efface the distinction between the object and its extended existence in memory. They involve the object in an experience of words as 'image'.

The Eiffel Tower presentations, then, are not mimetic. They efface identification of the Eiffel Tower because they have words all over them; they have to be read in and through time. But is the same true of the figures in the text?

11 45 29–5 14 Rue des Batignolles

These are the words and figures printed by the postmark covering the stamp on Apollinaire's postcard to his brother. But how imitative is this presentation, or re-creation? What are the effects of the 'souci de réalisme' that Apollinaire puts into the text here?[97] Does it offer the reader a single moment of recognition that he can relate to others in the artefact and use to involve himself in a simultaneity of extended interpretation? Only if we ignore the fact that Apollinaire's post office stamp is a textualisation of symbolic printed words and figures. The fact that this post office stamp consists, in Apollinaire's poem, exclusively of letters and figures in printer's ink on a page turns them into word-and-image, which is perceived differently from a post office stamp on a letter or a postcard, where letters and figures are not read, but taken for granted and are in fact often all but unreadable. The letters and figures of this fictional post office stamp, by being clearly legible as words and figures, are, paradoxically, the abolition — in expression, in reading — of the original or symbolic postmark. This abolition allows expressiveness in the familiar sign on an envelope or a card to be set free in the text. By stamping *out* the postmark as a concrete and functional event, Apollinaire gives his textualised postmark the power to express the action of memory in perception. It is the reverse of the situation whereby I write 'postmark': here, the context is familiar, the possibility of exploring the relation between objects, images and perception is not entered into. This evasion of displacement and expressiveness highlights the fundamental lack at the centre of any linguistic sign. As I suggested earlier, this lack is constituted in the difference between the perceptible elements of the signifier, and the *potentially* perceptible elements in the signified. However, by creating the fiction — in fact the appearance — of an equivalence between the signifier and the signified, Apollinaire allows the signifier to reign supreme and displacement to be explored. This displacement is indistinguishable from what we see and read, even though what we see *in* what we read is lost in the signifier, and in what is there on the page.

Similarly, the calligraphic creation 'T S F' both stamps out and evokes the way the signified extends in its reception. This also applies to the Eiffel Tower and the airwaves of the poem. There are words all over the object ('object'), and this constitutes the language of the poem as 'image'. The words that build up the visual word-representations of airwaves are *not* the words 'airwaves' or 'ondes'. Equally, the messages on the visually constructed word-airwaves do not express or represent the Eiffel Tower, despite the fact that the Tower is the (visual) context by which they present themselves as messages. As we saw, Renaud believes that these word-airwaves/messages are references to

172

a variety of separate conversations which the reader is able to move in and out of at will. But the reader cannot move around the text at will: he has to read his way around. In fact the word-airwaves/messages develop the process we saw initiated by the phrases 'Sur la rive gauche devant le pont d'Iéna', and 'Haute de 300 mètres'. This process is the presentation of the Eiffel Tower in terms of 'context' and its own unbounded enlargement in reading. Moreover, some of the 'messages' that make up this enlargement are blatantly obscure, secluded in an obscure specificity, and the reader loses his purchase on the Eiffel Tower in reading and in perception. The statement 'je me suis levé à 2h. du matin et j'ai déjà bu un mouton', in the shape of a spoke, is one of the word-airwave/messages from the second configuration in the text. It is an expression of a grotesque, Ubu-like jocularity: the textual speaker seems hardly to sleep or to stop drinking either sheeps' blood or bottles of Mouton wine. And yet the text does not provide the reader with the statement: 'Je me suis levé à 2h. du matin et j'ai déjà bu un mouton'. What he is in fact given to read is: 'Je/me/suis/levé/à/2h./ du/matin/et/j'ai/dèjà/bu/un/mou/ton'. Similarly, 'Ar/rê/tez/co/ cher' — from the first configuration — is not the same as: 'Arrêtez cocher!!'. The message is displaced in the reading process. The attempt to isolate a message produces a proliferation of reading itself. By saturating the reading space with the signifier in this way, Apollinaire confronts the reader in a quite new way with the fact of anteriority, the inescapable anteriority of perception in memory, and in relation to language. The reading of 'Lettre-Océan' articulates that which resists appropriation in thinking and in interpretation. It is a space without contours that marks the attempt to exhaust expressiveness in language. The text of 'Lettre-Océan' weaves itself into existence on the frontiers of the indecipherable, in that it produces messages that, in reading, break loose from all context, and have a significance that is fragmented, elusive, jocular, even broken down.

It is at this point that the fact that 'Lettre-Océan' consists of two Eiffel Tower configurations comes into play. An interpretation of the text in terms of a kind of mimetic simultanism (based on the desire to move in and around the text at will, and drawn, perhaps, from a naïve reaction to Apollinaire's 'souci de réalisme' in relation to his textual-ised missive) might have us believe that the first configuration rep-resents the picture on the front of the postcard, and that the second represents the message magically unstuck from the back and laid side by side with the picture on the front. Clearly, the demands Apollinaire makes on our imagination go beyond this. There are in fact no structural distinctions, either on the level of the signified or on the level of the signifier, between the two configurations. Both use disparate messages, or reference to disparate events, to set up the fiction of roving eyes and ears; equally, both use word-airwaves/messages that displace the object 'airwaves' or the signified 'ondes'.

In effect, in confronting the relation between the two configurations, we are confronted with a mobile, unavailable difference analogous to the difference between 'Arbre' and 'Lundi Rue Christine'. This relation is not one of narrative progression, nor does it produce a build-up to a conventional climax.[98] The word-picture on the left of the construct — the would-be picture on the front of a card — is *not* a picture, it is articulated in the dissolving fragments of the 'present', blotted out in the production of the 'present' in expression and in reading. The same applies to the message on the back, but here the fiction of an addressee is introduced, which means that now the *reader* is aimed at and involved as though *he* were being addressed, and the text definitively breaks the boundaries of a poet examining and extending the links binding him to the world. Writer is made reader, de-centred in the variety of stimuli making up the page or the moment, and in the unpredictability of any reader's response. In turn, the reader becomes 'addressee', and his privileged position as the one for whom everything on the text-stage happens is undermined.

This is intensified by Bohn's suggestion that the two side-by-side configurations can be read together as an explosive collapse into one another of a number of cards — message and picture — sent backwards and forwards between Apollinaire and his brother over a period of time.[99] But this temporal and spatial (con)fusion does not settle the problem of reception or give form to it — that is, the problem of the addressee and the control of experience. Rather, this is heightened by the replication of shape and design, the simultaneous complexity and minimisation of the difference between points and moments. In the text, the reader's experience of the present appears unmediated, and *is* so. By the same token, the recipient is de-specified, hovering in the poem between a reader and the figure of an addressee. We are neither part of a privately expressive, Apollinairian family code, nor in the dominant position of a reader-audience holding the reins of the performance.

Startlingly, but not surprisingly, this brings us back to a real postcard. The text and 'la mort du signe' that Goldenstein discerns in the calligram at large come to life as an expressive force at all the various points of their contact with the objective world and our consciousness of it.[100] As I implied earlier, Apollinaire is dealing with perceptions of real situations and real acts of communication. A real (or 'real') postcard itself exists in terms of displacement. The picture on the front of the card you buy is *not* the Eiffel Tower, it is the displacement of the Eiffel Tower in a photographic image — and photography, perhaps particularly on a postcard, *always* lies. Also, your own writing on the back of your card, like any telegram, *is* the displacement of the context and of the circumstances in which it is written. What Apollinaire's text implies — and seeks to respond to — is that the textualised postcard is *not*, simply because it is textualised, different from the real (or 'real') one. The 'real' postcard is *equally* an instance of displacement, of the impenetrable codification of its message, of a recipient de-specified in writing. It is a token, a space without contours, defined by constant change and a changing, over-determined function. It expresses the pursuit of a message, the headlong effort to codify what language expresses as it displaces experience and gives birth to it. The calligraphic creation 'Tarjeta Postal' — though the words are Spanish for postcard, the language of the country (Mexico) where the 'addressee', Apollinaire's brother Albert, finds himself — does *not* equate Apollinaire's text with a postcard, or define it as a mimetic representation of one. Equally, it does not free us from postcards, or objects at large, nor does it seek to. It suggests that messages on postcards, token statements in a transient context, derive *from* language, that they are a response to an experience of language and of what language does to our sense of images and the world. 'Tarjeta Postal' is a word or phrase that indicates a space, both textual and 'real', covered over with more words, shaping and reshaping indefinitely our involvement with objects and images.

What makes this challenging is that Apollinaire's poem not only has the power to represent the engrossing involvement with images and with 'image', it also traces in the boundaries that limit our capacity to identify with experience. As I reach the end of my brief reading of 'Lettre-Océan', I realise that the poem achieves its greatest impact through its appearance, the image of itself it creates, the way it *is*. Its circles and its circularity are its most expressive and potentially most dangerous feature; they invite us to wonder whether we merely receive images or engage in their construction as we look around us and consume. For the circles undermine symbolisation within the text, calling

175

G

into question the symbolic power of some of its elements. We have symbols of Mexico — the MAYAS and the 'Jeunes filles à Chapultepec' — bringing Central America into the here and now of reading. The circles, as we saw, can be thought to symbolise airwaves, and Daniel Delbreil and Françoise Dininman discern an enormous sundial with the Eiffel Tower casting a shadow and showing time.[101] But attempts to identify symbolic word-representations in the text — and thus identify with them, and establish a power to impose on events — are blocked. Each word-circle is in fact a pun, and as we have by now come to expect, this does not create a kind of liberating potentiality of equally valid and stimulating interpretations or poetic intentions. Instead, each layer of expressiveness *displaces* others: concentration does not entail easy interpenetration or indefinite access. Looking again at the concentric word-circles of the poem, it becomes clear that they can be read as representing the music, in the form of grooves on the record, from the gramophones commemorated in the text. Of course, these circles are also word-airwaves, the words of which make the signified 'airwaves' or 'ondes' inaccessible. Moreover, the concentric circles can also be read as a representation of the author-persona walking around in circles: 'Les Chaussures Neuves du Poète'. At this point, as Apollinaire specifies with his bold-type naming, the punning itself comes full circle, for the noise the poet's new shoes make is given a textual expression indistinguishable from the sound of static on a receiver: 'cré cré cré cré cré'. Everything adds up to the Eiffel Tower — or is it to itself; or is it to everything else?

This is much more than a joke at the expense of poetic aspirations to rise to modernity and to act as a recording of it. The circles and their dual centre ultimately incarnate the *desire* for symbolic representation and dominance. But in the wake of this unrealised desire, Apollinaire finds means to make 'image' out of image, shape out out of the aformal vastness of the 'present'; his inventiveness makes language where linguistic inventiveness is magnificently mined from within and from without. Apollinaire's calligraphy in the poem and his elaborate punning consist of a multi-contextual, over-determined signified that inevitably, *because* of the overload of information it carries, transforms itself into a multi-contextual, over-determined signifier, made up of phonetic concentric circles. In 'Lettre-Océan', the signifier *is* an overflow of meaning from the contours of the signified, it is expressiveness itself, barring reader and writer from communication and possession of their own history and sense of self. The signifier that Apollinaire constructs traces out the distinction between experience, words and displacement. Ultimately, Apollinaire creates a text in which memory, in the form of displaced expressiveness, overloads the signifier to such an extent that memory is indistinguishable from its own displacement as signifier. Apollinaire's signifier in 'Lettre-Océan' traces out the dissolving line between pure experience, and continuous experience of otherness, of alienation: 'cré cré cré cré cré cré'. We need not be afraid to make important poetic claims for this sequence of textualised phonemes in relation to the poem as a whole. It represents response as such, pure being, to such an extent that it is hardly a word — to such an extent that it can be nothing other than a 'word'.[102]

7—WHAT IS THE IDENTITY OF GUILLAUME APOLLINAIRE? 'COEUR COURONNE ET MIROIR'

'Lettre-Océan' leaves its reader in a mosaic-space of mobile words, an iridescent structure that makes its reference to the world unfamiliar, buried and sourceless in the traces left by watching, thinking and writing. It is a space that recurs consistently in Apollinaire's experience; it becomes anxiously familiar, at the same time as producing incandescent novelty. Apollinaire sees through to this space and invents words for it in the verse of *Vitam Impendere Amori*, produced three years later, after living through the war, in collaboration with André Rouveyre:

> La vitre du cadre est brisée
> Un air qu'on ne peut définir
> Hésite entre son et pensée
> Entre avenir et souvenir[103]

The difference between the textual vocabulary in this verse and in 'Lettre-Océan' is itself the 'context' of an experience of selfness that repeats itself irrevocably in Apollinaire's writing, and in the reading of his poetic fiction. The pane of glass, the merest token of an obstacle to immediacy, is broken, leaving only the frame, whose contours are effaced in the experience of the moment, or of the picture, which the frame does not enclose. Instead, Apollinaire lyrically observes — in effect, creates a language for — a moment between moments, a moment filled with melody, or with a word, an idea or a memory of a melody; or is it just the air he breathes and his sense that he is watching himself alive? The moment is 'there', the 'present', the point where the future *is*, where intervention is built out of sensation from the past. In this writing, Apollinaire discovers words that are between words and thought: words *and* thought, alternately and with no distinction. His writing represents an in-between space that *is* his sense of self. But it is a space sealed in the words that both create and observe it — in the sound of words as he writes or is it as he thinks of writing?

In 'Coeur couronne et miroir', Apollinaire finds new ways of overloading his words and of transforming them into an exclusive experience of words themselves, an all-exclusive signifier. He weaves the connection textually between this and an experience of identity that is not there but 'there' — there in so far as it re-emerges unpredictably at points that elude comparison. In 'Coeur couronne et miroir', the language that observes and creates this experience is based on an intricate visual punning of a kind that also operates in 'Lettre-Océan'. In 'Coeur couronne et miroir', Apollinaire exploits the dismantling, which he pursues throughout his poetic fiction, of a hierarchy of poetic and non-poetic language, by re-presenting the expressiveness of cliché. He develops a dynamic of equivalence and substitution in relation to word forms on the page. 'Mon coeur pareil à une flamme renversée' can be seen to be making use of the commonplace metaphors that equate love with the heart and with fire; in this context, a heart equated with an upside-down flame could be read as an expression of unrequited love, or anxiety in love. Apollinaire was later to adjust the cliché in a similar way in poem V of *Vitam Impendere Amori*:[104]

> Tu flottes sur l'onde nocturne
> La flamme est mon coeur renversé
> Couleur de l'écaille du peigne
> Que reflète l'eau qui te baigne   (l. 4)

Here, Apollinaire's adjustment of the cliché emphasises a tension between the cliché itself, its limited range, and the surfeit of stimuli expressing the *subtlety* of his experience or his memory: reflected comb, souvenir comb, reflected water, eroticism. But in 'Coeur couronne et miroir', the tension is between the simplicity of the cliché, and the overload of *pre-recognised* meanings and tokens it carries. Here, the cliché is a compressed entity, and highlights the signifier on the page. The letters that make up the statement 'Mon Coeur pareil à une flamme renversée' are shaped like a heart *and* like an inverted flame. This visual punning does not suggest that one context is immediately

Cœur Couronne et Miroir

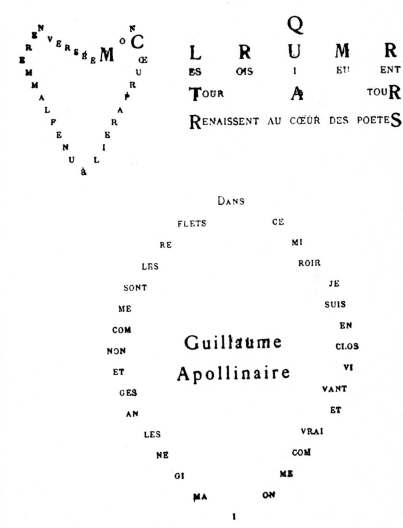

Heart (left): reading spirals — MON CŒUR PAREIL À UNE FLAMME RENVERSÉE

Crown (right):
LES ROIS QUI MEURENT
TOUR A TOUR
RENAISSENT AU CŒUR DES POETES

Mirror (bottom, circular):
DANS CE MIROIR JE SUIS ENCLOS VIVANT ET VRAI COMME ON IMAGINE LES ANGES ET NON COMME SONT LES REFLETS

Guillaume
Apollinaire

interchangeable with another; nor would this be a full explanation of the 'joke'. Once again, we have a barrier between (the) expressiveness (of the cliché) and its communication. The indistinguishability, which the pun produces, of the signified and the visual elements of the signifier *is* the signifier: it dismantles the function of designating, which in this case consists in the relation of the 'cliché' to a particular context. Not only this, but the 'cliché' can therefore not be read as an inadequate and — self-consciously or not — imprecise token expression of an emotional impulse. The joke is that the visual punning does not emphasise any power to redeploy circumstance, but instead it makes the expressiveness of this cliché what it *is* — a minimally adjusted cliché.[105]

Does this mean that the poem is trivial or a failure? What Apollinaire is in fact suggesting is that to explore the relation between experience and words rebuffs the user of language and involves the poet in the indivisible anteriority of both language and appearance. In 'Coeur couronne et miroir' this expresses itself in terms of an invading immediacy of the visual impact of words, which itself suggests a near-incapacity to affect the independence of words (clichés) as they are experienced by individuals. Equally, however, the overloaded signifier *is* expressive; new and unpredictable word forms are produced. But this novelty itself implies *incompleteness* in the idiom and the word form, its incapacity to create difference in experience through time, to come to grips with identifications, and to intervene in sensation rushing at us from the past. The novelty of the word form paradoxically expresses its incapacity to distinguish itself from the already expressed, from what excapes the possession of the language user. Yet the word form's novelty is a fertile moment in undominated history and uncontrollable novelty — otherness in the experience of self, which it is the prize of creativity to delve into.

The 'couronne' seems to offer the poet this prize. Symbol of kingship, as the heart is of love, it seems to take its place confidently between the threat or the challenge of passivity and cliché on the one hand, and the bold(-type) artist's signature in the third word form. But just as the heart/inverted flame grapples with its own incomplete coming-to-terms with our identifications, their structure and the clichéd comparisons we might make of them, so the crown is an imperfect and melting symbol. It expresses its own incapacity to encompass experience, and, as one element among three, it calls into question its own part in moulding the whole into any form of self-expanding narrative fulfilment. Once again, this undermining comes from the design as words, rather than as pictorial emblem, particularly on the level of the signified. While the crown suggests dominance, the message that makes it up is in tension with this promise, hollows it out rather than fulfilling it; the sovereign performance is in the hands of poets and not kings, new masters and different heroes not covered by the crown outline. Kings only survive in the reflected glory of an awaited resurrection through poets that have yet to write: 'Les rois ... renaissent au coeur des poètes'. And this undermining of the capacity of the form as symbol to impose its own terms is triggered by another Apollinairian manipulation of the signifier and the consequent mobile reading process. The capitals, while delineating a power to enclose, in fact muddle a coherent reading of the form as sentence and confuse the eye in its search for linguistic sense. 'Les rois qui meurent tour à tour renaissent au coeur des poètes'. The capitals outline a crown, but they can only be read if their function as capitals is undermined in their interaction with the lower-case letters. Ultimately, reading the promise of reincarnation through poetry blurs the contours of the kingship symbol; or to put it differently, a structure of dominance is dissolved in the formless process of the reading it produces. And the 'Quia' (Latin for 'because') forming the crux of the edifice concentrates the question asked about the relation of creativity in language to transcience, symbol to usage and exchange, intention to impact.

This questioning is not an expression of defeat. But neither need we be too eager to await a gesture of transcendence from Apollinaire as he composes his linguistic mirror.[106] What it suggests is an identity made unfamiliar with itself in language: 'Dans ce miroir je suis enclos vivant et vrai comme on imagine les anges et non comme sont les reflets dans ce miroir je suis ...'. In the manner of the Eiffel Tower configurations in 'Lettre-Océan', the reading of syllables separated from each other in the visual form they take on the page affects the extent to which this 'form' can be recognised; the 'oval mirror' is not the same one that would emerge from treating the words as a punctuated sentence in a paragraph. This dissolving recognition is also produced on the level of the signified and the decipherable; the level where the words form a sentence that can be uncoupled from its dependence on the signifier, and from the form it takes on the page. As such, the sentence refers to a vision of so-called pure identity and vision: 'comme on imagine les anges'. But this vision is imagined ('comme on imagine'), and moreover it is sealed off ('enclos', like a text) in a mirror — and reflections in a mirror do not reflect words, the emphatic words striven for at the centre of the word form. The pure vision is an illusion, beyond our grasp, but it becomes vital at the point where the writer as reader realises that such pure vision, or pure identity, is *not* the mirror-form in terms of which it is imagined, but the words that displace it. The name Guillaume Apollinaire is not the reflection in the mirror: 'non comme sont les reflets' that are neither 'vivants' nor 'vrais'; reflections are silent anyway but the word-space 'Guillaume Apollinaire' is one where we all but drown in the headlong effort to come to grips with the mobility of perceived forms. The emboldened letters 'Guillaume Apollinaire', being enclosed in a mirror that does not reflect them, being seen and read in the act of naming, trace the sense of 'I' into 'immediacy' and memory. A de-familiarising overlap emerges between this commonplace act of naming, and a heightened awareness, a keener observation of living and perceiving, a dispossession in the 'present'. 'Guillaume Apollinaire', 'vivant et vrai', like a wordless or pre-verbal reflection, is 'Entre son et pensée', involved *in* experience as it slips away from words or through them. But this space is a signifier — either the phrase 'Entre son et pensée' or 'Guillaume Apollinaire'. It both embodies and bars the way to the endless source of the formulated and the expressed, and our part in it.

In 'Coeur couronne et miroir', the identity of Guillaume Apollinaire *is* the traces it leaves in the resiliently particular, description-rebuffing relation of experience to language. We move from minimal adjustment, to self-hollowing promise, to a signifier and a name unidentical with themselves.[107] The identity of Ġuillaume Apollinaire is its effacement. It is also its power to re-present this continuous otherness, the repeatedly unfamiliar sense of self that emerges through time, images, identifications and words. And the power of Guillaume Apollinaire comes from an anxiety — the anxiety of language as language and the de-structed, unnamed dimensions of its resonance.

8—'VOYAGE'. PURITY. BEING

The interplay of immediacy and otherness, familiarity and dispossession, and the dangerous proximity of creativity and banality, continue in 'Voyage'. Here, the intermeshing of word and word form is textured in a particularly 'lyrical' way, and this lyrical texture outlines a way of drawing my reading of these poems to a close.

The idea of a journey stretches back through Baudelaire's 'Invitation au Voyage' to Romantic nostalgia and beyond. The crushing sense of transience and the promise of fulfilment are reincarnated in the fluttering feathers, the suggestive moonlit night, the still summer so bright that colours fade prior to the explosion of a sunset. The elements in the image as signified might suggest a Verlainian mood poem such as 'Beams' or 'Promenade sentimentale'.[108] Moreover, the poem as a whole responds to the desire dominant in Apollinaire since 1908 that poetry should find a new 'fausseté' and be unconcerned with psychological, social or historical truths. The freedom of the forms on the page bears witness to Apollinaire's will to create new roles for words and images, new experiences for readers and seers; at the same time 'Voyage' perhaps more than all the other ideograms of 'Ondes' vindicates Apollinaire's claim that such writing is 'une idéalisation de la poésie vers-libriste'.[109]

But this awareness of history is an untamed sensation that comes at us from the page. The nostalgia emanating from the images as signified — the distant forests and valleys, the ease and freshness of the air, a face that may never be seen again — is produced by a sense of lost specificity and lost source. The train opens the page out — it is any train moving across the countryside, towards all the destinations in the experience or the imagination of the reader and the writer. In being perceived, looked at and interpreted, the event is lost, and we lose our purchase on the resonances that are scrawled across the page.

But the invisible focus is controlled. There is no train but the one moving with increasing intensity across the page, sequestered in its boldness. The movement of the train/statement suggests the passage of time.[110] Within reading, it *is* time, not because we have access to time through it, or because the observation of trains gives us this access, but because access is banished in the bold disappearance of the train and the shape on the page. This banishment inaugurates a perception of time, and reinstates our exclusion *within* it. The moment passes and it is this that produces the signifier, born in the passing of sensation and evoking the power of history over images. It produces an awareness of perception; it transfixes it in the form on the page and in the abstract space of memory and the 'present'.

The increasing intensity of the signifier is inevitably a question-mark — one that dominates the page-span, but whose presence is as taunting, mobile and trivial as a puff of smoke. Once again, readers may feel gagged by the imaged tonality of the poem. But Apollinaire finds with

Voyage

A_{DIEU} AMOUR NUAGE QUI

FUIS REFAIS LE VOYAGE DE DANTE

ET N'A PAS CHU PLUIE FÉCON

OU   VA   DONC   CE   TRAIN   QUI   MEUR

DANS   LES   VALS   ET   LES   BEAUX   BOIS

O
D U
CE

L
A

T
I
U
N

E
T
D O
I
L
E
S

L
P E
I N E

N
E

J E

TÉLÉGRAPHE

OISEAU
QUI   TOMBER
LAISSE

SES AILES PARTOUT

?
E
L
A
LOIN   TENDRE ÉTÉ SI P
IS   DU

L   U

N   A
I
R
E   E T

C'   TON
EST   SA
VI   GÈ

QUE

V
O
I
S   P L U
S

ease the forms with which to write on the poem, in it and about it, and to engage with it further. He finds more words and forms for the reading and seeing his forms produce. The stars in the sky, in any event, sparkle sourcelessly. Here on the page, the constellations are given vestigial contours — the contours of language within image. The minimalist letters in the constellations and the spaces between them incarnate the indefinitely expressive failure of words to master images and perception. But the power of the letter-shapes is the capacity they produce to read images and to watch reading. The starlit, moonlit night *is* read: 'lu*e*naire'. Equally, the unusual first 'e' could be taken as an indecipherable calligraphic space overloaded with unmastered significance and otherness. This nexus involving the real moon, image and reading, and banishment, is itself a concentration of the split identity of the reader/ writer in the poem.[111] As in 'Arbre', he/she is either me or you ('je'/ 'tu'), the writer or the reader, the writer seeking an attitude to the images 'of' his sensation, from which he is excluded and for which the words he finds remain *creatively* as imaged as any pre-verbal, pre-expressed, yet processed perception. This identity is either active or sequestered, but in either event, it is *not* there, it is past, words, fragments. And this '*not*' is the purity of the language and its inroads into being. The stars and the train are not objects and events in nature, but experience and memories. Within them, we see and watch ourselves see and 'read' and sense.

This space, where signifiers yield their mobility and perception is continually reinstated in its realm between the eyes, silence and the pen, finds its most telling form in the *cut* in the page. The 'C' of 'C'est' does not indicate, it is a calligraphy that buries, both in time and space. As we read, we join Apollinaire and the poem is about us; we *are* readers, outside what we identify with, and the crescent cut, a black hole that opens out as the finger is pointed, raises the curtain on the race, or the dance, with image, creativity and death: 'C'est ton visage que je ne vois plus'.

NOTES

1 Roger Shattuck, *The Banquet Years*, revised edition (London, 1969), pp. 62–5, pp. 266–8, p. 272.
2 See *Méditations esthétiques*, OC, IV, pp. 47–9.
3 'L'avant-guerre. Essuyons nos yeux. Le génie renaît plus beau du bouquet ardent de la catastrophe.' (André Breton, *Les Pas Perdus*, Idées, Paris, 1979,

p. 24.) For an exploration of Apollinaire's interest in de Chirico, its development and implications, see William Bohn, *Apollinaire et l'homme sans visage: création et évolution d'un motif moderne* (Rome, 1984).

4 'Le grand déploiement de notre art moderne
  Mariant souvent sans lien apparent comme dans la vie
  Les sons les gestes les couleurs les cris les bruits
  La musique la danse l'acrobatie la poésie la peinture
  Les chœurs les actions et les décors multiples'
  Les Mamelles de Tirésias, 'Prologue', OP, p. 881.

5 'Zone', 'Les Colchiques', 'Crépuscule', 'La Maison des morts', 'Salomé', 'Merlin et la vieille femme', 'Le Larron', 'Les Fiançailles': OP, p. 39, p. 60, p. 64, p. 66, p. 86, p. 88, p. 91, p. 128.

6 This is an ambition he shares with Cendrars: 'pour Cendrars, tout l'héritage symboliste est à liquider définitivement,' writes Marcel Poupon: 'Apollinaire et Cendrars', *Archives des lettres modernes*, 103, Archives Guillaume Apollinaire, 2 (1969), p. 19.

7 'L'Emigrant de Landor Road', OP, p. 106, l. 53.

8 'J'atteignais l'âge mûr quand la guerre arriva': 'A L'Italie', OP, p. 274, l. 2.

9 Gabriel Arbouin, 'Devant l'idéogramme d'Apollinaire', in *Le Guetteur mélancolique* (Paris, 1952), p. 144.

10 Georges Braque, *Standing Female Nude* (1907–8), in Douglas Cooper and Gary Tinterow, *The Essential Cubism 1907–1920*, The Tate Gallery (London, 1983), p. 39; Pablo Picasso, *Les Demoiselles d'Avignon* (Paris, 1906–7), in Jaime Sabartés and Wilhelm Boeck, *Picasso* (Paris, 1955), p. 143.

11 See Shattuck, *The Banquet Years*, p. 266, p. 279; Marie-Jeanne Durry, *Guillaume Apollinaire — 'Alcools'*, 3 vols (Paris, 1956–64 and 1977), II, pp. 212–13.

12 So termed by Virginia Spate, *Orphism* (Oxford, 1979), pp. 160–274. As we know, Apollinaire derived the term 'Orphic' from his thinking on Cubism and 'le cubisme orphique'. (OC, IV, p. 25; CAA, p. 169.)

13 'Zone', OP, p. 39, 'Les Fenêtres', p. 168. Apollinaire added 'Zone' to the proofs of *Eau de Vie*, and changed the collection's name to *Alcools* in November 1912. In December, 'Zone' was published in *Les Soirées de Paris*. In January 1913, 'Les Fenêtres' appeared in *Poème et Drame*. Durry also points out how soon 'Les Fenêtres' appeared after 'Zone', and wonders about the significance of the presence of the two poems in the different collections. (Durry, *Guillaume Apollinaire — 'Alcools'*, II, p. 209).

14 Claude Debon gives an intricate thematic study of the concerns common to *Alcools* and 'Ondes', showing the continuity between the two, in her *Guillaume Apollinaire après 'Alcools'*, vol. 1, *Calligrammes — le poète et la guerre* (Paris, 1981).

15 Leroy C. Breunig, 'Apollinaire et le cubisme', *La Revue des lettres modernes*, Guillaume Apollinaire, 1 (1962), 7–24 (p. 22).

16 OP, p. 83. The italics in the quotation that follows are my own.

17 'Le tact est relatif mais la vue est oblongue': OP, p. 95.

18 'Tu lis les prospectus les catalogues les affiches qui chantent tout haut/Voilà la poésie ce matin et pour la prose il y a les journaux': OP, p. 39.

19 OC, IV, p. 493.

20 OP, p. 123.
21 André Billy, *Apollinaire vivant* (Paris, 1923), pp. 54–5.
22 CCA, p. 172; Robert Goffin, *Entrer en poésie* (Brussels, 1948).
23 Philippe Renaud, *Lecture d'Apollinaire* (Lausanne, 1969), p. 298, OP, p. 1079. See also C, p. 349.
24 CAA, p. 170.
25 Breton, *Entretiens* (Paris, 1969), p. 31.
26 'Le Musicien de St. Merry', OP, p. 188, l. 6.
27 One of the reasons for Apollinaire's pride in 'Les Fenêtres' is that he felt it was a climax in his effort to develop poetic syntax and simplify it. In a well-known comment, he describes this effort in the following way: 'J'ai fait mon possible pour simplifer la syntaxe poétique et j'ai réussi en certains cas, notamment un poème: "Les Fenêtres" ....' OC, III, p. 478.
28 'Il Pleut', OP, p. 203.
29 'Liens', OP, p. 167, l. 4.
30 'Liens', OP, p. 167, l. 17.
31 'Les Fenêtres', OP, p. 168, l. 18.
32 Renaud, *Lecture d'Apollinaire*, p. 351.
33 'Lettre-Océan', OP, p. 184.
34 'Les Fiançailles', OP, p. 132, l. 55. See p. 73 above.
35 Renaud, *Lecture d'Apollinaire*, pp. 352–3.
36 Renaud, *Lecture d'Apollinaire*, p. 352.
37 Greet and Lockerbie point to the mystery and the conceptual overtones that accrue to this capitalisation: 'to drop the definite article and capitalize all four nouns heightens the mystification by treating them as place names — or absolute ideas'. C, p. 353.
38 'Autant dire qu'il est impossible de *fixer* le vers dans une représentation stable; c'est un *perpetuum mobile* par l'effet de l'éclairage réciproque des mots-images qui le composent; loin de se laisser "voir" et "définir", ils fonctionnent comme des miroirs qui éblouissent l'esprit en renvoyant la lumière du Soleil central qui, précisément, en devient multiple.' Renaud, *Lecture d'Apollinaire*, p. 353. Renaud's italics.
39 'Aussi rejetterons-nous comme illusion l'idée que, dans ce genre de poèmes, tout s'explique et se résout par la magique énonciation des mots "simultanéité" ou, plus savamment, "simultanisme".' Renaud, *Lecture d'Apollinaire*, p. 357.
40 Interestingly, Greet and Lockerbie read in the 'multiples soleils' a reference to Delaunay's *Formes circulaires*. (C, p. 353.) Such a comparison, along with the title of the poem, emphasises the non-Futurist mode of 'simultaneous' expression that Apollinaire is striving for here.
41 Renaud describes the line in terms of 'mots-images' (p. 353), and the phrase is revealing in that it suggests an unquantifiable back and forth movement between expression and memory, words and perception. The signifier is the arena of this 'glissement'; it both incarnates it and eradicates it from view, it hovers between word and image, it is a word that does not circumscribe an image; it gives rise to an image for which there are no words, and to a shared reality penetrated by psychic experience. Perception and the sense of self inhabit this 'space' of the signifier.

Lacan's comments on the *lapsus* in his preface to the English language edition of *Le Séminaire de Jacques Lacan, Livre XI, (1964)* are helpful here. Awareness of forgetting is awareness of the unconscious, of the dimensionless imaginary. But this awareness places us *outside* the unconscious and threatens to cast us as the mere consumer of perception and stimuli. Such is the interplay inaugurated by the signifier. 'When the space of a lapsus no longer carriers any meaning (or interpretation), then only is one sure that one is in the unconscious. *One knows.* But one only has to be aware of the fact to find oneself outside it. There is no friendship there, in that space that supports the unconscious.'. (Jacques Lacan, *Four Concepts of Psychoanalysis*, translated by Alan Sheridan (London, 1979), p. vii. Lacan's italics.)

42 *Méditations esthétiques*, OC, IV, p. 18. See p. 30 above.

43 *Le Médaillon toujours fermé* was the title of the group of seven poems ultimately placed at the start of 'Lueurs des tirs' in *Calligrammes*. For a discussion of these poems, see Margaret Davies, '*Le Médaillon toujours fermé*', *Revue des lettres modernes*, 450–5, Guillaume Apollinaire, 13 (1976), 77–98.

44 'The puns juxtapose journalistic and poetic effects: at once ephemeral, banal objects, limited by time and space, and abstract but very suggestive concepts, they may also comment on the underlying theme of artistic creation, if time in which to create is seen as a kind of freedom': C, p. 353.

45 CAA, p. 118. See pp. 115–19 above.

46 OC, III, p. 478.

47 Greet and Lockerbie, in their pertinent analysis of Apollinaire's revisions of the poem, show Apollinaire's pursuit of juxtaposition and its place among other characteristic devices: 'thus one sees how, when revising, Apollinaire tends towards ellipsis, mystification, discontinuity, through an increasing emphasis on juxtaposition *per se*'. (C, p. 352.)

48 Renaud, *Lecture d'Apollinaire*, pp. 354–5.

49 Greet and Lockerbie see the shift in tense as a sign of 'temporal simultaneity'. (C, p. 352.) My own view is that there is a dynamic interplay in the poem between this sort of simultaneity and the text as sequence.

50 Greet and Lockerbie, in their reading of Apollinaire's revisions of the poem, see in the treatment of light an aspiration of the poet to become painter: 'one thinks of a painter whose medium is paint rather than words'. (C, p. 352.) Perhaps, though, the poem, among other things, is made in the difference between the two, the unrealised desire of one to become the other.

51 One such example of the cross-fertilisation of imaginary and concrete events in Apollinaire's thinking and writing is provided by Pierre Roy's account of the composition of 'Paysage', in *Les Soirées de Paris*, July/August 1914, and OC, III, p. 918.

52 'Et tous aigle phénix et pihis de la Chine/Fraternisent avec la volante machine': 'Zone', OP, p. 41, l. 69.

53 The poem thus answers Arbouin's fear that 'Lettre-Océan' in particular, and simultanist writing generally, might merely result in 'un langage d'initiés, un art d'initiés'. *Le Guetteur mélancholique* (Paris, 1952), p. 144.

54 CAA, p. 115.

55 Greet relates the line specifically to Chevreul's colour wheel, the restrictive nature of which was attacked by Delaunay. (C, p. 351.)

56 See pp. 51–3 above.

57 In another story told by Apollinaire, half a body, this time a human one, emerges as a divine poet-cripple. Justin Couchot, 'L'Infirme divinisé', remembers nothing and has no notion of dimensions. His vision is an endlessly rejuvenated transparency; he responds to all the levels on which life is produced and reproduced: 'Le monde entier et toutes les époques étaient ainsi pour lui un instrument bien accordé que son unique main touchait avec justesse.' (Le Poète assassiné, in Guillaume Apollinaire, Oeuvres en prose, 1, ed. M. Décaudin, Paris, 1977, p. 376.)

58 C, p. 351.

59 C, p. 355.

60 'Apollinaire's modernism differs from that of his Futurist friends by its lyricism.' (C, p. 354.)

61 OP, p. 188.

62 OP, p. 178, p. 180.

63 In fact, Greet and Lockerbie stress the relation of memory to creativity enacted in the poem, and contrast this with Cendrars's enterprise: 'the kind of cosmopolitan and sentimental poetry attempted by Cendrars in his Prose du Transsibérien is compared with the entirely different ubiquity conceived of by Apollinaire, which is based on the nature of the creative, remembering mind'. (C, p. 375.)

64 'Arbre', OP, p. 178, 1. 18; 'Lundi Rue Christine', OP, p. 182, 1. 47.

65 See Marcel Adéma, Apollinaire le mal-aimé (Paris, 1952), p. 174.

66 René Magritte, La Vie secrète IV (1928), in Magritte, ed. D. Larkin, with an introduction by Eddie Wolfram (London, 1972), fig. 24.

67 OP, p. 254.

68 'Apollinaire thinks of several friends in their pictorial or verbal words.' (C, p. 375.)

69 This illusion would be a movement on from the Symbolist notion of creative artifice which Greet and Lockerbie explore in relation to the mosque at Isfahan. (C, pp. 373–4.)

70 My own view, here, differs from Greet and Lockerbie's view of the poem as a whole, in that they see a 'nostalgia for lost possibilities' responded to in a 'steadfast awareness of his [Apollinaire's, man and poet] own identity'.

71 Apollinaire engages in the same process in the repetitions of 'Il y a' in the poem of that name in 'Obus couleur de lune', OP, p. 280. The reader, the writer and his friends also disappear in this poem amidst the camouflage of naming and indicating: 'Car on a poussé très loin dans cette guerre l'art de l'invisibilité', 1. 30.

72 C, p. 380.

73 OP, p. XLII.

74 Renaud, Lecture d'Apollinaire, pp. 369–70.

75 S. Themerson, Apollinaire's Lyrical Ideograms (London, 1968).

76 Linda da Molina Silva was the sister of a school friend.

77 Themerson, Apollinaire's Lyrical Ideograms, p. 27.

78 Guillaume Apollinaire, *Le Guetteur mélancolique, suivi de Poèmes retrouvés*, ed. M. Décaudin, Poésie (Paris, 1970), p. 188. 'A Linda' is placed on the same page as the previous poem in this series of *Quelconqueries*, 'Le Teint'.

79 I am reading the fourth word in the following quotation as 'luenaire', although the first ''e'' does not present itself clearly as such in the text; it could be assessed equally well as a non-legible calligraphic design. Greet and Lockerbie simply, and equally suggestively, leave a space here. (C, pp. 92–95.) See pp. 182–6.

80 There has been much discussion of the relation of reading to seeing on display in these texts. Lockerbie, in his introduction to C (p. 11), stresses the impossibility of 'tautology between a linguistic statement and the instant impression covered by a shape'. See also Michel Foucault, *Ceci n'est pas une pipe* (Montpellier, 1973), and for a discussion of it, Timothy Mathews, 'Figure/text', *Paragraph*, 6 (1985), 28–42, and Silvano Levy, *Foucault on Magritte: Similitude and Resemblance* (forthcoming). Drawing on Julia Kristéva's 'Le Mot, le dialogue et le roman', in *Sémeotiké, recherches pour une sémanalyse* (Paris, 1969), Jean-Pierre Goldenstein describes the problem of distinguishing the visual from the verbal in these texts, and of relating one to the other, as 'la quasi-impossibilité dans laquelle nous nous trouvons de penser une non-opposition hors de la logique 0–1', in *Revue des lettres*, 450–5, 1976 (Guillaume Apollinaire 13), p. 177. This is a review of Alain-Marie Bassy, 'Forme littéraire et forme graphique: les schématogrammes d'Apollinaire', *Scolies, Cahiers de recherches de l'Ecole normale supérieure*, 3–4, (1974–5), 161–207, who writes: 'admettons que plusieurs perceptions frappent simultanément nos sens . . . elles n'accèdent pas toutes simultanément à la conscience'. (p. 202) Willard Bohn, in his *The Aesthetics of Visual Poetry* (Cambridge, 1986), refuses to accept this: see p. 67 and note 36.

81 Bohn, *The Aesthetics of Visual Poetry*, pp. 47–8.

82 Bohn, *The Aesthetics of Visual Poetry*, pp. 69–84; Jean-Pierre Goldenstein, 'Pour une sémiologie du calligramme', in *Lecture et interprétation des calligrammes, Que vlo-ve?*, 29–30 (1981), separate pagination; for Alain-Marie Bassy's work and Goldenstein's response to it, see note 79.

83 Bohn, *The Aesthetics of Visual Poetry*, p. 66.

84 Bohn, *The Aesthetics of Visual Poetry*, p. 68.

85 OP, p. 253.

86 OC, III, p. 890. See also Bohn, *The Aesthetics of Visual Poetry*, pp. 64–6.

87 Renaud, *Lecture d'Apollinaire*, p. 371. Renaud's italics.

88 Renaud, *Lecture d'Apollinaire*, pp. 371–2. Renaud's italics.

89 Guillaume Apollinaire, *Le Guetteur mélancolique* (Paris, 1952), p. 144: 'il faut que notre intelligence s'habitue à comprendre synthético-idéographiquement . . .'.

90 Daniel Delbreil, Françoise Dininman and Alan Windsor, ' ''Lettre-Océan'' ', in *Apollinaire et la peinture, Que vlo-ve?*, 21–2 (1979), separate pagination. Bohn, *The Aesthetics of Visual Poetry*, pp. 9–45.

91 'La synthèse du calligramme comme création ''idéographique'', s'achève après la lecture entendue comme acte de déchiffrement et d'interprétation': Pénélope Sacks, 'La Mise en page du calligramme', in *Lecture et*

interprétation des calligrammes, Que vlo-ve?, 29–30 (1981), separate pagination (p. 6). Bohn argues the point in terms of an interplay between perception and conception in the interpretation of 'Lettre-Océan': 'from poster to painting to poem, simultaneous perception leads to simultaneous conception once the text has been decoded'. *(The Aesthetics of Visual Poetry*, p. 19, and also p. 67.) Bohn also argues this view in terms of Cubism, thus positing an ultimate synthesis in Cubist expression the existence of which I have argued against in chapters one and two: 'Comme le calligramme, le cubisme exige une participation active du spectateur. Comme le cubisme, le calligramme le récompense à la fin d'un moment précieux de conscience totale.' ('L'Imagination plastique des calligrammes', in *Lecture et interprétation des calligrammes*, separate pagination, p. 17.)

92 OC, IV, p. 351.

93 See Oswald Ducrot and Tzvestan Todorov, *Dictionnaire encyclopédique des sciences du langage* (Paris, 1972), pp. 131–3: 'la dénotation se produit non entre un signifiant et un signifié mais entre le signe et le *référent* ...' (p. 133). For a comment on the relevance of Jean-François Lyotard's distinction between 'sens' and 'signification' to the workings of reference in the calligram, see Timothy Mathews, 'Figure/text', p. 40.

94 For a discussion of Apollinaire's use of solid forms in his calligrams, as opposed to the word-outlines of 'Ondes', see Bohn, *The Aesthetics of Visual Poetry*, pp. 51–2, and p. 59.

95 Delbreil, Dininman and Windsor, ' "Lettre-Océan" ', p. 3 and p. 16.

96 Georges Schmits reads 'pad' as 'une réduction populaire de "padre" avec le sens de "petit père" ', in his ' "Lettre-Océan" ', *Savoir et Beauté*, 2–3 (1964), 2691–8.

97 Delbreil, Dininman and Windsor, ' "Lettre-Océan" ', p. 4.

98 My own view differs here from that of Greet and Lockerbie, who see the reader/viewer led into a 'natural climax' in that the 'second circular shape is bigger and more explosive than the first'. (C, p. 382.)

99 Bohn, *The Aesthetics of Visual Poetry*, pp. 19–20.

100 Goldenstein, *Revue des lettres modernes*, 450–5, Guillaume Apollinaire, 13, p. 175.

101 Delbreil, Dininman and Windsor, ' "Lettre-Océan" ', pp. 31–2.

102 Jean-Pierre Goldenstein notes the relevance of Derrida's concept of 'le supplément' to a study of the calligrams, and of the position Derrida arrives at with regard to writing: 'on peut d'autant moins faire abstraction du texte écrit pour se *précipiter* vers le signifié qu'il *voudrait dire*, que le signifié est ici l'écriture elle-même'. (Jacques Derrida, *De la Grammatologie*, Paris, 1967, p. 215; Goldenstein, *Revue des lettres modernes*, 450–5, Guillaume Apollinaire, 13, p. 181.)

103 OP, p. 162.

104 OP, p. 161. See also C, p. 392.

105 It is possible to argue that this manipulation of cliché, or this struggle with it, brings Apollinaire close to an 'écriture blanche' as characterised by Barthes in *Le Degré zéro de l'écriture*. On the one hand, Apollinaire rejects 'l'écriture artisanale', the creation of new forms that ultimately fail to challenge the accepted scope of Literature, or to explode the confines of

its performance. Equally, Apollinaire rejects the Mallarmean Murder of Literature, the attempt to remove history from language, as well as from the resonances of social interaction and unchallenged values. But Apollinaire does develop a transparent 'écriture' that seems to achieve the suppression of all style. It acquires a new 'instrumentalité', which is its power to represent 'image', to re-present the silence that rushes in with language and which exhales from 'le creux de l'homme. But like Barthes's 'écriture blanche', Apollinaire's ideogrammatic deployment of cliché in 'Coeur couronne et miroir' is open to attack from hardened responses and defunct metaphors — in this case the spectre of sentimentality. See Roland Barthes, 'L'Ecriture et le silence', in *Le Degré zéro de l'écriture*, Points (Paris, 1972), pp. 54–7.

106 Greet and Lockerbie see just such a gesture of transcendence in the design. Building, perhaps, on Bassy's reading of the oval shape as a halo or mandorla, they suggest that the poet strives for, and achieves, a kind of Mallarmean 'ideal Apollinaire who dwells in the absolute, beyond change'. (C, p. 393.)

107 My own view here differs significantly from that of Bohn who sees the transition in the poem as a double progression: 1. man—king—saint; 2. love—power—spirituality. (*The Aesthetics of Visual Poetry*, p. 56.)

108 Verlaine, *Oeuvres poétiques*, p. 54, p. 138.

109 OC, IV, p. 778. See also C, p. 394, where Greet and Lockerbie outline a continuity between the theme in *Alcools* of lost love and transience, and 'Voyage'.

110 Lockerbie, while discussing the connection between Apollinaire's fascination with trains and his obsession with the passage of time, highlights an expressive tension in 'Voyage' between the signified, where the train disappears, and the visual signifier, where the train seems to move closer and become larger. (S. I. Lockerbie, 'Forme graphique et expressivité dans les calligrammes', in *Lecture et interprétation des calligrammes*, separate pagination, p. 1, p. 6.)

111 My own view, then, is that it is very much possible to move on from the generally accepted interpretation of 'tu' in this peom as referring to the departed Marie Laurencin.

4—CONCLUSION

1—BEGINNINGS IN LANGUAGE. FICTION. WHAT DOES WRITING EXPRESS?

It seems that a concluding chapter to this exploration of Apollinaire's language needs to begin with some remarks that cannot avoid being introductory. To conclude is in some sense to explain what has happened, and yet to explain the problem that perplexes me and that Apollinaire confronts me with is to be constantly starting at the beginning, constantly confronting anew the necessity of inventing a beginning in language. Readers were told at the outset how this work would progress, and yet they may have become frustrated by the fact that the method I have adopted is at odds with their natural desire to see a particular poem become a crystallised, luminescent object in their own experience. Experience is of course not a solid object, of constant value, open to exchange; it is something to which we all contribute, and it is instigated in exchange. I have developed an approach to Apollinaire's texts that has not avoided the danger of being perplexing, that has represented the experience of reading Apollinaire as evading crystallisation, and that has invited us to re-evaluate constantly the positions we adopt in relation to reading and to language itself. This is to do more than merely engage in the critical procedure that recognises that the poems are so rich and varied in texture that each reading produces an altered, 'richer', and more nuanced experience for the reader. What we have been confronting is how Apollinaire seeks to discover his own arena in language, and the way in which he represents experience as being taken over and overrun by the forms of expression with which it engages.[1]

It is for this reason that, despite the variety of approaches that have already been developed (historical, biographical, stylistic), I have attempted to find new terms through which to grapple with this elusive and often baffling writing. Apollinaire's writing evades categorisation, and this is compounded by the way in which criticism itself has developed, by the way its objectives and its scope have altered. Once certain working critical concepts have been challenged, such as the possibility of stabilising the 'l'homme et l'oeuvre' relation, the work of fiction becomes increasingly impenetrable, and its relation to the rest of experience cannot be conclusively defined or fixed.

One reaction to this problem has been to embark on a sophistication of literary history. Another has been to follow through the thinking that presents the specificity of any fictional work as a problem in its own right, and it is basically this second line of action that this work is engaged in. In English criticism, I. A. Richards took on the challenge, in relation to poetry, of approaching a fictional work 'on its own grounds'. But the weakness of Richards's premise, as he outlines it in his *Principles of Literary Criticism*, lies in the assumption that it is possible to uncover terms of reference exclusive to poetry, through which the critic can specify the essentially poetic and distinguish it from other forms of expression.[2]

In 'Raisons de la critique pure', however, Genette approaches the same problem on the basis of a quite different experience of literature, and arrives at opposite conclusions.[3] Genette refers to a different critic operating at a different stage in the history of criticism to express his own approach. In discussing the critical theories Albert Thibaudet develops in *Réflexions sur la critique*, Genette suggests a critical approach of his own, capable of establishing and dealing with the exclusiveness of the literary object, and an essentially literary use of language.[4] But what distinguishes his approach from Richards's is the view that the essence of a literary product is that it escapes its own terms of reference, and that literary objects make the category 'literature' inaccessible.

Genette uses the term 'essence' to reverse the sense in which it is conventionally understood. He reworks Thibaudet's formulation of the essence of literature, which is in fact an essence divided into three related aspects of itself, the first of which is 'le génie'. Genette redefines 'le génie' by using brief references to Blanchot, Lacan, and Valéry, and by exploring further Thibaudet's own speculation that 'le génie' consists of a paradox involving the height of individualness, and the explosion of individuality. While presenting the height of individualness as an exclusive and intense engagement with writing, Genette also suggests that this meeting involves the disappearance of the writer in writing. For Genette, the confrontation of what Thibaudet thinks of as individualness with writing creates a language that distinguishes itself from dialogue because it regards how it operates as an open question, along with the definition of who consumes it and who uses it. These questions remain unanswered for the writer, who strives to invent a beginning in language, which has no beginning:

> 'Le génie, dit Thibaudet d'une manière un peu énigmatique, c'est à la fois le superlatif de l'individuel et l'éclatement de l'individualité.' Si nous voulons trouver le commentaire le plus éclairant de ce paradoxe, c'est peut-être du côté de Maurice Blanchot (et de Jacques Lacan) que nous devrons chercher, dans cette idée aujourd'hui familière à la littérature, mais dont la critique n'a sans doute pas encore assumé toutes les conséquences, que l'auteur, l'artisan du livre, comme disait encore Valéry, *n'est positivement personne* — ou encore, que l'une des fonctions du langage, et de la littérature comme langage, est de détruire son locuteur et de le désigner comme absent. Ce que Thibaudet nomme le génie, ce pourrait donc être ici cette absence du sujet, cet exercise du langage décentré, privé de centre, dont parle Blanchot .... 'L'écrivain, ajoute Blanchot, appartient à un langage que personne ne parle, qui ne s'adresse à personne, qui n'a pas de centre, qui ne révèle rien.'[5]

'Le génie', discovered in an obligation to express, explores the dissolving arena of identity, and the failure to meet with identity in the words that it produces: 'Ecrire est l'interminable, l'incessant ... L'écrivain appartient à un langage que personne ne parle, qui ne s'adresse à personne, qui n'a pas de centre, qui ne révèle rien. Il peut croire qu'il s'affirme en ce langage, mais ce qu'il affirme est toujours privé de soi.'[5]

What Thibaudet sees as the second aspect of the essence of literature also turns out to be, for Genette, a formulation of the way in which literary language withdraws from definition, and from a definitive differentiation between itself and other forms of language. This second 'essence' is the choice of 'genre', and Genette recognises that this concept has to be re-evaluated to some extent if it is to be relevant to the modern period in literature where the distinction between art forms is eroded in the continuing effort to galvanise modes of expression, and mould them to changing experiences of language itself:[7] 'Il n'est peut-être pas vrai, ou plus vrai, que les genres vivent, meurent et se transforment, mais il reste vrai que le discours littéraire se produit et se développe selon des structures qu'il ne peut même transgresser que parce qu'il les découvre, encore aujourd'hui, dans le champ de son langage et de son écriture.'[8] Genette accepts 'genre' as an aspect of the essence of literary writing, not because of the attempt it implies to formalise certain conventions and allow literature to be categorised, recognised and planned, but rather, because 'genre' inscribes the limits of the literary by representing what it is *not*. The categories of 'genre' are made unavailable by the process of writing itself, and as they disappear they are impossible to transgress. Thus from the point of view of 'genre', literary language presents itself as a barrier, since it encloses the user within its own unreadable laws and undermines the framework by which acts of intervention can be perceived.

And this is the significance, for Genette, of Thibaudet's third 'essence' in literature, 'le Livre'. 'Mais il faut savoir gré à Thibaudet de nous rappeler aussi fortement que *la littérature s'accomplit en fonction du Livre ...*', which means that 'le Livre', each work, is a new beginning in Literature, that literature is not a carefully built up category of expression and of the experience of expression; it is something the definition of which begins again with each instance of 'le Livre'.[9] The reader is invited to follow a language that builds up the text by effacing its terms of reference, and to engage with a language that creates the Book by setting up its relation to the rest of language as a pursuit and a question. Blanchot writes: 'la littérature va vers elle-même, vers son essence qui est sa disparition'.[10] He is coming to terms with the disappearance of the category 'literature' with each product of literature and contribution to it, the disappearance of the writer in every act of writing. The writer is both buried and excluded in the language that presents itself to him and through him.

2—BEING AND BLINDNESS. THEME AND IDENTITY

It was in order to approach Apollinaire's writing within these terms that I began this work with a discussion of 'L'Adieu'. My reader may have been surprised that I chose to begin with a poem that has attracted little critical attention, and that is so sparse in the textual elements that it manipulates — heather, picking, the death of autumn, memory.[11] But these four elements suggest preoccupations that are apparent throughout Apollinaire's work — not only in *Alcools*, but also in some of his more 'modernist' texts: preoccupations with death, diversity, the repercussions of expression. The sparseness of the poem, far from making it less stimulating, produces a concentration that undermines the attempt to strike an attitude in relation to the eternal experiences raised by the poem. 'L'Adieu' is unique; it evades definition, it frustrates our desire for crystallisation, even at the cost of evoking the banal and commonplace. As we saw, the absence of distinction between the identities moving in the poem contributes to creating an intransitive writing that allows Apollinaire to rework the appeal of the nostalgic mood-poem. An essential, all-pervading, diamond-hard nostalgia emerges, wiping out the past, devaluing the gestures that might bring it to life, and raising the curtain on the present. Equally, contact with the present is undermined. The specificity of 'J'ai cueilli' regresses and becomes past, re-presenting the structures in experience that have produced it and that it displaces. Contact with the present is hidden in words and is endlessly awaited. The reader is engaged in the drama of pursuing identity within the terms that make it unavailable. 'L'Adieu' is neither a farewell nor a hopeful gesture in relation to the future. The waiting incarnated by the poem is an extended moment of being and blindness.

I began this work with a discussion of 'L'Adieu' because this short poem allows us a sharp focus on the problematic status of Apollinaire's language. This enabled me to avoid doing what has often been done — discovering a thematic pattern that might tend to reduce the challenge of difference dividing one poem from others. Not that such a difference is readily available; it recedes in so far as each poem is thought of as a new beginning, a new effort to fix and draw in the relations binding memory to objects, perception to sensation, past to present. Each beginning triggers new configurations of these relations, and inaugurates new perceptions. But it has proved tempting to perceive many of the poems in *Alcools* in terms of what is perhaps its most obvious single theme: the theme of farewell, of separation, of alienation.

> Le gardien du troupeau chante tout doucement
> Tandis que lentes et meuglant les vaches abandonnent
> Pour toujours ce grand pré mal fleuri par l'automne
> ('Les Colchiques')

> Oh! l'automne l'automne a fait mourir l'été
> Dans le brouillard s'en vont deux silhouettes grises ('Automne')

> Au-dehors les années
> Regardaient la vitrine
> Les mannequins victimes
> Et passaient enchaînées ('L'Emigrant de Landor Road')

> Des enfants morts parlent parfois avec leur mère
> Et des mortes parfois voudraient bien revenir
> ...
> Puis dans le vent nous nous en retournâmes

> A nos pieds roulaient des châtaignes
> Dont les bogues étaient
> Comme le coeur blessé de la madone

> Dont on doute si elle eut la peau
> Couleur des châtaignes d'automne ('Rhénane d'automne')
>
> Une épouse me suit c'est mon ombre fatale
> Les colombes ce soir prennent leur dernier vol ('Signe')
>
> Non je ne me sens plus là
>   Moi-même
> Je suis le quinze de la
>   Onzième ('A la Santé')
>
> Passons passons puisque tout passe
> Je me retournerai souvent ('Cors de chasse')

Similarities and echoes of this kind have enabled many critics to abandon the individual text in favour of a prose-poetic, *Alcools*-in-general style of commentary that itself harbours many preconceptions about what is a suitable objective for poetry as a whole, and Apollinaire in particular:[12] 'La poésie d'Apollinaire vogue sur des images de mers, de fleuves, de ruiseaux, où l'eau reste un peu *l'eau des regrets*, puisque pareille à nous elle est l'image de la fuite'.[13] Using the well-known line from Lamartine as a point of perspective,

> Ainsi tout change, ainsi tout passe,
> Ainsi nous-mêmes nous passons
> Hélas sans laisser de trace
> Que cette barque où nous glissons
> Sur cette mer où tout s'efface.[14]

Durry begins to trace throughout the Apollinaire opus a dominant thematic structure established by the experience of transience that she isolates as the crucial element in Apollinaire's sensibility. She maintains this thematic structure through an underestimation of the difference and the difficult transition between the two poetic works *Alcools* and *Calligrammes*. Durry concludes that Apollinaire, through this transition, breaks the sound-barrier, as it were, by transforming the threat posed by transience into a positive confrontation with it — if it can be imagined that a 'positive' attitude to death in any way changes the reality of it. And in doing so, Durry is in effect obscuring the poetic dynamic Apollinaire creates in *Alcools*. She suggests that 'l'eau des regrets' is created by Apollinaire to express a kind of wandering identity that eludes itself even as attempts are made to confront it, and that this is an experience Apollinaire seeks to put behind him and to transcend. The step open to Apollinaire to achieve this, according to Durry, is to discover a solidity of identity through the realisation that transience itself is the *permanent* factor in existence: 'L'errant qui cherche et se cherche et qui se défait avant même de s'être trouvé, se saisit enfin dans sa fluidité devenue permanence comme celle de l'ombre.'[15]

What Durry claims that Apollinaire has discovered in this way is 'l'apaisement...de s'abandonner à un mouvement dans lequel rien ne bouge'.[16] A dubious desire, particularly as Durry also suggests that identity can be concretised and fixed in the words that seek to express it: '*se percevoir dans son identité* c'est moins demeurer fixe et stationnaire comme Le Pont Mirabeau, que demeurer en s'en allant, comme la Seine'.[17] Durry is defusing the complex relation between perception and the experience of self by identifying it with a 'poetic' image and a recognisably 'poetic' content. She argues that identity is open to being located and expressed by language, and that language ceases to be emphasised as a struggle with words and can be used to bring identity into contact with itself. For Durry, Apolliniare gets ever closer to such contact, and she finds support for this in the lines from 'Toujours' in the 'Case d'Armons' section of *Calligrammes*:

> Toujours
> Nous irons plus loin sans avancer jamais
>
> Et de planète en planéte
> De nébuleuse en nébuleuse
> Le don Juan des mille et trois comètes
> Même sans bouger de la terre
> Cherche les forces neuves
> Et prend au sérieux les fantômes[18]

She concludes from them that Apollinaire discovers and expresses himself as 'l'Amant de l'absolu, maître de l'espace et du temps, sans faire un pas il se meut à travers les astres chevelus, et ce qu'il possède dorénavant c'est le "Toujours"'.[19] Durry thus ensures self-protection for Apollinaire, in that she places (his) identity above and beyond any attack on its solidity and self-definition, and endows it iwth *absolute* power and mastery. Such a power would be menacing and dangerous for the rest of us were she not restricting her comments to an unexplained notion of 'poetic' experience.

Moreover, the dialectic of Apollinaire's work does not support the notion of a power to control history, and to abolish the difference between the sense of self and the response to images coming from the world. Indeed, 'Toujours' is not only constructed in expressions of power, novelty and virility. It also comes to terms with an inability to dissociate perception — the writer's reactions structured indefinitely in the past — from the images he has always 'seen', and from modes of expression that all manner of innovation seems to leave intact:

> Et tant d'univers s'oublient
> Quels sont les grands oublieurs
> Qui donc saura nous faire oublier telle ou telle pj rtie du monde
> Où est le Christophe Colomb à qui l'on devra l'oubli d'un continent
>   Perdre
> Mais perdre vraiment
> Pour laisser place à la trouvaille   (l. 9)

The creativity Apollinaire seeks is not simply to construct new languages, but an ability to forget the wealth of previous languages, and to improvise within this immense lapsus. But the 'toujours' suggests the impossibility of asserting a chosen beginning in the relations binding language, identity and the world.

>   Toujours
>   Nous irons plus loin sans avancer jamais   (l. 1)

The value of Durry's approach is her ability to trace Apollinaire's development from poem to poem, from biography to image, and from history to performance. What it fails to take account of is a poetic imagery that is not a reworking of a 'tangible' experience, aimed at establishing projected goals and desires; or an imagery that is not only aimed at producing transformed configurations of the world. The phenomenology of Apollinaire's images is abstract as well as uniquely concrete. It represents perception, the hidden structures that control what it receives, the process that creates our involvement with the present. It is not a distortion or a rewriting of experience, hovering between hallucination, the activity of the 'visionary', and projection. It is an imaginative expression that has no direct relation to objects and that does not accept that experiences can be fixed in the past, in perception or on the page. This kind of imagery is an immediate presentation, an incarnation of perception; yet it is not immediately readable. It takes shape in a moment; equally, it regresses in and as perception itself. It treads a borderline with the shapes of the present on one side, and the displacement of the past on the other.

Seen in this light, even a recurrent image is not a key to a specifiable experience, say, of time, transience or dominance. It is more an obsession, a dissolving arena within which a writer seeks to come to terms not only with certain configurations of experience or with specifiable desires, but with image as image, the familiar sense of otherness and novelty that evades encapsulation and dissolves the contours of the image even as it is composed and read. In this sense, the 'thematic' recurrence of images is not a means of establishing a directôn in writing, but part of the problem that the writing faces and creates for itself. Barthes argues that 'l'écriture est un langage durci qui vit sur lui-même et n'a nullement la charge de conférer à sa propre durée une suite mobile d'approximations, mais au contraire d'imposer, par l'unité et l'ombre de ses signes, l'image d'une parole construite bien avant d'être inventée'.[20] With every word spoken and written, we take part in social exchange, we are defined by its structures and our unquantified involvement with them. Thematic recurrences, rather than the establishing of an attitude to this mobility, intensify the confrontation with it that is the crucial experience of the *écrivain*. He seeks to invent an image of language in memory, to impose it on his audience and to involve them with it. He seeks 'new' forms to express an identity buried in the forms that already exist, 'new' forms to express the power of language displaced in its own history as 'parole'. and removed from his immediate grasp. Thus his 'écriture' is mined, undermined from within, fatally attracted to the forms of discourse from which it is under threat and whose immeasurably diverse impact he seeks to re-present and intervene in: 'ce qui oppose l'écriture à la parole, c'est que la première *paraît* toujours symbolique, introversée, tournée ostensiblement du côté d'un versant secret du langage'.[21]

Apollinaire, *écrivain*, is engaged in withdrawing from literature as a category of privileged communication, a category that fails to challenge the way in which language as such and its socio-historical forms present themselves and the experience of people. Yet the rejection of this communication does not unproblematically open out an access to an independent creativity:

> Admirez le pouvoir insigne
> Et la noblesse de la ligne:
> Elle est la voix que la lumière fit entendre
> Et dont parle Hermès Trismégiste en son Pimandre.[22]

The Orphic power brings forth a line that shapes itself to the irredeemably displaced. As Apollinaire explains in his notes following *Le Bestiaire*, it is the voice of light, incarnating psychic experience and memory, and outmanoeuvring the network of objects that make up our perceptual life in the present. But it is also an unarticulated cry: 'Bientôt, lit-on dans le *Pimandre*, descendirent des ténèbres... et il en sortit un cri inarticulé qui semblait la voix de la lumière.'[23] This combination of light and line, and including colour ('et quand la lumière s'exprime pleinement tout se colore'), invokes a paradoxical creativity.[24] This creativity is *not* separable from the continuity of colour *in* light, the involvement of seer in seeing, thinker in thought. This '*not*' binds 'la noblesse de la ligne' to the concrete, dimensionless ('inarticulé') reality of perception as it unfolds here and now. If Orpheus is the poet, then Eurydice is his own creativity, his power to give form to the unexpressed. On the brink of realising his desire to bring Eurydice into dialogue with him in the present, to recognise her as alive and his, Orpheus discovers that her presence does not identify her, she removes him from the words that bind him to her, her presence is in memory, which eludes touch and eludes dialogue.

3—THE SPECTRE OF THEMATISED EXPERIENCE REMAINS

But thematic structure remains an active notion within these poems and the responses they produce; it refuses to be dispelled. This is partly because many of these 'themes' evoke some of the major issues affecting all poets: transience, history, creativity, death.[25] Another reason is that within each poem, the 'theme', even as it dissolves as a self-contained element in the text, is itself part of the dynamic of language in which apollinaire is involved. 'Automne malade' is open to being interpreted as a poem about autumn and the nostalgia it gives rise to, rather than as a poem concerned with substitution, whether of object or theme. But at the same time, as we saw, the elements in the poem and the relation between them prevent us from visualising any particular autumn, and from accepting that the concrete impact of the poem derives from its autumnal associations alone. The end of autumn is not presented as the beginning of something else, but as a network of possible futures and images from the past. Perception and memory interpenetrate; animals and humans move in a space defined by the words and that the words fail to — refuse to — stabilise.

Although the poem opens with a direct address, the promise of an open dialogue with autumn is not kept. What is being addressed is autumn in the poem, a concentration in the writer's experience to which no specific autumn does justice, whose appeal is given no name, no place, whose significance recedes — or rather whose hold over the writer is fragmented and multiplied within the poem in the wake of the gesture of address with which it begins. Like the C of 'C'est' in 'Voyage', the metaphor of the pointed finger opens out a black hole and transforms the poem into a mobile space rich with the associations the language seeks to encompass ('richesse'), and incarnating the self-emptying of the writer ('blancheur').

> Automne malade et adoré
> Tu mourras quand l'ouragan soufflera dans les roseraies

As we saw, the internal conflicts in the opening 'address', like others in the poem, dispel particular autumns and focus our attention on the language, the abstract movement the reading triggers — on language as language. Equally, to point the finger at language is once again to 'indicate' a space that withdraws and cannot be said to incorporate experiences and memories. We know that the final lines of the poem mark language and undermine our identification with it: transience is incarnated in its failure to be assimilated in the language that gives it form, and in the fact that language substitutes itself for transience and the sense of self in time. In 'Automne malade', Apollinaire hardens his language (Barthes's 'un langage durci'); it withdraws its feelers into the world outside it, it sequesters itself and us with it in its privacy and our own. Since the poem substitutes itself for the configurations that prompt it, it is driven by something *not* contained in the language or in language, but by something in the 'space' around language, displaced and secluded. The urgency of this experience is intensified by the hardness of the poetic language that exludes it, and that gives it form in a realm of difference and otherness. The abstract qualities of the verse, its efforts to mould itself to the shapes of perception and memory, do not defuse its melancholia, but intensify it. The sense of depression and loneliness that comes out of the poem from all angles *is* the privacy it represents, and that it obliterates by transforming it into the text we read, gambling with communication and approximation.

And the 'I' in the poem is vestigial:

> Et que j'aime ô saison que j'aime tes rumeurs

— swallowed in the 'object' of his love, in the language that emerges in the wake of his absence. The 'je' is 'un cri inarticulé', both within the signified that gives it a context ('rumeurs'), and in terms of the signifiers that take its place in the text. The 'I' *is* the forms invented for it by the poet, and the 'light' they cast. The expressive power of this 'light' relies on the independence it creates, the anti-mimetic hardness of the poem, which also inaugurates a struggle for dialogue. This brings us back to 'nostalgia'. Apollinaire's approach to it is a galvanised one that invites us to pursue, or even to invent, our own sense of self, of difference *in* language and in relation to it. But difference is by turns discovered, threatened, and threatening. Involvement in perceptual and reading forms, and alienation from them, displace each other continually:

Soleil cou coupé

One of the processes that Apollinaire's poems initiate is, then, a potentially liberating one for us as readers; but this process is not unproblematic. It moves from thematic readability to abstract reading forms that yield the mobility of perception in so far as they displace it, and it then returns to the impact of appearance itself. The final lines of 'Rhénane d'automne' involve us in this process once again, and bring the third element of appearance sharply into play. This time the 'themes' involved are not only transience and nostalgia, but death, loss and the Christian mythology:[26]

> Oh! je ne veux pas que tu sortes
> L'automne est plein de mains coupées
> Non non ce sont des feuilles mortes
> Ce sont les mains des chères mortes
> Ce sont tes main coupées
>
> Nous avons tant pleuré aujourd'hui
> Avec ces morts leurs enfants et les vieilles femmes
> Sous le ciel sans soleil
> Au cimetière plein de flammes
>
> Puis dans le vent nous nous en retournâmes
>
> A nos pieds roulaient des châtaignes
> Dont les bogues étaient
> Comme le coeur blessé de la madone
> Dont on doute si elle eut la peau
> Couleur des châtaignes d'automne   (l. 38)

How does Apollinaire introduce the Madonna, and what does he tell us about her? What does the Christian reference tell us about Apollinaire's attitude to his own poem and to language? The Madonna's wounded or bleeding heart, along with the fairy-tale fantasy aspects of the poem as a whole, suggest childhood superstitions rather than Christian complexities: the mysterious beyond, the promise of indefinite contact with friends and relations from all generations. But the fantasy element in the poem, like the one in 'La Maison des morts', also suggests a more ambitious poetic project: an Orphic contact with the underworld, a power to resuscitate decaying modes of expression and to bring to life hidden concentrations of poetic potential.[27] Thus the Madonna's wound, *via* the spiky chestnut husks in the last stanza, links up with the crown of thorns, the crucifixion of God on earth and the pursuit of immortality.

But the bleeding heart of the Madonna ('le coeur blessé de la madone') is also a broken heart, a broken love affair, a broken mythology, a lost contact between devotion and the object of devotion. The curtain is raised on a world where sacrifice expresses the terms of existence rather than its transformation or the realisation of desires. The Madonna's wound can only be understood in terms of her presence in the poem: she is divorced from the symbolism by which she transcends the diversity of circumstance. She is transformed every time she occurs in experience, and one such occasion is the poem itself. Within the poem, the concrete sensations that bring her into the thoughts of the author-persona fail to define her, the links between the two are unspecified, their expressiveness is not identified with, and it is this sense of doubt that keeps the poem open to further and still further readings:

> . . . le coeur blessé de la madone
> Dont on doute si elle eut la peau
> Couleur des châtaignes d'automne

The Madonna is involved in a circular linguistic structure that creates no distinction between the terms in which she is introduced ('les bogues des châtaignes') and the terms in which she might be interpreted ('la couleur des châtaignes d'automne'). The associations linked with her find no form other than appearance or an arbitrarily charged sensation, where familiarity and otherness are indistinguishable: 'A nos pieds roulaient des châtaignes'. Purification by fire, or an intensification of physical existence — 'Au cimetière plein de flammes' — do not provide the poetic heroism that liberates us from the material, the circumstantial and the way they appear. In fact it is the raw material of perception that Apollinaire delves into here, the silent voice of reading in which the concrete and the imaginary intermesh and where interpretation adds to the texture of the images it confronts. Despite the voice it gives to departed beings, the poem ends by representing an involvement *in* experience that is tantamount to alienation, to a passive consumption of transience and a silent admiration of its diversity: 'Puis dans le vent nous nous en retournâmes'. The image of ourselves that Apollinaire holds up is not an image of lost identity, the power of the material over our creative potential. It is an image of the inaccessibility of identity, in language and around it; it is an image of identity fragmented as appearance, of the wound of alienation in relation to perception, reading and the world: 'Ce sont tes mains coupées'.[28]

4—ALIENATION AND RESISTANCE

The paradox of alienation and involvement in relation to the text is explored by Blanchot in the section of Le Livre à venir entitled 'La Disparition de la littérature'.[29] Blanchot begins by locating the artist in terms of his (the artist's) sense of his own irrelevance in relation to the radical new demands made by a world in progress — a question Apollinaire addressed himself to from 1908 on. Blanchot describes an awareness that art may no longer be the form in which the great chapters in human endeavour are written. Art gives way to action and to fulfilment within the historical process.[30] But Blanchot goes on to argue that this situation is not simply a function of the artist in the 'modern' world, but a function of the artist's relation to his work. It is the critics who are surprised by the poet's rejection of the poet-hero role. The poet himself, while not withdrawing from the transformation — the radicalisation — of the world, is concerned with his own activity as something that expresses and even re-presents ('accomplit') the relations that produce it. And these relations, in Blanchot's thinking, precede — are dimensionlessly anterior to — the part they play in historical development; they precede their ossification in the mobile approximations of social exchange. The artist searches for the source of his own work: 'l'étrange mouvement qui va de l'oeuvre vers l'origine de l'oeuvre, l'oeuvre elle-même devenue la recherche inquiète et infinie de sa source'.[31] The artist seeks the source of his motivation to write and of his relation to language. But the work itself is the barrier that abolishes the source of the work by incarnating it; the work fixes the relations that produce it, if only because of the activity of critics. There is no source other than the relations in the text, which remains an object that is read, however much it withdraws from the anecdotes of literary history. Thus what we may call an alienating unity emerges between the work and its 'source', producing the text and assimilating identity itself.

Apollinaire's 'Automne' is a good example of this 'unity': it expresses a process by which the text attempts to break loose from its forms, its reading, the barrier to its 'source' that it sets up.[32] This 'unity' is quite different from the appearance of unity established by a concentration on the thematic coherence of *Alcools*. Thematic unity turns out to construct a mirage of heroic self-expression, an illusion of self discovered and established in expression. The peasant in 'Automne', who moves in as obsessional an autumnal atmosphere as the diverse and dissolving figures in 'Rhénane d'automne', is dissociated from this mirage through a song of infidelity, a broken ring and a broken contract.

But his dissociation is itself a nostalgic one, and 'Automne' remains a poem with the recognisable features of a poem about autumn, just as 'Automne malade' does, and just as Apollinaire's writing, from the earliest to the latest, continues to present itself as having 'themes'. In 'Automne' the presence of the theme of 'autumn', the interplay of unity and diversity with which it presents the world, constitute the air writer and reader breathe in the poem.

> Et s'en allant là-bas le paysan chantonne
> Une chanson d'amour et d'infidélité
> Qui parle d'une bague et d'un coeur que l'on brise   (l. 4)

The peasant's song, even though it dismantles collaboration with a theme-myth and expresses the peasant's alienation, is written in the language of the poem, the language we so freely and blandly recognise as thematic and autumnal. The peasant's broken ring and flowing infidelity are the image of his identity-in-difference. But to break the contract that places the peasant in the employ of the autumnal, nostalgic view of disillusion and frustration is to dismantle the language that gives rise to this sense of difference — the only language available, at this point, with which to represent alienation, and to mark the beginning of an (other) awareness of it. The terms of the peasant's contract within the language of the poem allow his identity-in-alienation to be expressed and recognised. The flowing melody of infidelity breaks the peasant's service to frozen relations and fixed characteristics, but it binds him to them as well. The image of his existence and its 'source' is both pursued and fragmented, and as the peasant moves away from the poem, this image begins to emerge around the poem and from its depth; simultaneously, it is sequestered and buried in the restricted, autumnal resonances of the language:

> Oh! l'automne l'automne a fait mourir l'été
> Dans le brouillard s'en vont deux silhouettes grises   (1.7)

Thus these 'thematic', 'autumnal' points of view are tyrannical. They assert a tyranny of the point of view that can only be overthrown in modes of expression that are associated with it and that cannot evade upholding it. The poet's privileged and visionary powers are undermined. Similarly, for the Cubist painter, the object remains in the picture, however vestigially and conceptually, within the process and the product aimed at sweeping aside dominance of the object in perception. Nostalgia in *Alcools* is an expression of an inability to absorb without losing the perceptions that define identity and bring it into being. It is a lament, a lament over the fact that language is only language and has lost the Orphic powers it once had:

> J'ai eu le courage de regarder en arrière

Here, 'Les Fiançailles' does not mean what it says, it cannot contain the desires it projects. Apollinaire does not gain a hindsight that absorbs experience and constitutes identity as a subject, nor does he assume the lyre of Orpheus and breathe air into the silenced voices of poetry. Neither can he achieve what even Orpheus could not: to bring Eurydice back to life along with all the hidden structures of obsession and expressiveness that structure identity in the past. The 'je' is not at the centre of an experience that belongs to it, that it can define in language and that it controls. The backward look is belied in the writing of the sentence and abolished in its reading. The 'I' so majestically asserted in the sentence is exploded by the time the section draws to a close. Having invented a moment in time where he imagines he can look back and discover the subject in his experience, Apollinaire rewrites that moment as though it had never existed, as though the gesture of discovery were still to be made, and as though language were still to be used:

> Et les roses de l'électricité s'ouvrent encore
> Dans le jardin de ma mémoire   (1.47)

Conversely, Apollinaire here has kept his creativity alive. The dissolution of focus and domination in the continuity of perception and image *is* the experience of language and of history. Apollinaire's efforts to bring lyric poetry into the twentieth century are not based on a desire to place his own 'poetic' experience at the centre of the world. By confronting alienation and difference, he begins to resist

— and his targets are perspective and the illusion of detachment from history.

> Et l'on tissait dans sa mémoire
> Une tapisserie sans fin
> Qui figurait son histoire

'L'Emigrant de Landor Road' achieves a level of lyrical storytelling that embeds the circle of alienation, perspective and the sense of self in the intensely painful experiences we all know and fear.[33] The poem is both intimate and intimidating. Intimidating, because it seems to be aimed at no reader, it offers no context of response, change or liberation; attitudes and positions dissolve, the reader is swallowed in a massive decay of powers of ubiquity:

> Des cadavres de jours rongés par les étoiles
> Parmi le bruit des flots et des derniers serments   (1. 52)

But on the other hand, the headless mannequins (1. 13), the droves of shadows lingering listlessly (1. 6), the hands holding light that are transformed into birds in the sky (1. 7), all the silenced bric-à-brac of the tailor/'brocanteur' along with the incarnations of unpredictable turn-abouts in memory, even the cliché of the tapestry of life — all these create an 'image' with which we cannot identify but with which we do. It is an image of dispossession implanted in everything we see, encounter and interpret; it both triggers and represents a seamless flow of otherness that germinates in the dimensionless arena of perception. It is an image woven by others that takes us in; it has no outlines along which the words 'theirs' and 'mine' would gather significance. But it is an image that Apollinaire has imagined, it 'rivalises' with the sourceless image of anxiety, desire, the sense of self and other ('sa mémoire'). In language, the image hangs on to the creativity undermined in language; it represents and resists.

5—DOMINANCE?

Language does not explain the world, it is a product of the world; we do not control the links binding us to the world and to language, we are overrun by them. The moment or the process of expression both incarnates these links and their control of us, and wipes them from view and from appropriation. This was the relevance of my reference, during the course of my reading of 'Automne malade', to Barthes's notion of intransitive writing:

> Or cette parole est une matière (infiniment) travaillée; elle est un peu comme une sur-parole, le réel ne lui est jamais qu'un prétexte (pour l'écrivain, *écrire* est un verbe intransitif); il s'ensuit qu'elle ne peut jamais expliquer le monde, ou du moins lorsqu'elle feint de l'expliquer, ce n'est que pour en mieux reculer l'ambiguïté: l'explication fixée dans une *oeuvre* (travaillée), elle devient immédiatement un produit ambigu du réel, auquel elle est liée *avec distance*....[34]

The world and the historical moment are a pretext for the writer's exploration of them and of his own experience in language; these dimensionless relations are the 'pre-text' the *écrivain* seeks to represent his involvement with, for it is through these relations that his identity comes to life in an interplay of history and perception. But in writing, the *écrivain* fails to encompass these relations and his own identity within them; for the pre-text is articulated as text, it *is* the text. The *écrivain*'s language produces images of perception that displace it, and the images draw us in and abolish their relation to others ('un langage durci'). The *écrivain*'s writing is 'un produit ambigu du réel', because his exploration of the involvement of his language with the world is both placed and displaced *in* the process of writing and *reading*. The *écrivain*'s writing challenges the values of the social moment, but it is drawn into them by the fact that it is read and interpreted. Intransitive writing, while seeking to challenge the values of the moment, is a product of them in so far as it seeks to represent its involvement with them, which is yet to be appropriated and yet to acquire form. The relations that contextualise experience and establish identity remain *hidden* — and it is this that intransitive writing confronts.

Thus the identity of the writer is experienced as a lack. A writer obsessed with experience as it is discovered in language is faced with a choice. Does he continue to represent intransitively the terms of identity-as-lack, or does he seek to wall in this lack, to transcend and dominate it? Moreover, how important is such a distinction in our appreciation of poets and poetry? Certainly the relation of past to present, transience to mastery, decay to novelty are crucial to an understanding of the transition from *Alcools* to *Calligrammes*, and it is in terms of these concepts or themes that Jean-Pierre Richard approaches the experience of lack in Apollinaire's work. Richard's account of Apollinaire's development in 'Etoiles chez Apollinaire' is instructive.[35] Within what he himself terms 'le lié lyrique' of *Alcools* in particular, he is able to isolate images one from another and in so doing, to attribute mythological significance to them. His aim is not simply to indicate the 'themes' informing Apollinaire's poetry, but to evoke the implicit impulses and desires they contain. The initial structure he perceives is a structure of stellar nostalgia, voluptuous tenderness and betrayal, transience and lack:

> Ainsi se construit une première constellation rêveuse: étoile, chair infidèle, ruisseau lointain, nudité, eau lactée, nuit maternelle, jours anciens, grelottement, tremblement y forment un réseau ambigu de la volupté et de l'absence. A travers leurs échos et leurs rapports s'indique une certaine idée de la solitude humaine. Sans déchirure aucune — ce qui permet le développement mélodique, le lié lyrique du langage — l'être s'y trahit d'abord comme *défaut*.[36]

The themes of drunkenness and erotic effervescence combine in Richard's reading of Apollinaire's early poetic experience with a maternal, fluid and yielding intimacy. But this state of being borders on melancholia, although, for Richard, its feminine, carnal fluidity opens out receptiveness in the poet; he has no power over transience and betrayal. Richard looks to the 1907–8 poems to uncover the textuality of Apollinaire's desire for an independent creative power — or the phenomenology of his desire for one:

> Ainsi se construit un deuxième régime de l'image: liée au soleil (et non plus à la lune), au futur (et non plus au passé), à la virilité (et non plus à la fémininité), à l'exaltation d'un moi qui s'élance hors de lui-même par secousse, par flamme, par éclats (loin de toute fluidité), l'étoile est l'une des réalités sensibles où s'investit avec le plus de force le rêve apollinarien de créativité absolue; elle supporte pleinement le projet d'une illumination, d'une *annexion totale des choses par l'esprit*.[37]

Richard's writing invites us to respond to Apollinaire's work on a variety of different levels: we think of the nature of poetry generally, of other individual poets and their purpose, as well as what psychoanalysis can tell us about sensation and desire. Yet his analysis seems guided by a single crucial motive. Richard clearly believes that Apollinaire's experience of language culminates in an apotheosis of self-expression. For Richard, Apollinaire's desire is for a heroic language capable of manipulating his experience at will and transcending representation.

Richard recognises that these poetic ambitions, the sense of poetic power that he sees developing in Apollinaire's work, cannot be directed at the social world we inhabit. The poetic and the historical are different orders of experience. Apollinaire as cosmic stage-manager is, for

Richard, an expression of imaginative capacities and desires: '...il est le metteur en scène des drames de l'espace.... Mais attention: cet engagement reste tout intérieur, mental, il n'implique aucune démarche réelle, il exclut toute activité physique....'[38] Yet, to an important extent, any act of writing is different from physical actions, whether it is 'about' such actions or not. To circumscribe imaginative experience in this way is to leave unanswered the question of how a writer's desires in language relate to his sense of self and his desires in relation to others. Moreover, Richard himself links imaginative to concrete experience in a way which, disturbingly, seems to remove from the latter any element of threat or danger: 'Si bien que le projet poétique d'Apollinaire semble très exactement s'accomplir au moment où l'éclat d'obus vient frapper sa tempe, creusant dans sa tête "ce trou presque mortel et qui s'est étoilé"'.[39] Once again, Richard is dealing with imagined capacities, and with Apollinaire's 'Tristesse d'une étoile' in particular.[40] But to establish such a framework and to work within it leaves the way open to asserting that poetic/imaginary dominance includes the material, political moment and encompasses it in a poetic act of will. Indeed Richard goes on to respond to the war poems as a whole in terms of an interpenetration of poetic achievement and national, historical fulfilment. Apollinaire's writing at this stage is 'une activité chargée d'accoucher à la fois la victoire et l'avenir'. The equivalence is developed still further: 'Apollinaire...regroupe...les thèmes de l'étoile, de l'artillerie, du futur, de la créativité géniale sous une seule mythologie professée de la *fécondité*.'[41]

Thus for Richard, a poetic identity overrun by transience, tenderness and betrayal is solidified in Apollinaire's work in an indefinite broadening of creative power. This power not only spans the destructive and the fertile, it is equal to the immensity of political and historical events. Creative imagination is able to impose its own mythologies and, in Richard's reading of the Apollinairian desire, to assert an impregnable, quasi-Futurist mobility and independence provided by images and the manipulation of them. Lack is transcended by transfiguring images into myths in this way, and by developing a mythology of the image as such. In effect, in Richard's perception, Apollinaire achieves the impossible: his desire is to create an absolute equivalence between signifier and signified, and to create an imaged language that, in a recast, re-imagined world, realises and enacts what it refers to.

> Un Icare tente de s'élever jusqu'à chacun de mes yeux
> Et porteur de deux soleils je brûle au centre de deux nébuleuses

Where we saw eroded lines of perspective involving an eroded focus on identity itself, Richard interprets these lines from 'Les Fiançailles' as a focus *on* identity, a creative embracing of identity that removes it from the tangible and the circumstantial, and gives it a cosmic independence and grandeur: 'Le moi y est focal par rapport aux nébuleuses, c'est vers lui que se dirige l'effort icaréen de découverte, c'est de son embrasement que procède le feu stellaire....'[42] This Richard-Apollinaire perception gives rise to a mythology of dominance that breaks loose from imagination and encompasses the world: 'Ces étoiles allumées au ciel à coups de canon, ce sont ainsi les nouveau-nés, les enfants, les futurs petits hommes que le pansexualisme apollinarien convie tous les français à mettre au monde.'[43]

6—DOMINANCE AND TRANSPARENCY

The aspiration to such ubiquitous power may strike us as naive. Control of the world through images as such, and images of violence in particular, might appear illusory, and its pursuit both insensitive and reckless. But Richard may be justified in his assessment of an Apollinairian pursuit of (poetic) virility and omnipotence. We might respond to Richard's indication that Apollinaire seeks to marry war with non-war as highlighting the potential oppressiveness of Apollinaire's poetic ambitions.[44] The attempted abolition of the barrier between signifier and signified might be an integral part of the unique sense of poetic freedom that emanates increasingly from Apollinaire's language, which we would therefore need to approach with increasing caution. We would want to be suspicious of any suggestion that the power to create new forms implied an impulsive disregard for the relationship binding images to individual existences and to history.

Certainly, it is impossible to ignore that Apollinaire poems exist that are difficult to read other than as attempts to establish dominance, whether real or imaginary:

> Je lègue à l'avenir l'histoire de Guillaume Apollinaire
> Qui fut à la guerre et sut être partout
> Dans les villes heureuses de l'arrière
> Dans tout le reste de l'univers
> Dans ceux qui meurent en piétinant dans le barbelé
> Dans les femmes dans les canons dans les chevaux
> Au zénith au nadir aux 4 points cardinaux
> Et dans l'unique ardeur de cette veillée d'armes[45]

214

Here, Apollinaire seems to render inert the equation that brings together language, sexuality and identity, and to present it as resolved. The language of 'Merveille de la guerre' presents itself as an atemporal, acontextual texture in terms of which Apollinaire induces a vision of himself and his name in a future that is in fact an expanded, hyper-responsive present. This future is seen as transcending history, as an endless affirmation of the world, regardless of whether the 'world' is death, dying soldiers, or of whether this hyper-sexualisation of the world is in effect the abolition of any difference between women, cannons and the phallus. This affirmation depends on conveniently, even suicidally, failing to distinguish between the fact that the world presents itself in terms of images, and the fact that images can be the weapon by which history is distorted and the present manipulated. 'Merveille de la guerre' is an 'aesthetification' of the realities of oppression. It is a poem in which the dissolution of an attitude to alienation is experienced as poetic fulfilment, and in which the pursuit of liberation through a poetic confrontation with history and politics is superseded by a merely linguistic transformation of oppression into images of liberation.

To what extent do we need to think of 'Merveille de la guerre' as exemplifying all the poems Apollinaire wrote as a soldier? Are they all expressions of a desire for power, for a wilful suppression of difference and the constrictions of circumstance? Should we think that Apollinaire's pre-war desire for a unified modernism is satisfied by his experience of war and the diverse and explosive images it produces? Certainly, 'Merveille de la guerre' is not the only poem in *Calligrammes* that expresses enthusiasm for the images of war, the prospect of war, and the incarnation of 'le nouveau' that it purports to offer. 'La Petite Auto' begins by depicting Apollinaire's sudden return from Deauville on hearing of the outbreak of war.[46] But the text quickly dissolves its own anecdotal element within the sense of the immanence of war and of a productive and expansive experience associated with it. For all its jagged, unpredictable intransitivity,[47] the poem presents the future in terms of an expectation of supremacy and an indefinitely extendable identity:

Je m'en allais portant en moi toutes ces armées qui se battaient
...
Hauteurs inimaginables où l'homme combat
Plus haut que l'aigle ne plane
L'homme y combat contre l'homme

215

> Et descend tout à coup comme une étoile filante
> Je sentais en moi des êtres neufs pleins de dextérité
> Bâtir et aussi agencer un univers nouveau   (l. 12, l. 21)

Nor is 'Merveille de la guerre' the only poem in *Calligrammes* to equate the existence of a soldier with the prospect of sexual satisfaction, or to equate women with the instruments of war:

> La boucle des cheveux noirs de ta nuque est mon trésor
> Ma pensée te rejoint et la tienne la croise
> Tes seins sont les seuls obus que j'aime
> Ton souvenir est la lanterne de repérage qui nous sert à pointer la nuit
>
> En voyant la large croupe de mon cheval j'ai pensé à tes hanches[48]

Not the least striking aspect of this writing from 'Merveille de la guerre', 'La Petite Auto' and 'Fusée' is the experience of unambiguous transparency it puts on display. We are left in no doubt about the experience Apollinaire is referring to. Objects remind us of a lover's body; with Apollinaire, we think of situations that emphasise a lover's absence; we recognise the ideal of heroism; we imagine scenarios of passionate activity and historical significance, and we become involved as spectators and even leading protagonists in upheavals that are both imagined and concrete. Images of war are presented as snatches from a consistently optimistic, improvisatory and ludic experience of war itself. This textual transparency is striking in relation to *Alcools*, where acts of expression are often juxtaposed with the unreadably obscure; complex allusions make history impenetrable, and, as we saw, the present is displaced as expression. 'Les Fenêtres' also steers us into the indecipherable, but the structure of its composition, in common with that of the poems we are looking at now, also suggests an expansive, all-inclusive overview that makes experience open to assimilation, readable and transparent. It appears that the development of this transparency is taken further in Apollinaire's war poems, and that they acquire the power to move at will from concrete to imaginary, experience to creativity, image to myth.

It is, then, Apollinaire's own effort to 'simplifier la syntaxe poétique', to extend the range of stimuli available to his reader and to himself as he writes, that is here again under scrutiny. But the writing in *Calligrammes*, pre-war or not, does not merely de-emphasise writing itself in relation to the 'shared' experiences it directs us at. It also confronts the reader with transparency as such. The transparency created in the service of affirmation and the fabrication of a responsive and dominated

216

world turns out to give 'form' to an irony at the heart of illusion: it *is* the way it appears to be. The artifice of the images and the mobility with which they respond to the diversity they themselves evoke transform the text into a network of image as such ('image'), which acts on us as appearance itself ('une beauté qui s'offre et qui s'évanouit aussitôt').[49] Perception itself is represented, the mobility of image in the text is the mobility itself of eye and mind across surfaces. Eyes and looks are everywhere in the opening lines of 'Merveille de la guerre'; interpretation and evaluation are removed in the silent voice of reading:

Que c'est beau ces fusées qui illuminent la nuit
Elles montent sur leur propre cime et se penchent pour regarder
Ce sont des dames qui dansent avec leurs regards pour bras et coeurs   (l. 1)

Equally, the perceiver loses his contours, experience is not dialogue with itself, contexts are not discovered. Artifice controlled by the author turns into the illusion that the world and the structures of our response are revealed in the immediacy of an image or of a graceful movement. It is this illusion that the transparency of these texts confronts. Having provided the affirmation of a ubiquitous perception with 'form', transparency turns out to be a 'context' of alienation:' from A to B and back again'; from the desire to establish identity in extended image, to the invisibility of identity; image as the receptacle for psychic shocks, to image as the 'source' of alienation.[50]

Writing that spans these two forms of transparency, and the displacement of one in the other, is produced by Apollinaire in 'Il y a' and 'Du Coton dans les oreilles'.[51] In 'Il y a' each line, apart from the last two, begins with the demonstrative phrase 'il y a', giving the poem the appearance of a series of affirmative statements about the world, a web of explosive, cultural, erotic and war stimuli. But at the same time, the repeated demonstrative gestures preclude any difference of emphasis between them, so that the writer's experience of the poem, and the reader's, is defined in equal terms and with equal emphasis by each one. Identity is dismembered, displaced from the centre of command; with each line, the simultaneity of the language reinstates the search for an attitude, and the desire to distinguish perception from passivity. The variety of configurations created by the juxtapositions ensures that shocks to psychic experience are enjoyed if not encompassed, until the overload produces a melting of all contours in the poem and an invisibility emerges, the transparency of pure perception, pure alienation. *Via* Eastern mysticism and military camouflage, the poetic identity is re-formed as nostalgia for itself and for lost friends:

Ils pensent avec mélancolie à ceux dont ils se demandent s'il les
 reverront
Car ils ont poussé très loin durant cette guerre l'art de l'invisibilité   (1. 29)

The calligraphy of 'Du Coton dans les oreilles' is equally ambiguous.
It might be read, along with the pre-war ideograms, as an attempt to
encapsulate the fleeting and explosive transience characteristic of much
intense experience, and perhaps of war experience in particular.[52] All
notional sense of perspective is abandoned, the page is opened out and
provides Apollinaire with the arena in which to meet the arbitrary
variety of a world in complete upheaval. Even the curiously inappropriate flippancy in the poem as a whole seems to give the writing
persona a sense of keeping up with the pace:

> Tant et tant de coquelicots
> D'où tant de sang a-t-il coulé
> Qu'est-ce qu'il se met dans le coco
> Bon sang de bois il s'est saoulé
> Et sans pinard et sans tacot
> Avec de l'eau
> Allô la truie[53]

In the calligraphic opening, the word 'vif' explodes from the page and
the linear ordering of words in a sentence is disrupted and made to look
like the débris of a sentence thrown through the air. The megaphone
amplifying its orders above the din of shattering fragments and falling
shells is emphasised by being addressed as well as by being given the
shape of a megaphone and having the letters that spell it tear across
the page with the intensity of an explosion or of the letters 'vif'. In
effect, neither the writing nor the experience it opens itself out to is
unproblematic. The expectation that the immediate, readable transparency of the poem provides the writer with control over images and
events coming at him is undermined by the writing itself, which demands that the relations between identity and experience be constantly
re-evaluated, redrawn and reread. The transparent writing effaces any
dominant angle of reflection along its path, and the fragmentation of
moments of recognition turns the page into a texture of alienation. The
transparency of the text not only makes indefinite diversity readable,
it also emhasises the writing for what it is: writing. In this way it
re-presents the experience of *attempting* to keep up with images. The
rhetorically addressed megaphone, 'O mégaphone', the voice of command, does not create a demonstrable perspective, vocal or written,
that would provide what is happening on the page with a consumable

form or direction. More than anything else, the megaphone is a letter — 'O' or 'Omega' — it triggers as well as represents the transparent effacement of identity *in* experience and *in* language. And the letter/phrase 'Omega'/'O mégaphone' is in fact a calligraphic construction of gradual disappearance, and the entire page is dominated by a literal question mark.

7—FUTURISM AND ORPHISM. 'GUILLAUME APOLLINAIRE'

An answer to the problem posed by the war poems seems, then, in sight. It appears that we need no think of them exclusively as a collaboration with the images of oppression, embarked on in order to buy mastery and dominance from the manifestations of oppression. They do not confuse liberation with tyranny. We can regard such criticism as illusory, in the same way as we are suspicious of Durry's and also Richard's contention that Apollinaire's war writing is a successful attempt to separate experience from memory, to conquer transience and initiate the future. We can forget the disquietingly inappropriate language of 'Merveille de la guerre' and 'La Petite Auto', and suggest that the overall purpose behind the war poems is to effect a further step in the shift away from lyrical appreciations of lack to a representation of access to identity barred in the self-evident clarity in which the present is experienced. War, by an accident of history, happens to be the circumstance that coincides with this stage in Apollinaire's development. Moreover, Margaret Davies and others have pointed out the difficulty of dissociating oneself from the nationalist fervour that swept over Europe on both sides of the confrontation leading to the Great War. Apollinaire especially would have been anxious to become involved with this fervour and to justify conclusively his claim to being legally and respectably French, rather than an illegitimate Pole.[54]

But the problem refuses to go away. Is Apollinaire in control of the illusion of transparency, or is he exploited by it, and thus exploiting his readers? Raymond Jean suggests the latter. In his section on Apollinaire in *La Poétique du désir*, he argues that Apollinaire's writing in *Alcools* as well as in *Calligrammes* represents an inability to confront the involvement of existence in history, and of identity in the political structuring of society.[55] He argues that this is not only discernible in what he regards as Apollinaire's enthusiastic attraction to the experience of war, but also in the continuous references in *Alcools* to exile.

For Jean, Apollinaire's use of the language of exile means that, from its very beginnings onwards, Apollinaire's writing is not concerned with bringing lyric poetry into the modern generation, in the sense of confronting the socio-historical dynamics of language and identity. For Jean, Apollinaire's obsession with exile, and correspondingly, with cosmopolitanism, is indicative of a writing that expresses what Jean sees as a politically self-destructive desire to reify identity in a rejuvenated vision of the power and intensity of nationalism:

> Or, ce cosmopolitanisme dans lequel on l'enferme, Apollinaire ne le récuse pas. Il l'assume au contraire avec une extrême complaisance. Il entre dans le jeu de l'exotisme qui lui est assigné et peuple ses poèmes comme ses récits de toute une mythologie de tziganes, bohémiens, allemands, juifs, cosaques, etc., à laquelle il intègre ses propres fantasmes généalogiques, prenant en charge dans son oeuvre toutes les formes de ce que Barrès appelle à la même époque le *déracinement* et développant une 'contre-idéologie' poétique qui s'oppose moins à l'idéologie nationaliste dominante d'alors qu'elle n'en est le reflet renversé.[56]

What Jean finds disturbing in Apollinaire's writing is that, by not confronting the process by which ideology structures the present, it actually obscures and mystifies the action of ideology, and that it acquiesces to the interests of that ideology: 'Ainsi, le discours cosmopolite repris par Apollinaire à son époque, devient 'générateur' d'un langage nouveau et reste lisible dans l'oeuvre au moment même où il cesse d'y être idéologiquement déchiffrable.'[57]

Just as Apollinaire's familiarity in his writing with the imagery of exiles and outcasts is supported by an ideology of nationalist fervour and aggression, so his pursuit of 'modernism' is responded to by Jean as an illusory liberation, a barring of access to the terms that make up the present. For Jean, the Futurist anti-aesthetic forms the basis of Apollinaire's 'new' approach to the present. In his view, the Futurist elements that begin to appear in Apollinaire's language and in his thinking about language are an expression of an overall Apollinairian desire to suppress history in language: Apollinaire's eulogy of Futurism, *L'Antitradition futuriste*, cannot be regarded as a sudden or isolated dramatic change in Apollinaire's approach to expression, but rather as an attitude that represents a structuring element in the whole of the writing: 'il s'agit de la production d'une *forme-sens* dont les manifestations traversent l'oeuvre toute entière'.[58] With implicit references to Merlin the 'enchanteur', *L'Esprit nouveau et les poètes* and 'Sur les Collines', Jean describes the involvement of Apollinaire's writing with Futurist thinking in these terms:

La notion d'*antitradition* s'appuie chez lui sur la conscience effectivement 'prémonitoire' d'un art capable de faire 'flamber l'avenir' et 'apparaître le temps de la magie', surgir des 'milliards de prodiges' et la 'grande force' du désir, en tirant des *moteurs* nouveaux du double mouvement de *destruction* et de *construction* qui est (avec la violence), celui même de l'histoire et de la civilisation de son temps. C'est, à la limite, une idéologie de la *suppression de l'histoire* (ce qui est dit en toutes lettres dans le Manifeste-synthèse de l'*Antitradition futuriste*), au profit d'une inscription systématique sur la page ainsi laissée blanche de tous les *signes* 'des grandes explosions imminentes'.[59]

Of course, there are many indications that by the time war broke out, Apollinaire had already tempered his enthusiasm for the Futurist approach. In the February 1914 issue of *Les Soirée de Paris*, he levels the same charges at Futurist writing as had been levelled at Impressionist painting, namely, that for all its attacks on conventional rhetorical and typographic innovations, it fails to make a definitive break from a mimetic, subservient approach to the concrete world: 'Les mots en liberté de Marinetti amènent un renouvellement de la description et à ce titre ils ont de l'importance, ils amènent également un retour offensif de la description et ainsi ils sont didactiques et anti-lyriques.'[60]

Nevertheless, the ludic theatricality of a poem such as 'A l'Italie',[61] with its exhortations to further aggression and increased nationalist fervour, is reminiscent of the performances dramatising war that Marinetti staged in London with much notorious popularity.[62] We need only to compare such an approach to the Vorticist account of the machine, and the machinery of war, and to think of the Vorticist exposure of the politics of war in *Blast*, to wonder whether the creative perusal, the creative encompassing of experience that Apollinaire seems to attempt in his later writing, is not itself manipulated by images, and by a failure to grasp the significance of the events in the history that he, Apollinaire, was living through.[63]

The argument that Futurism is the crucial element behind Apollinaire's poetic purpose in the direction from *Alcools* through to *Calligrammes* is an important one. It is impossible to ignore the view that Apollinaire's writing in *Alcools* expresses alienation and the unbuilding of identity in language and in memory, whereas the war writing attempts to 'transcend' alienation by transforming images of destruction, image itself, into the material of creative construction. We ignore Jean's argument at the risk of abdicating our own right as readers to pursue dialogue even in the context of its suppression, and at the risk of undermining our capacity to question what the world has to offer and what language presents us with. The Futurist mythology is one that needs to be resisted. Jean's argument is attractive in that it exposes the naïvety of any project seeking to use language to transcend time, to divorce experience from memory. We need to be suspicious of any project that attempts to equate language with experience rather than to represent the displacement that language exemplifies and fails to encompass. Jean's critique is valuable in that it approaches language in terms of a confrontation with an absolute difference, for if we accept this critique, we accept that the difference between language (over which we seek to gain control) and experience (which we seek to analyse and formulate) is the object of a constant pursuit, and that its inaccessibility is that of identity itself.

If Futurism exploits the artist and the consumer by 'aesthetifying' objects and events, then we can assess the dynamism of an author of the period by measuring his distance from it. By opposition to the Futurist textual independence, which seeks to discover a ubiquitous, all-embracing perception, *representation* is the dynamic element in relating perception to expression. The 'perception' we have been concerned with throughout these pages is an involvement *in* the world with every action, every act of seeing and of language. Language replaces it, but perception remains immeasurably *before* any articulation, and before any form it takes in the present. This 'form' is produced in representation, which articulates perception in terms of novelty, 'otherness' and displacement. While this response to concrete and familiar sensations may surprise us and make reading more difficult, it allows a space to emerge in which language can be questioned, analysed, and redirected. By both representing and incarnating the dimensionless anteriority of perception in relation to expression, many of Apollinaire's poems invite us to think of language as having a creative or manipulative power that needs to be continually reassessed.

But 'Merveille de la guerre', as we saw, does not emhasise a reassessment of language and image. It derives creativity from the distortion of perception in consciousness and expression. The perceiving 'Guillaume Apollinaire' in the text is protected not only from, but *within*, the images he receives in the present, and he designates such images as instruments of his creativity. The sensation of *not* being penetrated by things, the 'que moi qui suis en moi' with which the poem ends (1.43), is not so much a de-centering exploration of the mobile space between perception and the birth of image, but far more a further sense of excitement in the attempted creation of life out of death:

Conclusion

Pourtant c'est aussi beau que si la vie même sortait des mourants   (l. 11)

In relation to this, 'Coeur couronne et miroir', from the 'Ondes' section of the collection, emphasises the paradoxical nature of the creativity Apollinaire develops in *Calligrammes* as a whole. As we saw in the previous chapter, the 'Guillaume Apollinaire' in 'Coeur couronne et miroir' does not discover a reflection of himself; he faces a language where the named mirror does not reflect, but produces a displacement that exchange and the illusion of transparency do not give direction or dimension to. Unlike in 'Merveille de la guerre', this lack is not only a metaphor, even a dominant metaphor, in the poem. It *is* the sensation of perception itself, traced on the page in the letters and shapes of the text, and incarnated in its reading. Rather than providing an answer, contextualisation, in the form of a name, produces source-less reflections, signifiers that fragment the sense of self. Context is both self-evident and without contours, and it is this tension that I have been calling alienation. In doing so, I have not been concerned with maladjustment or a self-indulgent unwillingness to act. Alienation creates the opportunity to question images and their power to define. But this questioning is itself articulated in terms of images.

The 'Guillaume Apollinaire' in 'Merveille de la guerre' and the 'Guillaume Apollinaire' in 'Coeur couronne et miroir' appear to represent opposite poles in the same creative paradox, opposing approaches to the challenge of alienation. By the same token, Futurism cannot be regarded as the only model for the interpretation of Apollinaire's 'esprit nouveau' to the exclusion of the 'Orphic' conception of art he developed in relation to Delaunay and to a lesser extent Picabia and Duchamp. Although Apollinaire hoped to extend the notion of Orphic art to include all progressive art forms, its involvement with Cubism and its rejection of it give it a quite specific historical and conceptual background. As we saw, Cubism is an analytical praxis; it is critical of the action of appearance in perception and in the production of images. Unlike Futurism, it does not see in appearance the framework in which experience can be liberated from its involvement with the historical process. But neither does Cubism seek to bypass or transcend the fact that perception is faced with appearance. Its attempts to present the object from all angles produce a texturised artefact that represents our involvement *with* objects, with image as such, and with words (newspaper titles, alphabetical fragments, etc.).

Although Delaunay rejects the Cubist concentration on the object,

223

his approach, as we saw, involves a sophistication of representation of a kind that is inconceivable without the Cubist innovations. Delaunay's aim is to remove the object from its function of focusing seeing and painting, and in turn to dissociate colour from the function of qualifying objects. For Delaunay, colour is the object analysed in the process ('métier') of painting. But colour is also the terms in which the world presents itself; it is the form taken by our response to matter itself, it is the framework of our desire to see into the world and seek discoveries in it: 'le sens de la vie poétique donnée à la matière se traduit par la matière même: la couleur'.[64] To paint the world is to paint light. To use colour is to paint colour. The distinction disappears between making a picture with colour and making a picture of colour.

To paint with colour is to paint with light itself, and for Delaunay, as we saw, this confronts the viewer with the very act of thinking and removes from it the function of establishing points of view. Apollinaire is committed to this approach to light, and recognises not only what it owes to Cubism, but also the rediscovery of representation, the 'pure' representation that it involves:

> Avec ces deux mouvements, Cubiste et Orphisme, nous sommes en pleine poésie et en pure lumière.
> J'aime l'art de ces jeunes peintres car j'aime par-dessus tout la lumière.
> Et tous les hommes aiment par-dessus tout la lumière car ils ont inventé le feu.[65]

Thus writes Apollinaire in 1913. Fire purifies us of our involvement with objects and with matter. But equally, fire is matter. Moreover, fire is not light, but gives form to light, it re-presents light. The relation Delaunay sets up between light and colour, light and the syntax of light, is based on displacement. To use colour is to represent light, and perception. But light is not the equivalent of thinking or of perception. Equally, colour is not light; it is made of light, and it fragments our perception of light: this is represented in colour and contrast. But on the other hand, colour is the 'light' we see; it represents and initiates our involvement with the world. Colour is light, by being different from light. To see is to see representation. The fire invented by man is the power to create new forms, but these forms have power only if they display their relevance to the human condition. They give rise to new discoveries, not only new configurations of seeing and thinking, but new incarnations of the fact of representation itself: 'représenter est à la base de la vie plastique, représenter ne veut pas dire copier ni imiter, mais *créer*.[66] To represent is not only to confront sensation, but to create a new impetus in the analysis of experience, the world and the present. Like the 'Guillaume Apollinaire' in 'Coeur couronne et miroir' in relation to the man holding the pen, representation both *is* and is *not* what we are.

8—REPRESENTATION. THE SIGNIFIER. PROGRESS

Nos yeux sont la sensibilité entre la nature et notre âme.[67]

This is a form that Delaunay's thought takes in Apollinaire's editing of it in the article 'Realité peinture pure' in *Der Sturm*, December 1912. This 'sensibilité', the acute sense of 'I' in the world, is nowhere if not in colour on canvas. Representation is what we are. The present is the 'present'; consciousness is displaced in language and in sensation itself; anteriority has no form other than the 'present'. This 'Orphic' approach is both positive and critical. It does not seek to minimise, as Futurism claims to, the difference between consciousness and unconscious, context and identity. Its colours and its contrasts are a representation of this difference. The difference between context and identity, the displacement of identity in 'context', is unyielding; it is also mobile, and this mobility and its representation are a source of creativity in Delaunay's and Apollinaire's art. The emphasis on a lack of access to identity does not abandon formal anarchy merely to oscillate between paranoia (experience as invasion) and alienation (experience as exclusion). Rather, the sense of alienation is transformed into a praxis of simultaneous construction and deconstruction: deconstruction in the displacement we encounter in perception; construction of forms that express displacement, a language that maintains itself in the present. Representation is the language of alienation and of radical resistance. It is a language in which identity is continuously something other than itself, and experience continuously other, and in which this process is both incarnated and observed.

Representation is language on the level of the signifier. It puts quotation marks around 'image', 'context', even 'identity'. The signifier is the 'form' that expresses/displaces the phenomenon of passing: the passing of sensation through the eye, experience through to memory. But it is clear that the articulation of memory and 'identity' — of existence and exchange in the real world of the present — takes place on the levels of signifier and signified simultaneously. Genette writes that 'le langage ne peut "exprimer" le réel qu'en l'articulant, et cette articulation est un système de formes, aussi bien sur le plan signifié que sur le plan signifiant'.[68] In what way, then, can representation be regarded as language on the level of the signifier? Barthes and Derrida among others have pointed out that the relation of signifier to signified is not as arbitrary as Saussure implies. Clearly, the relation of signifier to object is arbitrary, but the relation, which produces the sign, of signifier to concept is a 'fait accompli' to the user of language. It is the product of a series, a history of decision-events that take place between the levels of the signifier and the signified, language as such and language as exchange, and that create the conventions by which language communicates.[69] Simultaneously, these decision-events are not available to consciousness as language is used: 'mon coeur pareille à une flamme renversée'. This is what the emphasis on language as signifier represents. It is the signifier itself that represents the relation of signifier to signified: it effaces access to the developing relation between the two, just as language displaces the world in its articulation of it; just as articulation constructs a displaced world, sets it in motion, and un-builds memory in its relation to the present and to expression. It is this experience that Apollinaire invites us to confront in 'Voyage'. The exploded signifier not only articulates identity as unnameable and uncentred, it is an active involvement in this; the signifier sets in motion an active and alive 'identity', buried *in* image, *as* image and the experience of it, and expressed within the star-'lit' sentence in the lower part of the poem-drawing: 'C'est ton visage que je ne vois plus'.

Representation, displacement, resistance — these are crucial elements in Apollinaire's impressive creativity. Apollinaire frequently leaves us with the sense of a writing that stretches the limits of subjectivity to the point of discovering the dispossession of identity and experience in language and the world. The aggressive, optimistic disillusion that comes out of 'La Victoire' is an expression of an endless attempt to master novelty and confront otherness.[70] It is the language of discovery, and also of acceptance. The forms we seek and that are to give expression to our desire for progress are in constant movement. The phenomena we seek to identify with rush rapidly into history; the links binding us to them will be none the less strong for having decayed. It is *this* process that constitutes our language indefinitely in advance of our efforts to make it ours:

> Ces chemins de fer qui circulent
> Sortiront bientôt de la vie
> Ils seront beaux et ridicules
> Deux lampes brûlent devant moi
> Comme deux femmes qui rient
> Je courbe tristement la tête
> Devant l'ardente moquerie
> Ce rire se répand
> Partout
> Parlez avec vos mains faites claquer vos doigts   (1. 48)

The images on which we pin our desires both dissolve and ossify. *This* is the moment when the drive for language re-emerges. All languages are good enough for the project of removing egoism from the poet's activity and of involving us all in the struggle to take hold of our experience. We need forms — any forms, old, new, transient — to give shape to the leap we need to make to unite ourselves with our existence in time and in the present. This leap takes place with every second, for it is the world that is threateningly, gloriously unfaithful:

> La mer gémir au loin et crier toute seule
> Ma voix fidèle comme l'ombre
> Veut être enfin l'ombre de la vie
> Veut être ô mer vivante et infidèle comme toi   (1. 64)

Apollinaire leaves us with an insatiable desire to read continuously and to write with passion: with a passionate hatred for what language fails to dominate and for the way it dispossesses, and with a passionate desire to create *in* language a world that looks like the world and gives dialogue to our aspirations:

> La Victoire avant tout sera
> De bien voir au loin
> De tout voir
> De près
> Et que tout ait un nouveau nom   (1. 88)

This world is one where we would be able to see, and be free to touch and give.

Reading Apollinaire (and writing about him) forces continual alterations of attitude on us, and a development of any attitude we adopt to fix his writing. It lives as we do, as we perceive, remember and read. As I seek to bring this episode in my involvement with Apollinaire to an end, his own parting expressions of faith are suddenly present in the arena: the twin statements of *L'Esprit nouveau et les poètes* and

'Les Collines'.[71] His own expressions of optimism and his own belief in progress are far more powerful than any versions of it that we can provide.

In both these pieces, Apollinaire pins his existence on developing an attitude of exploration through which individuals can meet, and through which diversity is made productive. Self-expression and the freedom to explore are to produce forms flexible enough to communicate without stifling. The world Apollinaire believes in is a post-war world where experimentation is coupled with responsibility, novelty with the expressiveness of classical forms. The pursuit of novelty that provides Apollinaire's final sense of purpose is one whose positive impetus seems secure. Its aim is to enlarge the wealth in our experience, and to intensify the critical pursuit of progress it embodies: 'L'esprit nouveau qui s'annonce prétend avant tout hériter des classiques un solide bon sens, un esprit critique assuré, des vues d'ensemble sur l'univers et dans l'âme humaine, et le sens du devoir qui dépouille les sentiments et en limite *ou plutôt en contient les manifestations.*'[72] And to create this world of positive exploration, the artist must find the strength to prophesy it:

> Tant que les avions ne peuplaient le ciel, la fable d'Icare n'était qu'une vérité supposée. Aujourd'hui ce n'est plus une fable...
> L'esprit nouveau exige qu'on se donne de ces tâches prophétiques...
> Les jeux divins de la vie et de l'imagination donnent carrière à une activité poétique toute nouvelle.[73]

To break through into the endless new discoveries to be made in the world and in our perception, a *new* world must be created: 'C'est que poésie et création ne sont qu'une même chose; on ne doit appeler poète que celui qui invente, qui crée....'[74] New worlds, the new discoveries yet to be made *in* the world 'que les savants scrutent à chaque carrefour de la matière' — these discoveries must be prophesied if they are ever to become real, and open to the critical and exploring gaze.[75] Only through a gesture as radical as prophecy can the world be freed from the appearance that bring it to life in the present, but that hide its development and its diversity in the anti-progressive clothes of the past.

> Je me suis enfin detaché
> De toutes choses naturelles
> Je peux mourir mais non pécher
> Et ce qu'onn a jamais touché
> Je l'ai touché je l'ai palpé[76]

228

Conclusion

I began this work with one farewell — 'L'Adieu' — and it draws to its conclusion with another. Not only because 'Les Collines' is among the last of Apollinaire's poems to be written, but also because Jaqueline Apollinaire-Kolb saw expressed in these lines the achievements and the grandeur Apollinaire should be remembered for: they can be read on his tombstone.[77] The lines are a statement of immense confidence, of power to touch the invisible, to plunge his hands in the yet-to-be-discovered, in the ever-deeper levels of the present and its structuring through time. It is a power that Apollinaire *asserts* in these lines — a power, he reminds us, that he has created through relating to the cultural display of the previous eleven years since the eruption on the scene of *Les Demoiselles d'Avignon*. It is the power to dismantle appearance, to see without perspective, to discover the non-objective, abstract expression in which imagination and the fact of perception are incarnated:

> Et j'ai scruté tout ce que nul
> Ne peut en rien imaginer
> Et j'ai soupesé maintes fois
> Même la vie impondérable
> Je peux mourir en souriant   (l. 96)

'Les Collines' itself seems to *be* the language Apollinaire knows he has created; it seems to uphold, as he writes it or rereads it, the claim he makes for it and for his life-in-writing. Its verse moves to a place where we confront optimism and human progress as the reality of the next seconds. The concepts on which this optimism is built weave themselves transparently into the mind's eye as it sees, remembers and watches the words move in and out of experineces that we recognise and that breathe life into words. A new urgency is given to the desire to explode surface appearances and the limitations they impose on perception:

> Profondeurs de la conscience
> On vous explorera demain
> Et qui sait quels êtres vivants
> Seront tirés de ces abîmes
> Avec des univers entiers
>
> Voici s'élever des prophètes
> Comme au loin les collines bleues
> Ils sauront des choses précises
> Comme croient savoir les savants
> Et nous transporteront partout

La grande force est le désir
Et viens que je te baise au front
O légère comme une flamme
Dont tu as toute la souffrance
Toute l'ardeur et tout l'éclat   (l. 51)

Nothing is allowed to remain within a nameable category; concepts find life in vision and in the simplicity of touch: 'Et viens que je te baise au front'. In the bright illusion of simplicity, Apollinaire internalises the world-in-transience, and discovers implanted in it the transparency of his desires as they slip outwards through his perception and structure it.

Transparency, simplicity — these are in effect the material of creativity and its measure, the limits beyond which it cannot go, beyond which it destroys itself. 'Les poètes ne sont pas seulement les hommes du beau. Ils sont encore et surtout les hommes du vrai....'[78] Apollinaire is not involved in creating an escapist world, a world cutting its links with others in an illusion of spontaneous birth. He turns to surprise as a major tool in the hands of the artist, not because he wants to open out worlds that have never been seen, or because he wants to flex his creative muscles as an individual artist, but because he wants to give birth to the world as it *is*, and to what it hides. 'Le nouveau' explores regions of silenced progressive potential *in the world* ('à chaque carrefour de la matière'), not in the subjective fantasies of an individual, or his delusions of independence:

C'est que la poésie et création ne sont qu'une même chose; on ne doit appeler poète que celui qui invente, celui qui crée, *dans la mesure où l'homme peut créer*.... Les poètes ne sont pas seulement les hommes du beau. Ils sont encore et surtout les hommes du vrai, en tant qu'il permet de pénétrer l'inconnu, si bien que la surprise, l'inattendu est un des principaux ressorts de la poésie d'aujourd'hui.[79]

The 'sens du devoir' exemplified by 'l'esprit nouveau' consists of the desire to open out the world and reveal it as it *is*, as it is seen and cont^xined in the formless receptacles perception.

'Le vrai', the penetration of the unknown, the transparency in and through which natural appearance is dismantled — all this does not only involve Apollinaire, and us with him, in visions of transformation and knowledge; the dismantling of appearance involves the clothes, the attitudes and roles of identity itself. The transparent material of creativity involves an immense self-emptying, an absorption *by* the endless texture of the world, ploughing paths across perception. The measure of the new creativity is the extent to which the artefacts it produces dissolve *as* diversity, novelty, and the images of progress it seeks to delve into. What the poet produces is flooded *by* the world as it is and as it hides. Creation is self-emptying to the point of self-destruction:

> Un chapeau haut de forme est sur
> Une table chargée de fruits
> Les gants sont morts près d'une pomme
> Une dame se tord le cou
> Auprès d'un monsieur qui s'avale   (l. 181)

But there is no such 'point' arrested in time:

> Le bal tournoie au fond du temps
> J'ai tué le beau chef d'orchestre
> Et je pèle pour mes amis
> L'orange dont la saveur est
> Un merveilleux feu d'artifice   (l. 186)

Creative survival re-emerges in the killing of the Master, in shared discovery, and in an explosion of colour and image that no single individual can identify with, or even identify other than as the world revealing itself *again*, and *again* germinating in the language that uses all the means that can be discovered to appropriate it. The poet Apollinaire sees reflected in his desires has no greater ambition than to imagine *with* the world and *in* the world; he maintains an identity that lives, that continues, that is moved in the space where perception internalises, but is left powerless faced with events and memories that remain 'other':

> Et j'entends revenir mes pas
> Le long des sentiers que personne
> N'a parcourus j'entends mes pas
> A toute heure ils passent là-bas
> Lents ou pressés ils vont ou viennent   (l. 156)

Both farewells — this one and 'L'Adieu', with which we began — leave a space after the farewell gesture, after the last grasp or after the moss has collected in the letters carved in the stone, a space that is *now*. To prophesy is to imagine the world revealed and self-rejuvenating. The other side of prophecy is the present, the transformation of one second into the next. The farewells open out in a capacity to survive and to *give*:

C'est de souffrance et de bonté
Que sera faite la beauté
Plus parfaite que n'était celle
Qui venait des proportions
Il neige et je brûle et je tremble (l. 171)

The capacity to survive, to exchange life with the world, to sense forms still more expressive than the classical ones, is the capacity to create a language and to create gifts that dissolve in the diversity that leaks through them. In the transparency through which gifts are made and received, the 'I' suffers and is sacrificed to gifts offered and accepted:

Une autre fois je mendiais
L'on ne me donna qu'une flamme
Dont je fus brûlé jusqu'aux lèvres
Et je ne pus dire merci
Torche que rien ne peut éteindre (l. 146)

In imagination and creative exchange, the creating 'I' is silenced by the immense spontaneity and the dimensionless otherness that come at us from out there, build up our perception and fragment our sense of it. The 'I' *is* the signifiers that populate our awareness, and that incarnate our contact with the present in a self-revealing and *displaced* novelty. Creativity is measured in the extent to which anteriority is given life, to which the yet-to-be-discovered glows, to which novelty and the unknown draw disappearing images of our experience, of our pleasure in surviving in otherness. Creativity runs along the line where living and absence mix and produce colour, decay, symbolisation:

Je viens ici faire des tours
Où joue son rôle un talisman
Mort et plus subtil que la vie (l. 83)

The signifier: a poor word perhaps, out of its depth, entrenched in the systems that produce it, but a word nonetheless; an instrument, aimed at naming the impossible, at naming what is *there*, or there in Apollinaire's textuality, there in the unknown *incarnated* before our eyes, in the transitions of our memory, and *represented* in Apollinaire's words as we read. The signifier: as abstract a notion as 'there'; to prophesy is to be confronted with it, words must be found to represent it, and to express the experience of it. It opens out and displaces the creative identity that represents and survives in the moments of rejuvenation and absence that build it. The signifier, merely a word, perhaps too obsessively used in this work, is made to confront the bright streak of perception as it is articulated in Apollinaire. An instrument: Apollinaire himself used any and every instrument, any sign langauge or clicking of the fingers to achieve the breadth and purity of expression he sought.[80] The extent to which the signifier, or any other term or attitude, fails to appropriate Apollinaire's language is a representation of what his language is confronted with. It is also a gap that is unbreached, repeatedly vast, giving 'form' to his suffering; within it, words are constantly given back to the texts and to the world, back to what is there and new, alive in its otherness and transience:

> Des bras d'or supportent la vie
> Pénétrez le secret doré
> Tout n'est qu'une flamme rapide
> Que fleurit la rose adorable
> Et d'où monte un parfum exquis   (l. 221)

NOTES

1 According to this approach, Apollinaire's language does not emphasise the distinction between poetic and non-poetic, nor does it seek to establish ever more firmly the distinction between them. It is a comment on existence within language as a whole, and a heightened awareness of it. This approach is fundamentally different from the conclusion arrived at by Chevalier in the last pages of his stylistic analysis of *Alcools*. See Jean-Claude Chevalier, *'Alcools' d'Apollinaire — Essai d'analyse des formes poétiques* (Paris, 1970), pp. 268–73.

2 I. A. Richards, *Principles of Literary Criticism*, (London, 1976).

3 Gérard Genette, 'Raisons de la critique pure', in *Figures II* (Paris, 1969), pp. 7–22.

4 Albert Thibaudet, *Réflexions sur la critique* (Paris, 1939).

5 Genette, *Figures II*, p. 13, Maurice Blanchot, *L'Espace littéraire* (Paris, 1955), p. 17. In *Le Livre à venir*, Idées (Paris, 1971), Blanchot, while not dealing directly with 'un langage décentré', raises the related concepts of the lack of literary essence, and of the poet as the one 'en qui se fait chant la possibilité, l'impossibilité de chanter...'. He also raises the notion of language as 'exercice' in a comparison of Valéry and Kafka. (pp. 290–95.)

6 Blanchot, *L'Espace littéraire*, p. 17. A similarly problematic obligation to express is suggested by Beckett in his dialogues with Georges Duthuit in *Proust. Three Dialogues with Georges Duthuit* (London, 1965), p. 103.

7 'Un livre n'appartient plus à un genre...': Blanchot, *Le Livre à venir*, p. 293.

8 Genette, *Figures II*, p. 15.

9 Genette, *Figure II*, p. 16. Genette's italics.

10 Blanchot, *Le Livre à venir*, p. 285.

11 Marie-Jeanne Durry, *Guillaume Apollinaire — 'Alcools'*, 3 vols (Paris 1956–64 and 1977), II, pp. 154–6.

12 OP, p. 60, p. 104, p. 106, p. 120, p. 125, p. 141, p. 148.

13 Durry, *Guillaume Apollinaire — 'Alcools'*, III, p. 228.

14 Alphonse de Lamartine, *Oeuvres poétiques complètes*, ed. Guyard, Bibliothèque de la Pléiade (Paris, 1963), p. 64.

15 Durry, *Guillaume Apollinaire — 'Alcools'*, III, p. 228.

16 Durry, *Guillaume Apollinaire — 'Alcools'*, III, p. 229.

17 Durry, *Guillaume Apollinaire — 'Alcools'*, III, p. 229. My italics.

18 OP, p. 237, l. 1.

19 Durry, *Guillaume Apollinaire — 'Alcools'*, III, p. 229.

20 Roland Barthes, *Le Degré zéro de l'écriture*, Points (Paris, 1972), p. 18.

21 Barthes, *Le Degré zéro de l'écriture*, p. 18. Barthes's italics.

22 *Le Bestiaire*, OP, p. 3.

23 OP, p. 33.

24 'Cette "voix de la lumière", n'est-ce pas le dessin, c'est-à-dire la ligne [i.e. the 'noblesse de la ligne' in Apollinaire's poem]? Et quand la lumière s'exprime tout se colore. La peinture est proprement un langage lumineux.' (OP, p. 33.) Delaunay was attracted to this notion of the drawn line combining with colour. In terms of his own art, we might say that he 'line' is created between colours; the painter-practitioner discovers the contrasts that allow light to be re-presented, and perception and the world to yield their own colours. (CAA, p. 150, p. 188.)

25 Indeed, it should be pointed out that 'thematic' approaches to apollinaire's work exist that do seek to respond to those global issues in such a way as to reveal questions Apollinaire might ask about his own experience of language. Scott Bates's *Apollinaire* (New York, 1967) deals with the historically appropriate 'themes' of Christ and Antichrist, the Traveller and the City. Burgos treats the 'themes' of 'éloignement', 'séparation', 'agrandissement' in a way that shows how each involves its opposite, and that allows him to evoke their relation to perception. See Jean Burgos, 'l'Univers imaginaire d'Apollinaire', *La Revue des lettres modernes*, 276–9, Guillaume Apollinaire, 10 (1971), 35–67, (pp. 37–8, p. 55).

26 OP, p. 120.

27 OP, p. 66.

28 It is well known that hands were a part of the anatomy that Apollinaire found particularly expressive, and he often used 'ma main' or a variant as a signing-off formula in letters.

29 Blanchot, *Le Livre à venir*, pp. 285–95.

30 Blanchot, *Le Livre à venir*, pp. 285–86.

31 Blanchot, *Le Livre à venir*, p. 289.

32 OP, p. 104.

33 OP, p. 105.

34 Roland Barthes, 'Ecrivains et écrivants', in *Essais critiques* (Paris, 1964), p. 149. Barthes's italics.

35 Jean-Pierre Richard, 'Etoiles chez Apollinaire', in *De Ronsard à Breton: Hommages à Marcel Raymond* (Paris, 1967) pp. 223–4.

36 Richard, 'Etoiles chez Apollinaire', p. 227. Richard's italics.

37 Richard, 'Etoiles chez Apollinaire', p. 230. My italics.

38 Richard, 'Etoiles chez Apollinaire', pp. 229–30.

39 Richard, 'Etoiles chez Apollinaire', p. 230.

40 OP, p. 308, l. 6.

41 Richard, 'Etoiles chez Apollinaire', p. 233.

42 Richard, 'Etoiles chez Apollinaire', p. 228.

43 Richard, 'Etoiles chez Apollinaire', p. 234.

44 'La notion suggérée d'activité virile...qui rejoint, sous le signe de la constellation, l'idée de guerre à celle d'espérance non-guerrière.' Richard, 'Etoiles chez Apollinaire', p. 233.

45 'Merveille de la guerre', OP, p. 271, l. 31.

46 OP, p. 207.

47 'Et des bergers gigantesques menaient
    De grands troupeaux muets qui broutaient les paroles
    Et contre lesquels aboyaient tous les chiens sur la route   (l. 29)

48 'Fusée', OP, p. 261, l. 1.

49 'Merveille de la guerre', OP, p. 271, l. 13.

50 Andy Warhol, *From A to B and Back Again* (New York, 1975). Warhol's paintings cast an interesting light on Apollinaire's ideograms. There, the fictional product *is* the mass-produced object and its domination of perception through advertising. In Warhol's Campbell's soup tins and Apollinaire's ideograms, the union of the signifier and the signified, while opening out new areas of creative freedom and providing 'short-cuts to reality', as Jean-Claude Chevalier would say, also produces images that resist being identified with, that invite identification with the familiarity of alienation itself. See Jean-Claude Chevalier, 'La Poésie d'Apollinaire et le calembour', *Europe*, 451–2 (1966), 56–76, (p. 75).

51 OP, p. 280, p. 287.

52 'N'en doutons pas: l'impressionnisme d'Apollinaire, qui se fait jour notamment dans certains calligrammes presque contemporains de 'Liens', répond en grande partie à ce besoin de saisir le fugace et de le fixer, non seulement par les mots mais par la forme'. Michel Décaudin 'Apollinaire à la recherche de lui-même', *Cahiers du Sud*, 386 (1966), 3–12 (p. 9).

53 OP, p. 288.

54 Margaret Davies, *Apollinaire*, Biography and Criticism, 5 (London, 1964), p. 248. See also Toussaint-Luca, *Guillaume Apollinaire, souvenirs d'un ami* (Monaco, 1964), pp. 78–9.

55 Raymond Jean, *La Poétique du désir* (Paris, 1974).

56 Jean, *La Poétique du désir*, p. 345. Jean's italics.

57 Jean, *La Poétique du désir*, p. 346.

58 Jean, *La Poétique du désir*, p. 349. Jean's italics.

59 Jean, *La Poétique du désir*, p. 347. Jean's italics.

60 OC, III, p. 884.

61 OP, p. 274.

62 See Richard Cork, *Vorticism*, 2 vols (London, 1976), I, pp. 225–6.

63 *Blast*, ed. Wyndham Lewis (London, 1914 and 1915). For a discussion of the Vorticist approach to 'Man and the Machine', see Richard Cork, *Vorticism*, II, pp. 323–76. See also Percy Wyndham Lewis, *Vorticist Design* (c. 1914), p. 328, *Portrait of an English woman* (1914), p. 331 and Charles Nevinson, *On the Way to the Trenches* (c. 1910–15), p. 486. For an expression of

Wyndham Lewis's attitude to war and the politics of war, see *Vorticism*, I, pp. 268–69.

64 CAA, p. 173.

65 CAA, p. 166. See also CA, p. 275, and *Méditations esthétiques*, OC, IV, p. 26.

66 CAA, p. 173. Delaunay's italics.

67 CAA, p. 156. See also CA, p. 268–9.

68 Genette, *Figures II*, p. 19. Genette's italics.

69 Barthes argues that the relation of signifier to signified can be marked as ≡ (indistinguishable) but not = (identical). Barthes, *Le Degré zéro de l'écriture*, suivi de *Eléments de sémiologie*, Paris, 1953, p. 122.) Jacques Derrida discusses the relation of signifier to signified, 'l'idéalité du sens' and 'l'image accoustique', 'le monde', 'le vécu' and 'la trace' in *De la Grammatologie* (Paris, 1967), pp. 92–5.

70 OP, p. 309.

71 Scott Bates discusses the close ties between the two pieces in ' "Les Collines", dernier testament d'Apollinaire', *La Revue des lettres modernes*, 69–72, Guillaume Apollinaire, 1 (1962), 25–39.

72 OC, III, p. 900. My italics.

73 OC, III, pp. 906–7.

74 OC, III, p. 907.

75 OC, III, p. 906.

76 'Les Collines', OP, p. 171, l. 91.

77 See Bates, ' "Les Collines", dernier testament d'Apollinaire', p. 39. This stanza and the next one quoted are both on the tombstone.

78 OC, III, p. 907.

79 OC, III, p. 907.

80 'La Victoire', OP, p. 311, l. 57. The experience of poetry that Apollinaire pushes to its limits is a hybrid made up of an indefinite number of components — perhaps Blanchot's 'méchant hybride de lecture et d'écriture'. The texts Apollinaire reads are the sourceless images in perception, and writing is his language flowing through them and penetrated by them. The urgent, uncompromising affirmation that Apollinaire needs all his confidence to visualise within his own writing is an affirmation of a vast and daunting equality. Blanchot also seeks to rise to 'la tâche de préserver et de libérer la pensée de la notion de valeur, par conséquent d'ouvrir l'histoire à ce qui en elle se dégage déjà de toutes formes de valeurs et se prépare à une toute autre sorte — encore imprévisible — d'affirmation'. Maurice Blanchot, *Lautréamont et Sade*, Arguments, 19, Paris, 1969, p. 11, p. 14.

List of works consulted

This is not a complete bibliography of works published on Apollinaire: such information can be found in the review *Le Flaneur des deux rives* (1954–5), in the numbers of *La Revue des lettres modernes* devoted to Apollinaire and edited by Michel Décaudin, and, more recently, in the issue devoted to Apollinaire studies of the *Carnets bibliographiques de la Revue des lettres modernes*, edited by Peter Hoy (Paris, 1985). I list here the primary texts I have consulted, the works on Apollinaire I have found most useful, and the literary and critical texts that have contributed to my own approach.

The dates given after books below refer to the date of publication of the editions used. In the case of multiple entries, works are listed in the order of original publication.

—GUILLAUME APOLLINAIRE, PRIMARY TEXTS

Oeuvres complètes, ed. Michel Décaudin, with portraits and facsimiles compiled by Marcel Adéma, 4 vols. (Paris, 1965)

Oeuvres poétiques, eds. Marcel Adéma and Michel Décaudin, Bibliothèque de la Pléiade (Paris, 1965)

Oeuvres en prose, I, ed. Michel Décaudin, Bibliothèque de la Pléiade (Paris, 1977)

Alcools, with a portrait by Pablo Picasso (Paris, 1913)

Alcools, a parallel text translated by Anne Hyde Greet, with a forword by Warren Ramsey and commentary by Anne Hyde Greet (Berkeley & Los Angeles, 1965)

Alcools, ed. A. E. Pilkington (Oxford, 1970)

Alcools, ed. Garnet Rees, Athlone French poets, 8 (London, 1975)

Calligrammes, poèmes de la paix et de la guerre (Paris, 1918)

Calligrammes poèmes de la paix et de la guerre, préface by Michel Butor, Poésie (Paris, 1966)

Calligrammes, Poems of Peace and War, a parallel text translated by Anne Hyde Greet, introduction by S.I. Lockerbie and commentary by Anne Hyde Greet & S.I. Lockerbie (Berkeley & London, 1980)

Le Guetteur mélancholique, eds. Robert Mallet & Bernard Poissonier (Paris, 1952)

Le Guetteur mélancholique, suivi de *Poèmes retrouvés*, notice by Michel Décaudin, Poésie (Paris, 1970)

Chroniques d'art 1902–1918, ed. Leroy C. Breunig (Paris, 1960)

Les Peintres cubistes, eds. Leroy C. Breunig & Jean-Claude Chevalier, Miroirs de l'art (Paris, 1965)

2—WORKS ON APPOLLINAIRE, ON OTHER POETS AND ON AREAS RELATED TO APOLLINAIRE, INCLUDING THE VISUAL ARTS

Adéma, M., *Guillaume Apollinaire le mal-aimé* (Paris, 1952)

—— *Guillaume Apollinaire*, Vies perpendiculaires (Paris, 1968)

Adéma, P., and Décaudin, M., *Album Apollinaire*, Bibliothèque de la Pléiade (Paris, 1971)

Balakian, A., *Surrealism, The Road to the Absolute*, revised and enlarged ed. (New York, 1970)

Barr, A. H., Jr., *Cubism and Abstract Art* (reprinted New York, 1966)

Barre, A., *Le Symbolisme* (Paris, 1911)

Bates, S., *Apollinaire*, Twayne's World Authors, 14 (New York, 1967)

Beaumont, E. M., Cocking, M., & Cruickshank, J., eds., *Order and Adventure in Post-romantic French Poetry: Essays Presented to C. A. Hackett* (Oxford, 1973)

Berry, D., *The Creative Vision of Guillaume Apollinaire*, Standford French and Italian Studies, 25 (Saratoga, 1982)

Billy, A., *Apollinaire vivant* (Paris, 1923)

Bohn, W., *Apollinaire et l'homme sans visage: création et évolution d'un motif moderne*, Avanguardie Storiche, 8 (Rome, 1984)

—— *The Aesthetics of Visual Poetry* (Cambridge, 1986)

Bornècque, J.-H., *Verlaine par lui-même* (Paris, 1966)

Bowie, M., *Mallarmé and the Art of Being Difficult* (Cambridge, 1978)

Bowra, C. M., *The Creative Experiment* (London, 1949)

Breunig, L. C., *Guillaume Apollinaire*, Colombia Essays in Modern Writers, 46 (New York, 1969)

Buckley, H. E. *Guillaume Apollinaire as an Art Critic*, Studies in fine arts: criticism, 11 (Michigan, 1981)

Cadou, R.-G., *Le Testament d'Apollinaire* (Paris, 1980)

Caizergues, P., *Apollinaire journaliste. Textes retrouvés d'Apollinaire*, 2 vols., Bibliothèque des lettres modernes, 30, Bibliothèque Guillaume Apollinaire, 11 (Paris, 1981)

Carmody, F.-J., *The Evolution of Apollinaire's Poetics*, University of California Publications in Modern Philology, 70 (Berkeley & Los Angeles, 1963)

Chevalier, J.-C., *'Alcools' d'Apollinaire — Essai d'analyse des formes poétiques*, Bibliothèque des lettres modernes, 17, Bibliothèque Guillaume Apollinaire, 3 (Paris, 1970)

Cocteau, J., *La Difficulté d'être* (Paris, 1947)

Cooper, D., & Tinterow, G., *The Essential Cubism 1907–1920*, The Tate Gallery (London, 1983)

Cork, R., *Vorticism*, 2 vols. (London, 1976)

Davies, M., *Apollinaire*, Biography and Criticism, 5 (London, 1964)

Debon, C., *Guillaume Apollinaire après 'Alcools'*, Bibliothèque des lettres modernes, 31, Bibliothèque Guillaume Apollinaire, 12, 2 vols. (Paris, 1981)

Décaudin, M., *La Crise des valeurs symbolistes* (Toulouse, 1960)

—— *Dossier d''Alcools'*, Société de Publications romanes et françaises, 67 (Paris, 1960)

List of works consulted

Durry, M.-J., *Guillaume Apollinaire — 'Alcools'*, 3 vols. (Paris, 1956–64)

Francastel, P., ed., *Du Cubisme à l'art abstrait*, les cahiers inédits de Robert Delaunay (Paris, 1957)

Gleizes, A., & Metzinger, J., *Du Cubisme* (Paris, 1912)

Goffin, R., *Entrer en Poésie* (Brussels, 1948)

Golding, J., *Cubism, a History and an Analysis, 1907–1914* (London, 1959)

Greet, A. H., *Apollinaire et le livre de peintre*, Interférences, art, lettres, 4, Bibliothèque Guillaume Apollinaire, 9 (Paris, 1977)

Guillaume, P., *Sculptures nègres*, précédées d'un avertissement de Guillaume Apollinaire (Paris, 1917)

Jacaret, G., *La Dialectique de l'ironie et du lyrisme dans 'Alcools' et 'Calligrammes' de G. Apollinaire* (Paris, 1984)

Jean, R., *La Poétique du désir* (Paris, 1974)

Joll, J., *Intellectuals in Politics* (London, 1960)

Laborie, P., *Robert Desnos: son oeuvre dans l'éclairage de Arthur Rimbaud et de Guillaume Apollinaire* (Paris, 1975)

Lista, G., *Futurisme. Manifestes — proclamations — documents* (Lausanne, 1973)

Longrée, G. H. F., *L'Expérience idéo-calligrammatique d'Apollinaire* (Liège, 1984)

Morhange-Bégué, C., *'La Chanson du mal-aimé' — Essai d'analyse structurale et linguistique*, Bibliothèque des lettres modernes, 18, Bibliothèque Guillaume Apollinaire, 4 (Paris, 1970)

Morice, C., *La Littérature de tout à l'heure* (Paris, 1889)

Nadal, O., *Verlaine* (Paris, 1961)

Orrecchioni, P., *Le Thème du Rhin dans l'inspiration de Guillaume Apollinaire*, Thèmes et Mythes, 3, Bibliothèque Guillaume Apollinaire, 1 (Paris, 1956)

Oster, D., *Guillaume Apollinaire*, Poètes d'aujourd'hui, 227 (Paris, 1975)

Pia, P., *Apollinaire*, Ecrivains de toujours, 20 (Paris, 1965)

Pierre, J., *Le Futurisme et le Dadaisme*, Histoire générale de la peinture (Lausanne, 1967)

Renaud, P., *Lecture d'Apollinaire*, Letterata (Lausanne, 1969)

Richter, M., *La Crise du logos et la quête du mythe — Baudelaire, Rimbaud, Cendrars, Apollinaire*, translated by Jean-François Rodriguez, Langages (Neuchâtel, 1976)

Rosenblum, R., *Cubism and Twentieth Century Art* (New York, 1960)

Rouveyre, A., *Souvenirs de mon commerce* (Paris, 1921)

—— *Apollinaire* (Paris, 1945)

—— *Amour et poésie d'Apollinaire* (Paris, 1955)

Sabartés, J., and Boeck, W., *Picasso* (Paris, 1955)

Seitz, W., *Claude Monet* (London, 1960)

Shattuck, R., *The Banquet Years*, revised ed. (London, 1969)

Somville, L., *Dévanciers du surréalisme — les groupes d'avant-garde et le mouvement poétique 1912–1925*, Histoire, idées et critique littéraire, 116 (Geneva, 1971)

Spate, V., *Orphism, the Evolution of Non-Figurative Painting in Paris, 1910–1914*, Oxford Studies in the History of Art and Architecture (Oxford, 1979)

Stamelman, R. H., *The Drama of the Self in Apollinaire's 'Alcools'*, North

Carolina Studies in the Romance Languages and Literatures, 178 (University of North Carolina, 1976)

Steegmuller, F., *Apollinaire, Poet among the Painters* (London, 1963)

Taylor, C., *Futurism: Politics, Painting and Performance*, University Studies in the Fine Arts: The Avant-garde, 8 (Michigan, 1974)

Themerson, S., *Apollinaire's Lyrical Ideograms* (London, 1968)

Timms, E., & Kelley, D., *Unreal City: urban experience in modern european literature and art* (Manchester, 1986)

Tisdall, C., & Bazzolla, A., *Futurism* (London, 1977)

Toussaint-Luca, *Guillaume Apollinaire, souvenirs d'un ami* (Monaco, 1964)

Vriesen, G., & Imdahl, M., *Robert Delaunay: Light and Color* (New York, 1967)

3—ARTICLES

(i) SPECIAL SERIES, PRINCIPAL REVIEWS AND PERIODICALS DEVOTED TO APOLLINAIRE

Archives des lettres modernes:
Archives Guillaume Apollinaire
1 Caizergues, P., 'Apollinaire et la démocratie sociale', ALM, 101 (1969)
2 Poupon, M., 'Apollinaire et Cendrars', ALM, 103 (1969)
3 Goose, M.-T., 'Une lecture du "Larron"', ALM, 112 (1970)
4 Couffignal, R., '"Zone" — structure et confrontation', ALM, 118 (1970)
5 *La Bréhatine*. Cinéma-drame par André Billy et Guillaume Apollinaire, eds. by Claude Tournadre and Alain Virmaux, ALM, 126 (1971)
6 Follet, L. & Poupon, M., 'Lecture de "Palais"', ALM, 138 (1972)
7 Fröhlicher, P., '"Le Brasier" d'Apollinaire — lecture sémiotique', ALM, 208 (1983)
8 Renaud, P., 'Les Trajets du Phénix de la "Chanson du mal-aimé" à l'ensemble d'*Alcools*', ALM, 209 (1983)

Cahiers du Sud, 386 (1966)

Europe, 451–2 (1966)

Le Flâneur des deux rives, 1–7, 8 (1954–5)

Journées Apollinaire: Actes du colloque de Stavelot
1 Apollinaire et l'Ardenne stavelotienne (1958)
2 Apollinaire et les 'Rhénanes' (1960)
3 Apollinaire et ses amis (1963)
4 *Apollinaire et la musique*, Actes du Colloque de Stavelot 1965 (Stavelot, 1967)
5 *Du Monde européen à l'univers des mythes*, Actes du Colloque de Stavelot, 1968, ed. Michel Décaudin, Bibliothèque Guillaume Apollinaire, 5 (Paris, 1970)
6 *Apollinaire inventeur de langages*, Actes du Colloque de Stavelot 1970, ed. Michel Décaudin, Bibliothèque Guillaume Apollinaire, 7 (Paris, 1973)
7 *Regards sur Apollinaire conteur*, Actes du Colloqué de Stavelot 1973, ed. Michel Décaudin, Bibliothèque Guillaume Apollinaire, 8 (Paris, 1975)

List of works consulted

8 *Apollinaire et la peinture*, Actes du Colloque de Stavelot 1975, *Que vlo-ve?*, 21–2 (1979)

9 *Lecture et interprétation des calligrammes*, Actes du Colloque de Stavelot 1977, *Que vlo-ve?*, 29–30 (1981)

10 *Apollinaire et les arts du spectacle*, Actes du Colloque de Stavelot 1980, *Bérénice*, 3 (1982)

11 *Naissance du texte apollinarien*, Actes du Colloque de Stavelot 1982, *Que vlo-ve?*, 2, 6–7 (1983)

12 *Expérience et imagination de l'amour dans l'oeuvre d'Apollinaire*, Actes du Colloque de Stavelot 1984, forthcoming.

La Revue des lettres modernes

1 Apollinaire, le cubisme et l'esprit nouveau, 69–70 (1962)

2 Cinquantenaire d'*Alcools*, 85–9 (1963)

3 Apollinaire et les surréalistes, 104–7 (1964)

4 *Les Mamelles de Tirésias, L'Hérésiarque et Cie*, 123–6 (1965)

5 Echos de Stavelot, 146–9 (1966)

6 Images d'un destin, 166–9 (1967)

7 1918–1968, 183–8 (1968)

8 Colloque de Varsovie, 217–22 (1969)

9 Autour de l'inspiration allemande et du Lied, 249–53 (1970)

10 Méthodes et approches critiques, 1, 276–9 (1971)

11 Méthodes et approches critiques, 2, 327–30 (1972)

12 Apollinaire et la guerre, 1, 380–4 (1973)

13 Apollinaire et la guerre, 2, 450–5 (1976)

14 Recours aux sources, 1, 530–6 (1978)

15 Recours aux sources, 2, 576–81 (1980)

16 'La Chanson du mal-aimé' encore et toujours, 677–81 (1983)

Revue des sciences humaines, 84 (1956)

(ii) INDIVIDUAL ARTICLES

Bassy, A.-M., 'Forme littéraire et forme graphique: les schématogrammes d'Apollinaire', *Scolies, cahiers de recherches de l'Ecole normale supérieure*, 3–4 (1973–4), 161–207

Bates, S., ' "*Les Collines*", dernier testament d'Apollinaire', RLM, 69–70, Guillaume Apollinaire, 1 (1962), 25–39

Blanchot, M., 'La Voix narrative', *La Nouvelle revue française*, 142 (1964), 675–85

Bohn, W., 'Apollinaire inédit — l'énigme de Giorgio de Chirico', RLM, 576–81, Guillaume Apollinaire, 15 (1980), 121–32

—— 'L'imagination plastique des calligrammes', *Que vlo-ve?*, 29–30, (1981) separate pagination

Breunig, L.C., 'The Chronology of Guillaume Apollinaire's "Alcools" ', *Publications of the Modern Language Association of America*, 67 (1952), 907–23

—— 'Apollinaire et le cubisme', RLM, 69–70, Guillaume Apollinaire, 1 (1962), 7–24

—— 'Apollinaire's "Les Fiançailles" ', *Essays in French Literature*, University of Western Australia (1966), 1–32

Breunig, L. C. & Chevalier, J.-C., 'Apollinaire et "Les Peintres cubistes"', RLM, 104–7, Guillaume Apollinaire, 3 (1964), 89–112

Burgos, J., 'Apollinaire et le recours au mythe', in *Du Monde européen à l'univers des mythes*, Actes du Colloque de Stavelot 1968, ed. Michel Décaudin, Bibliothèque Guillaume Apollinaire, 5 (Paris, 1970), 118–27

—— 'Pour une approche de l'univers imaginaire d'Apollinaire', RLM, 276–9 (1971), Guillaume Apollinaire, 10 (1971), 35–67

—— 'Naissance d'un langage: Apollinaire correcteur de lui-même', in *Apollinaire inventeur de langages*, Actes du Colloque de Stavelot 1970, ed. Michel Décaudin, Bibliothèque Guilllaume Apollinaire, 7 (Paris, 1973), 21–38

—— 'L'Exploration de l'imaginaire apollinarien', projet d'étude, RLM 450–5, Guillaume Apollinaire, 13 (1976), 183–91

Butor, M., 'Monument de rien pour Apollinaire', in *Répertoire III*, (Paris, 1968), pp. 269–305

Debon, C., 'Les calligrammes d'"Ondes" ou la musique des formes', *Que vlo-ve?* 29–30 (1981), separate pagination

—— '"L'Ecriture cubiste" d'Apollinaire', *Europe*, 638–9 (1982), 118–27

Delbreil, D., Dininman, F., & Windsor, A., '"Lettre-Océan"', *Que vlo-ve?*, 21–2 (1979), separate pagination

Chevalier, J.-C., 'La Poésie d'Apollinaire et le calembour', *Europe*, 451–2 (1966), 56–76

—— 'G. Apollinaire. Rôle de la peinture et de la poésie dans l'élaboration d'une poétique', RLM, 217–22, Guillaume Apollinaire, 8 (1969), 97–107

Clark, J. G., 'Delaunay, Apollinaire et "Les Fenêtres"', RLM, 183–8, Guillaume Apollinaire, 7 (1968)

—— 'La Poésie, la politique et la guerre: autour de "La Petite auto", "Chant de l'honneur", et "Couleur du temps"', RLM, 450–5, Guillaume Apollinaire, 13 (1976), 7–63

Coquet, J.-C., 'Sémantique du discours poétique: "Les Colchiques" de Guillaume Apollinaire', *Littérature*, 6 (1972), 66–77

Davies, M., *'Vitam Impendere Amori'*, RLM, 249–53, Guillaume Apollinaire, 9 (1970), 69–93

—— 'L'Avenir dans l'oeuvre poetique d'Apollinaire', in *Apollinaire inventeur de langages*, Actes du Colloque de Stavelot 1970, ed. Michel Décaudin, Bibliothèque Guillaume Apollinaire, 7 (Paris, 1973), 141–65

—— '"Le Médaillon toujours fermé"', RLM, 450–5, Guillaume Apollinaire, 13 (1976), 77–98

—— 'Apollinaire, la peinture et l'image', *Que vlo-ve?*, 21–2 (1979), separate pagination

—— 'Non comme sont les reflets', *Que vlo-ve?*, 2, 6–7 (1983), separate pagination

Décaudin, M., 'Apollinaire à la recherche de lui-même', *Cahiers du Sud*, 386 (1966), 3–12

Delesalle, S., 'La Modernité dans le langage d'Apollinaire', *Europe*, 451–2 (1966), 105–12

Derrida, J., 'La Différance', in *Théorie d'ensemble*, Tel Quel (Paris, 1968), 41–66

Dupeyron, G., 'Espace et temps dans la poésie de Guillaume Apollinaire', *Europe*, 450–1 (1966), 192–201

List of works consulted

Goldstein, J.-P., review of Alain-Marie Bassy, 'Forme littéraire et forme graphique: les schématogrammes d'Apollinaire', RLM, 450–5, Guillaume Apollinaire, 13 (1976), 173–82

—— 'Pour une sémiologie du calligramme', Que vlo-ve?, 29–30, (1981), separate pagination

Goldenstein, J.-P., & Adam, J.-M., ' "D'un monstre à Lyon" ou la dé-monstration de l'écriture', in Regards sur Apollinaire prosateur, Actes du Colloque de Stavelot 1973, ed. Michel Décaudin, Bibliothèque Guillaum Apollinaire, 8 (Paris, 1975), 142–62

Hackett, C. A., 'Rimbaud and Apollinaire', French Studies, 19, 3 (1965), 266–77

Hubert, R. R., 'Apollinaire et Picasso', Cahiers du Sud, 386 (1966), 22–7

Jean, R., 'Apollinaire et Nerval', Cahiers du Sud, 347 (1958), 106–16

—— 'L'Erotique d'Apollinaire', Cahiers du Sud, 386 (1966) 13–21

Jutrin, M., 'Guillaume Apollinaire et Marcel Schwob: une affinité', RLM, 576–81, Guillaume Apollinaire, 15 (1980), 69–75

Kelley, D., 'Defeat and Rebirth: the city poetry of Apollinaire', in Unreal City: urban experience in modern literature and art (Manchester, 1986), 80–96

Lacan, J., 'Le stade du miroir comme formateur de la fonction du je', in Ecrits, 2 vols., Points (Paris, 1970 & 1971), I, 89–97

——'L'Instance de la lettre dans l'inconscient ou la raison depuis Freud', in Ecrits I, Points (Paris, 1970), 248–89

Laparcherie, J.-G., 'Ecriture et lecture du calligramme', Poétique, 50 (1982)

Lawler. J., 'Music and Poetry in Apollinaire', French Studies, 10 (1956), 339–46

Levaillant, J., 'L'Espace dans Calligrammes', RLM, 217–22, Guillaume Apollinaire, 8 (1969), 48–63

Levy, S., 'Foucault on Magritte: similitude and resemblance', forthcoming

Lockerbie, S. I., 'Alcools et le symbolisme', RLM, 85–9, Guillaume Apollinaire, 2 (1963), 5–40

—— 'Le rôle de l'imagination dans Calligrammes. Première partie: "Les Fenêtres" et le poème créé', RLM, 146–9, Guillaume Apollinaire, 5 (1966), 6–22

—— 'Le rôle de l'imagination dans Calligrammes. Seconde partie: les poèmes du monde intérieur', RLM, 166–9, Guillaume Apollinaire, 6 (1967), 85–105

—— 'Qu'est-ce que l'Orphisme d'Apollinaire?', in Apollinaire et la musique, Actes du Colloque de Stavelot 1965, ed. Michel Décaudin (Stavelot, 1967), 81–7

—— 'Forme graphique et expressivité dans les Calligrammes', Que vlo-ve?, 29–30 (1981), separate pagination

Marrow, A., 'Form and Meaning in Apollinaire's Picture-poems', Australian Journal of French Studies, 5, 3 (1968), 295–302

Mathews, T., 'Figure/text', Paragraph, 6 (1985), 28–42

Noszlopy, G. T., 'Apollinaire, allegorical imagery and the visual arts', Forum for Modern Language Studies, 9, 1 (1973), 49–74

Renaud, P., ' "Ondes", ou les-métamorphoses de la musique', in Apollinaire et la musique, Actes du Colloque de Stavelot 1965, ed. Michel Décaudin (Stavelot, 1967), 21–32

Richard, J.-P., 'Etoiles chez Apollinaire', in De Ronsard à Breton: Hommages à Marcel Raymond (Paris, 1967), 223–4

Riffaterre, M., 'Poétique du néologisme', *Cahiers de l'Association internationale des études françaises*, 25 (1973), 59–76

Sacks, P., 'La Mise en page du calligramme', *Que vlo-ve!*, 29–30 (1981), separate pagination

Schmits, G., '"Lettre-Océan"', *Savoir et Beauté*, 2–3 (1964), 2691–8

—— 'Le simulacre de la voyance dans quelques poèmes d'Apollinaire', in *Apollinaire inventeur de langages*, Actes du Colloque de Stavelot 1970, ed. Michel Décaudin, Bibliothèque Guillaume Apollinaire, 7 (Paris, 1973), 39–70

Somville, L., 'Apollinaire et le cubisme: une adhésion raisonnée', *Que vlo-ve!*, 21–2 (1979), separate pagination

Tournadre, C., 'A propos de "La Victoire"', in *Apollinaire inventeur de langages*, Actes du Colloque de Stavelot 1970, ed. Michel Décaudin, Bibliothèque Guillaume Apollinaire, 7 (Paris, 1973), pp. 167–80

4—WORKS OF GENERAL CRITICISM, THEORY, ETC.

Auerbach, E., *Mimesis*, trans. William R. Trask, Princeton Paperbacks (New Jersey, 1968)

Barthes, R., *Le Degré zéro de l'écriture*, suivi de *Eléments de sémiologie* (Paris, 1953)

—— *Essais critiques* (Paris, 1964)

—— *Le Degré zéro de l'écriture*, suivi de *Nouveaux essais critiques*, Points (Paris, 1972)

—— *S/Z*, Points (Paris, 1972)

—— *Le Plaisir du texte* (Paris, 1973)

Benjamin, W., *Illuminations*, ed. Hannah Arendt, trans. Harry Zohn (London, 1973)

Blanchot, M., *La Part du feu* (Paris, 1949)

—— *L'Espace littéraire* (Paris, 1955)

—— *Le Livre à venir*, Idées (Paris, 1971)

—— *Sade et Lautréamont*, Arguments, 19 (Paris, 1969)

Butor, M., *Essais sur le roman*, Idées (Paris, 1969)

—— *Les Mots dans la peinture*, Les Sentiers de la création (Geneva, 1969)

Culler, J., *Structuralist Poetics* (London, 1975)

Derrida, J., *De la Grammatologie* (Paris, 1967)

Ducrot, O., & Todorov, T., *Dictionnaire encyclopédique des sciences du langage* (Paris, 1972)

Eagleton, T., *Marxism and Literary Criticism* (London, 1976)

—— *Criticism and Ideology*, (London, 1976)

Foucault, M., *Les Mots et les choses, une archéologie des sciences humaines*, Bibliothèque des Sciences humaines (Paris, 1966)

—— *Ceci n'est pas une pipe* (Montpellier, 1973)

Freud, S., *Project for a Scientific Psychology* (1887)

—— *The Interpretation of Dreams* (1900)

—— *Introductory Lectures* (1916–17)

—— *Beyond the Pleasure Principle* (1920)

List of works consulted

— *The Ego and the Id* (1923)
in *The Standard Edition of the Complete Psychological Works of Sigmund Freud*, ed. James Strachey, 24 vols. (London 1953–74), I, IV, V, XV, XVI, XVII, XIX
Genette, G., *Figures II* (Paris, 1969)
— *Mimologiques* (Paris, 1976)
— *Introduction à l'architexte* (Paris, 1979)
Kirk, G. S., *The Nature of Greek Myths* (London, 1974)
Lacan, J., *Les quatres concepts fondamentaux de la psychanalyse*, Le Séminaire, Livre XI, 1964 (Paris, 1973)
— *The Four Fundamental Concepts of Psychoanalysis*, trans. Alan Sheridan (London, 1979)
Lévi-Strauss, C., *La Pensée sauvage* (Paris, 1962)
Lyotard, J.-F., *Discours, Figure* (Paris, 1971)
Picon, G., *L'Usage de la lecture* (Paris, 1960)
Poulet, G., *La Distance intérieure, Etudes sur le temps humain*, 2 (Paris, 1952)
Raymond, M., *De Baudelaire au surréalisme*, nouvelle édition revue et remaniée (Paris, 1940)
— *Vérité et poésie*, Langages (Neuchâtel, 1964)
Richard, J.-P., *Littérature et sensation* (Paris, 1954)
— *Poésie et profondeur* (Paris, 1955)
— *L'Univers imaginaire de Mallarmé* (Paris, 1961)
— *Onze études sur la poésie moderne* (Paris, 1964)
Richards, I. A., *Principles of Literary Criticism*, Routledge Paperbacks (London, 1976)
Sartre, J.-P., *Baudelaire*, Idées (Paris, 1980)
Starobinski, J., *Portrait de l'artiste en saltimbanque* (Geneva, 1970)
Thibaudet, A., *Réflexions sur la critique* (Paris, 1939)

5—LITERARY WORKS INCLUDING MANIFESTOS

Apollonio, U., ed., *Futurist Manifestos* (London, 1973)
Aragon, L., *Le Paysan de Paris* (Paris, 1926)
— *La Peinture au défi* (Paris, 1930)
Artaud, A., *Le Théâtre et son double* in *Oeuvres complètes*, IV (Paris, 1964)
— *L'Ombilic des limbes*, précédé de *Correspondance avec Jacques Rivière* et suivi de *Le Pèse-nerfs* et autres textes, Poésie (Paris, 1975)
Barrès, M., *Sous l'oeil des Barbares* (Paris, 1892)
Barzun, H.-M., *L'Ere du drame — essai de synthèse poétique moderne* (Paris, 1912)
Baudelaire, C., *Oeuvres complètes*, I, ed. Claude Pichois, Bibliothèque de la Pléiade (Paris, 1975)
Beckett, S., *Proust. Three dialogues with Georges Duthuit* (London, 1965)
Breton, A., *Manifestes du surréalisme*, Idées (Paris, 1972)
— *Las Pas perdus*, Idées (Paris, 1979)
— *Les Vases communicants*, Idées (Paris, 1977)
— *Positions politiques du surréalisme*, Méditations (Paris, 1972)

—— *Le Surréalisme et la peinture*, suivi de *Genèse et perspective artistiques du surréalisme*, et de *Fragments inédits* (New York, 1945)

—— *Entretiens* (Paris, 1969)

Cendrars, B., *Du Monde entier, Poésies complètes: 1912–14*, Poésie (Paris, 1967)

Corbière, T., *Les Amours jaunes*, suivi de *Poèmes retrouvés* et de *Oeuvres en prose*, Poésie (Paris, 1973)

Desnos, R., *Corps et biens*, Poésie (Paris, 1968)

Eluard, P., *Capitale de la douleur*, suivi de *l'Amour la poésie*, Poésie (Paris, 1966)

Flaubert, G., *L'Education sentimentale* (Paris, 1969)

Gide, A., *Les Nourritures terrestres*, suivi de *Les nouvelles nourritures*, Folio (Paris, 1979)

Gourmont, R. de, *Pensées inédites*, préface de Guillaume Apollinaire (Paris, 1920)

Hugo, V., *Oeuvres poétiques*, 3 vols., ed. Pierre Albouy, Bibliothèque de la Pléiade (Paris, 1964–74)

Huysmans, J.-K., *A Rebours*, suivi de *Le Drageoir aux épices*, Fins de siècles (Paris, 1975)

Jacob, M., *Le Cornet à dés*, Poésie (Paris, 1967)

Jammes, F., *Clairières dans le Ciel*, Poésie (Paris, 1980)

Jarry, A., *Ubu Roi*, etc., eds. Noël Arnaud & Henri Bordillon (Paris, 1978)

Laforgue, J., *Les Complaintes* et *Les Premiers Poèmes*, Poésie (Paris, 1979)

Lamartine, A. de, *Oeuvres poétiques complètes*, ed. Marius-François Guyard, Bibliothèque de la Pléiade (Paris, 1963)

Le Blond, M., *Essai sur le naturisme* (Paris, 1896)

Maeterlinck, M., *Serres chaudes* (Brussels, 1890)

Mallarmé, S., *Oeuvres complètes*, eds. Henry Mondor & G. Jean-Aubry, Bibliothèque de la Pléiade (Paris, 1951)

—— *Correspondance*, eds. Henry Mondor & Lloyd Austin, II (Paris, 1965)

Marinetti, F.-T., *Le Futurisme* (Paris, 1911)

Michaux, H., *L'Espace du dedans* (Paris, 1966)

Pausanias, *Guide to Greece*, trans. Peter Levi, 2 vols. (London, 1979)

Ponge, F., *Le Parti pris des choses*, précédé de *Douze petits écrits*, suivi de *Proêmes*, Poésie (Paris, 1972)

Proust, M., *A la Recherche du temps perdu*, eds. Pierre Clarac & André Ferré, Bibliothèque de la Pléiade, 3 vols. (Paris, 1954)

—— *Contre Sainte-Beuve*, Idées (Paris, 1979)

Rachilde, *Les Hors-nature* (Paris, 1897)

Reverdy, P., *La Plupart du temps*, Poésie, 2 vols. (Paris, 1969)

—— *Sources du vent*, précédé de *La Balle au bord*, Poésie (Paris, 1971)

—— *Note éternelle du présent, écrits sur l'art 1923–1960* (Paris, 1973)

Rimbaud, A., *Oeuvres*, ed. Suzanne Bernard (Paris, 1960)

Rouveyre, A., *Le Gynécée*, glose de Remy de Gourmont (Paris, 1909)

Royère, J., *Soeur de Narcisse nue* (Paris, 1907)

Salmon, A., *Souveniers sans fin*, 3 vols. (Paris, 1955–1961)

Scali, G., ed. *La cultura italiana del '900 attraverso le riviste*, IV: *Lacerba, La Voce* (1914–16) (Turin, 1961)

List of works consulted

Tzara, T., *Vingt-cinq-et-un-poèmes* (Paris, 1946)

—— *L'Antitête* (Paris, 1933)

Valéry, P., *Oeuvres*, ed. Jean Hytier, 1, Bibliothèque de la Pléiade (Paris, 1957)

Verlaine, P., *Oeuvres poétiques complètes*, ed. Y.-G. Le Dantec, Bibliothèque de la Pléiade (Paris, 1938)

—— *Choix de poésies*, préface de François Coppée (Paris, 1897)

Warhol, A., *From A to B and Back Again* (New York, 1975)

Wilde, O., *The Picture of Dorian Gray*, ed. Isobel Murray, The World's Classics (Oxford, 1981)

Index

of writers, painters, individual poems and other works by Apollinaire, excluding *Alcools* and *Calligrammes*

Index

List of illustrations